THE ORIGINS
OF STALINISM

Pavel Campeanu

The origins of

STALINISM

FROM LENINIST REVOLUTION TO STALINIST SOCIETY

Translated by Michel Vale

M. E. Sharpe, Inc.
Armonk, New York and London, England

Available in the United Kingdom and Europe from M. E. Sharpe,
Publishers, 3 Henrietta Street, London WC2E 8LU.

Published simultaneously as vol. xv, no. 3-4 of *International Journal of
Sociology*.

Library of Congress Cataloging in Publication Data

Câmpeanu, Pavel.
    The origins of Stalinism.

    "Published simultaneously as International journal of sociology,
vol. XV, no 3-4"—Verso of t.p.
    1. Communism—Soviet Union—History—20th century.
2. Stalin, Joseph, 1879-1953. I. Title.
HX313.C26   1985   335.43 '0947   85-18410
ISBN 0-87332-363-7

Printed in the United States of America

In memory of my close friend, Jerry Kline

CONTENTS

AUTHOR'S NOTE

A few years ago I sent some American academic colleagues a thesis I was working on. I hoped to obtain their critical comments. To my surprise, they arranged, in my absence, to have it published as *The Syncretic Society* (M. E. Sharpe, 1980).

At the time they were arranging for publication, they were cautious in trying to correctly determine my official position in Romania as well as my past affiliations and relationships. Additionally, the same caution led them to choose a pseudonym instead of identifying me by name as the author of *The Syncretic Society*.

The present volume offers me the opportunity to express to them my sincere thanks and gratitude. Their positive reaction to my theoretical formulations surprised and pleased me.

The information about the author that appears in the present volume was, like the text, given to the publisher by me and I take full responsibility for its accuracy.

PAVEL CAMPEANU

THE ORIGINS
OF STALINISM

INTRODUCTION

How did it come to pass that the first great anti-imperialist revolution of the modern era ultimately gave birth to but another imperialism of a new kind? One possible answer is that certain defining characteristics of neo-Stalinist imperialism were linked with certain defining characteristics of the 1917 Russian revolution. It is primarily with this still insufficiently explored hypothesis that the present book will be concerned.

The choice of subject was inspired in the first place by the current state of neo-Stalinism, and how it is portrayed by its present critics. Although Orwell's predictions were not borne out, 1984 confronted us with a Stalinism whose distinctive markings have been engraved ever more deeply upon its countenance. Its longevity and stability have earned for it a place in history, while its sheer territorial expanse, along with the political weight it is able to bring to bear across the globe, is testimony enough of its international significance. Immersed in crisis, now all but perpetual, the opposition Stalinism has traditionally engendered has shifted its epicenter from without to within the society itself. Oppositional thought, bent on eradicating Stalinism from the fairways of human history, has proven itself infinitely more prolific and inventive than reflective thought, more properly concerned with comprehending its nature.

The crisis of Stalinism is also a measure of the crisis in the critical theory of Stalinism, even as paradoxically the latter renders the former more bearable. One current of this criticism, drifting into journalism, tends to reduce Stalinism to the historical agents who at different times have incarnated it, while another part excels in prophecies proclaiming precisely when, how, by whom, and by what other social order Stalinism will be replaced. Both are equally heedless of the central problem, namely that of the actual workings of this society, so darkly known to us, although they thoroughly govern the behavior of its leaders and through their malfunctionings reveal its most vulnerable sides.

Observation of key individuals is no substitute for the study of structure, and the truism that the future is ever upon us cannot justify an ignorance of the present; thus the central question brooks no evasion—namely what is Stalinism? Yet the answer to this general question is contingent upon a second, more specific question implicit in the first: how did Stalinism come to be? What are its origins and what were the decisive moments in the historical process of its genesis and evolution into what it is today?

The quest for the origins of Stalinism has traditionally moved in certain preferred directions. One of the most popular would reduce the history of Stalinism to Stalin's political biography. Western criticism of a conservative cast prefers a reduction of another sort, making Stalinism the faithful material embodiment of Marxist, Leninist, or even Marxist-Leninist thought, thereby confirming the ideological legitimacy that Stalinism claims for itself. A fundamentally contrary point of view resorts to the category of chance, always an easy way out of a problem: Stalinism is simply the historical fruit of a particular constellation of chance events. Finally, another approach enjoying broad popularity sees Stalinism as merely one episode in the long unbroken line tracing the history of Russian despotism.

Most such approaches succeed in pinpointing one real source of Stalinism; all overlook or underestimate the importance of its principal source. Stalin was the creation, not the creator, of a period of severe constraints, of which he was the expression, with an application as consistent in principle as it was grievous in its consequences. The reality and ideology of Stalinism are no more related to Marxism than science fiction is to futurology. When Stalinism is reduced to a mere variant of the tsarist tradition in new trappings, the history of Russia is reduced to a single dimension and, by implication, Stalinism becomes the fatalistic outcome of an unbroken historical process. Any one-dimensional approach which sees Stalinism solely from the perspective of its historical continuity or discontinuity merely compounds the confusion marking the state of our knowledge about it. Continuity and discontinuity were intermingled in the molding of Stalinism; the main term of reference, however, is not the autocracy, which runs through the history of Russia like an unbroken thread, but the radical break that the Russian revolution of 1917 effected in the history of mankind. As for the agents of chance—circumstances and individuals—they no doubt left their imprint on the physiognomy of the process that led to the birth of Stalinism; we cannot rule out the possibility that other individuals and other circumstances might have given this process a different physiognomy without, to be sure, necessarily modifying its substance.

This view is by no means speculative; a reading of the facts of history will tell the same tale. It is clear enough that there are countries where Stalinism has been established or has evolved without Stalin, without the prelude of Russian history, sometimes even without the aid of a specious Marxist legitimacy, and involving quite different personalities and quite different circumstances. But it might appear somewhat inconsistent to imply that, though the landmarks may be comparable, history nonetheless does not repeat itself. Indeed the non-Russian versions of Stalinism thrust themselves upon the world not only independently of the conditions mentioned, which were peculiar to Russia, but also as a consequence of revolutionary upheavals with features of their own, distinct from those of the Russian revolution. Why then should we suppose that the latter was more important than the other factors cited in the genesis of Stalinism in Russia and elsewhere?

This question too will be illuminated in the course of this book. Our central hypothesis will be that the revolutionary upheavals that culminated in a Stalinist social order in various countries around the globe do indeed, despite their considerable diversity, bear some very essential resemblances both among themselves and to the Russian revolution. Our main emphasis therefore will be on the nature of the Russian revolution as manifested in its historical functions, i.e., its defining characters, rather than on a mere empirical rendering of events.

As the Marxist anthropologist Maurice Godelier points out, apropos of the capitalist system, to see the origin of a social formation entails going beyond a simple narrative of events to unearth the significant factors in a historical process, making use of appropriate concepts (which themselves undergo elaboration) possessing a maximum explanatory power.

Between Stalinism's roots in tradition and the circumstances immediately surrounding its emergence lies an array of historical events almost beyond number, varying widely in their scope and in their consequences. These events coalesced the flow of history into the process that culminated in Stalinism. The key determining circumstances of this process are several, some historical and some theoretical, each important enough to alter radically the course of history. The historical circumstances were three: the transformation of capitalism into imperialism, the victory of the Russian revolution in 1917, and the constitution of postrevolutionary society and its survival within the basic pale laid down by the revolution that gave it birth. The theoretical circumstances are two in number: one is positive: namely the reality of imperialism thrusting itself upon human consciousness and the elaboration on this basis of a revolutionary strategy unprecedented in history. The second was negative: the lack (from which we still suffer today) of a coherent theory explaining the society created by a Leninist revolution.

Our knowledge of these various factors, and of the ways they have come to intersect, is uneven. We will be concentrating mainly on two areas: (a) in what ways the nature of the revolution and its various characters were conditioned by the nature and variegated character of imperialism; and (b) how postrevolutionary and pre-Stalinist society was conditioned by the nature and characters of the revolution and, further, by its own inability to achieve an adequate theoretical understanding of itself.

In analyzing these conditioning processes I will be making use of the general concept of objective necessity in two senses: with focus on its internal transformation, wherein linear, univocal necessity tends to give way to antinomic necessity and of the tendency for the category of historical possibility to assume a determining role. A brief clarification of the terms of our argument will perhaps be useful.

Univocal necessity

The central idea of Marxism lies in searching for the hidden wellsprings of historical events in those events themselves. Neither men's wills nor chance, but objective necessity ultimately gives history its direction. Marx obtained this key philosophical idea from Hegel, for whom human actions were determined by a power beyond and independent of men's own consciousness and wills. That power is objective necessity, which, though counterposed to individuals as subjects, is in principle not inaccessible to individual consciousness. While Marx got his idea of the objective nature of necessity from Hegel, it was Feuerbach who bequeathed to him the idea that necessity was also determined. Equipped with these general premises, Marx put forth an original definition of objective necessity, namely, necessity, itself determined, determining in turn the flow of history. The crucial intersection between necessity and the individual lies in the social process of production, made up essentially of two basic components: the productive forces, essentially human labor power and the technical means of production, and the relations of production, essentially the system of stable relations among human agents in the process of production. In Marx's view, man's evolution as a social being is in the last instance determined by the necessary connection between the nature of the forces of production and the nature of the relations of production. It is the "imperfect fit," so to speak, between these two components which gives rise to social conflict, and provides the basis for the transition from one mode of production to another; but within any given stable mode of production, it is the relations of production which in the last instance are determining.

The interaction between the forces and the relations of production is marked by a fundamental contradiction that is the product of their unequal mobility, which means that over time, measured in epochs, they fall out of phase with one another, giving rise to conflict. Whereas the productive forces strain toward a constant self-transformation, the relations of production tend to perpetuate themselves in kind. Put in other terms, they are structurally conjunctive and functionally disjunctive.

Marx developed this broad historical design through his thorough study of the capitalist system in England. He identified capital's *raison d'être* as the pursuit of a maximum profit. Under capitalism, society, its structures, and the structures of production itself are continuously accommodated to the pursuit of this end. Consistent in its immediate applications, capitalism loses this congruence over the long term. To maximize its profits, capital is constrained to transform the structures of production to the point where they come into irremediable conflict with the social structures supporting the dominance of capital. Technological progress itself turns against its initiator. Capitalist property relations, which had required the full play of productive forces, now require that they stagnate (at least relatively so). Objective necessity, reflected in the steady development of the productive forces, ultimately enjoins the abolition of capitalist property relations, and the means of production, alienated from the producers, can and must be restored to them. With this stage achieved, necessity assumes a social form, exacerbating the conflict residing in the opposition between the fundamental constituents of society: the producers proletarianized, now polarized against the nonproducing proprietors. The specific form of this conflict is revolutionary class struggle.

Once in movement, capitalism has steered its ineluctable course toward an anticapitalist revolution that will be the most radical in the history of man: instead of replacing one form of private ownership of the means of production, it will abolish all private ownership and in its place effect the gradual appropriation of the means of production by the producers themselves. The historical mission of launching, leading, and carrying through this revolution to its completion falls necessarily to the proletariat in its quality as the necessary antithesis to the capitalist class. By abolishing every form of private control over the means of production, the working class lays the objective foundations for the abolition of class society in general.

The forces of production and the relations of production are the two terms basic to our analytical model. The connection between them is described by a multiplicity of univocal tendencies, e.g.:

(a) Their specific functions are not interchangeable; each has its own role to play.

(b) Their interaction takes place strictly within a closed system, and factors external to that system play no material role; the workings of the system take place therefore within a single dimension.

(c) The two terms stand essentially in a temporal, i.e., earlier–later, relation to one another; movement is linear.

(d) As the two terms differ in their mobility a discrepancy arises: the forces of production tend to develop at a more dynamic pace than the relations of production; the dynamics of the system tend unambiguously in one direction.

(e) This lag appears invariably in social life and consciousness as a dichotomous conflict; thus the social manifestation of the structural disjunction is simple and unequivocal.

(f) The solution is immanent to the conflict: the relatively greater mobility of the forces of production must in the long run win out over the relative inertia of the relations of production; hence the historical epilogue is unambiguous.

Our model may render the concept of univocal necessity plausible, but this does not necessarily mean that it will be useful as a tool of analysis. I will attempt to demonstrate this quality later on in examining the historical circumstances that gave rise to objective contradictory necessity. In concentrating on his concrete subject, Marx omits a number of historical potentialities in his analysis which, although they may have appeared improbable at the moment, were nonetheless not impossible: e.g., the factors external to the connection between the forces and relations of production became determinant; the dynamics shifted and the relations of production assumed the lead; roles consequently changed, the relations of production becoming determinant and the forces of production determined; the discrepancy produced by this inversion was unable through its own forces, to break through to the social plane, where it could assume the form of a specific conflict; as other factors surmounting these obstacles came into play, the emergent conflict was no longer dichotomous but rather polymorphous, and the outcome that was immanent to the dichotomous conflict over the long term gave way to a variety of possible outcomes; the movement of history lost its essential single direction and became itself much more determined by probability than reined in by univocal necessity.

Our description of the historical potentialities neglected by Marx is merely a description of post-Marxian capitalism, the capitalism that was to become dominant after his death. The principal limitation in Marx, therefore, was not in his analysis, but in what he was analyzing. He had studied the world as capitalism had made it, and the first anticapitalist revolution was to break out in a world profoundly different from it. That world was the world of imperialism.

Antinomic necessity

Under the impact of necessity, human societies change their structures. But a society thus modified can in turn alter the structure of objective necessity, in that the latter accommodates to its object. Thus the imperialist system embraced societies representing a broad historical, economic, and cultural diversity in the antagonistic unity that was proper to itself. Almost all the countries of the world have been drawn into this divisive process: upon the identity they derive from their own history, another identity is forcefully superimposed by the international imperialist system. It is this objective phenomenon—contemporary societies being pulled in two contrary directions—that I have attempted to describe through the term antinomic necessity. The prime cause of this internal rending of objective historical necessity is the reality of imperialism; its prime effect (as concerns our subject) is the possibility of anticipatory revolution. The internal contradiction that is the defining trait of imperialism—an apparent unity in a divided world and a torn economy—finds its echo in antinomic necessity.

Imperialism drew broadly on the achievements of past history as it developed into a system of world domination. The world it penetrated was on the verge of losing the equilibrium between its advanced sector and its backward sector. By virtue of the law of unequal development, the world economy spared international capital the effort of having to introduce the inequality that was an inherent part of its nature. It needed only to organize the inequality inherited from the past in accordance with its own interests. To that extent imperialism is merely the extension of the disparities arising from isolation to a world scale, and inequality, the product of unfortunate historical circumstances, became the fundamental precondition if the new international system was to function and reproduce. The world community created by that system was itself the negation of its own apparent unity; if it broke the isolation of former times, it was only to reproduce, control, and channel the consequences of that isolation. Initially an effect of the law of unequal development, imperialism became by an absurd twist, its perfect substitute. What history had produced spontaneously in its turnings, imperialism, using an economic and political strategy, carried further, and underdevelopment shifted categories: from a cause, it became a means to an end.

The key aim of this strategy is to maintain, expand, and control unevenness in industrial development across the globe. In making the step from the domestic market, where free competition was still wont to rule, to the monopolistic practices of international imperialism, the unseen hand of capital changed its role from promoter of industrialization at home to the enemy of industrialization in the rest of the world.

Stirred by its own achievements, but in like manner by the resistance it encounters both at the center and at the periphery, imperialism seeks to diversify its methods of rule. Leninism was essentially the theoretical realignment of the anti-imperialist current to take account of these changes, some of which had a decisive influence on the nature of the Russian revolution. Thus:

imperialism discovered that live labor power was the best source for reaping extravagant profits and, moreover, was a raw material that all underdeveloped countries had in abundance;

as a consequence, rather than squarely opposing industrialization, imperialism found it more advantageous to steer it in a direction that was consonant with its own interests, making the periphery a productive complement of the economy at the center;

thus imperialism contributed to the development of a peripheral proletariat, which experienced in a most direct fashion the burden of this inequitable exchange;

this peculiar predicament of the working class created a broad area where the interests of imperialism meshed with the interests of the indigenous possessing classes.

External rule in the underdeveloped countries strengthened its domestic social base within them. The boundary lines between external and internal become blurred. External contradictions, while remaining determinant, merge with contradictions arising internally. In those countries most affected by this development, with Russia heading the list, the necessity of industrialization encountered a double obstacle: international imperialism and the mixed relations of production prevailing in the domestic economy. Through the workings of antinomic necessity, the drive to industrialize and the obstacles placed in its path gave way to a conflict with roots both within the society and beyond it. There were now no longer two, but many, parties to this conflict, and to resolve it a revolution would have to be both national and international at one and the same time. But not only had the terms of the confict multiplied, roles too underwent a reshuffling, and the most important role change had to do with the bourgeoisie. In Russia, this class, by nature the very incarnation of industrial civilization, opposed industrialization. The keystone of success for Lenin's strategy linking an industrial revolution to an anticapitalist revolution was a bourgeoisie that was nationally and socially sterile. With the bourgeoisie, the prime mover of industrialization, having abandoned that role, it perforce fell to other social forces, the bourgeoisie notwithstanding.

The chain of factors involved grew longer, and their roles became more complex. The elimination of underdevelopment was contingent on the defeat of international imperialism, while the latter in turn was contingent on the defeat of the national possessing classes, most notably the bourgeoisie. Classical industrialization had been simply antifeudal; under the sway of imperialism, and the antinomic necessity of which it was the embodiment, industrialization in certain underdeveloped countries was destined to be antifeudal, anti-imperialist, and anticapitalist at the same time.

Lawful links appeared between the nature of the necessity posed by history and of the revolution aimed at carrying through that necessity to its fulfillment. Antinomic necessity created the possibility of a revolution invested with a plurality of fundamental characters, each enjoying in turn its period of ascendancy. But it was the anticapitalist character of the revolution that gave it its anticipatory quality, insofar as it was prepared to abolish a social class not *after* but *before* that class had accomplished the mission marked out for it. That the anticipatory aims of a revolution should be accomplished spontaneously is highly improbable; therefore, the anticipatory revolution had to have a strategy as well. Ultimately, antinomic necessity would reassert itself in the antinomy which contrasted this revolution achieved with its bastard child, the Stalinist social order.

Antinomic necessity is at its most transparent in the world imperialist system: the economy of the center is guided by the need to adapt underdevelopment at the periphery to its own needs, while the nations at the periphery are guided by the need to eliminate economic underdevelopment by freeing themselves from their subjugation to the needs of the center. The two opposing tendencies are driven by unequal forces: as a result, the internal need to eliminate underdevelopment is for all practical purposes frustrated by the external need, i.e., the need of the center, to consolidate it. For the underdeveloped countries, compelled effectively to swallow imperialist domination, industrialization remains but an alien possibility. Although industrialization is indispensable to the internal logic of the economies of these countries, it is intolerable to the logic of imperialism.

The peripheral societies are thus the object of two opposing constraints that leave their mark on social, economic, and political structures, and on international relations. These constraints may be represented schematically as follows.

Internal necessity	**External necessity**

Social structures

1. Generalization of capitalist relations of production	1. Preservation of the predominance of precapitalist relations of production
2. The bourgeoisie becomes the dominant class	2. Preeminence of the classes of the old order maintained

Economic structures

1. Primitive capitalist accumulation	1. Transference of a large portion of the surplus product and necessary product abroad
2. Bourgeoisie initiates industrialization	2. Abandonment by the bourgeois class of its industrializing mission in favor of a crippled development subordinated to imperialist interests

Political structures

1. National bourgeoisie militantly anti-imperialist and antifeudal	1. National bourgeoisie collaborates with foreign imperialism and reactionary feudalism
2. Alliance of the bourgeoisie with the popular masses against the former dominant classes	2. Alliance of the bourgeoisie with the former dominant classes against the popular masses

International relations

1. Promotion of international relations of equality	1. Accommodation to international relations of domination and subordination
2. Support to other underdeveloped countries against imperialism	2. Support to imperialism against other underdeveloped countries

This schema describes the situation in prerevolutionary Russia especially aptly. It gives some insight, if only very partial, into the way in which antinomic necessity was able to redefine the role of the bourgeoisie and render an anticipatory anticapitalist revolution objectively possible. Like objective necessity of any other sort, antinomic necessity moves from its quiescent stage to a manifest stage as it imposes a particular structure on the social conflict. It serves as a discriminant of social forces that take up their demands in different or even opposing ways as they pursue their own interests. Where these differences or oppositions cannot be absorbed by social structures, the social conflict swells until it erupts into violent revolution and the structures break under its pressure.

In a social conflict generated by antinomic necessity there is neither unity nor dichotomy, nor is there the linear evolution proper to social conflicts borne by univocal necessity. By incorporating external factors and internalizing their consequences, antinomic necessity broadens the premises of the social conflict, which becomes less clearly defined, i.e., it assumes many characters, all intermeshed, tending in several directions at once. So long as imperialism maintains its dominance, its conflict with the peripheral economies will tend to reproduce their underdevelopment. In a parallel process, the internal conflict in these economies tends spontaneously to undermine this subjugation and eliminate the mixed relations of production so as to clear the way for industrialization. The two conflicts move in opposing directions. Antinomic necessity assumes the form of a conflict between these two subsidiary conflicts. Rather than concentrating the transformative energies of the conflict, this division dissipates them, thus objectively favoring the status quo. Antinomic necessity throws the world into a turmoil, all the while enforcing its stagnation.

In the peripheral societies these tendencies carry considerable weight and assume specific forms. In their case, in contrast to the classical industrial revolutions, the prime source of social conflict lies in the inertia of the productive forces rather than in their mobility. But the objective chances both of conflict and of consensus are enhanced, inasmuch as the relations of production are reproduced not in tension with the progressive of productive forces, but in concordance with their stagnation, relatively speaking. This antinomy merely brings out the antinomy inherent in imperialist domination. It is the latter that in the last instance pulls the underdeveloped world into two opposing directions: toward its integration in the world economic system, on the one hand, and on the other, toward its technological isolation on a national, regional, or continental scale.

There is a third possibility: rejection of the vexed dilemma imposed by imperialist domination, and assimilation of existing technologies in consonance with national interests. In some countries the bourgeoisie has proven incapable of pursuing this end, and then the only social class able to act in its place is a nascent proletariat—not because circumstances have created in it the political will to undertake such a mission, but because of the very nature of the proletariat as a class. From the vantage point of subsequent history, and indeed of Leninism, the possibility of effecting this switch of functions represents the crucial moment in the reassignment of roles among the social forces in peripheral societies. As regards the necessity of industrialization, the proletariat becomes, using Merton's term, a functional surrogate for the bourgeoisie. But the proletariat in underdeveloped countries is hardly optimally equipped to bear this transference of roles. Immense difficulties are involved, most notably the objective immaturity of the proletariat as a class, which handicaps its ability to acquire the consciousness and organization that alone will enable it to carry through this mission successfully.

To the industry of underdevelopment corresponds an underdeveloped proletariat. Still immature, its immaturity extends over many levels. It is quantitative in that the proletariat constitutes a very small proportion of the entire population; it is qualitative in that it has still not completely severed its links with the countryside and hence the line separating it from the peasantry is still indistinct; and, at the same time, it is a historical immaturity, reflecting a relative inexperience in class struggle, although such experience is crucial if it is to assume a leading role in the anti-imperialist revolution. Finally, it is a political and cultural immaturity: the proletariat is the youngest class in these societies, it is superexploited, and the overwhelming majority of workers are but first-generation. All these things then help to explain why the proletariat is unable to build effective organizations and acquire a consciousness of its own.

In Marx's vision, the proletariat, to accomplish its historical mission—that of abolishing capitalist relations of production—must have achieved sufficient maturity at all these levels. But in peripheral societies, where the general contradictions of imperialism have been internalized by the proletariat, reality paints a different picture. Its historical mission has become compounded, yet it is called upon to accomplish this compound task while still in the full flush of its immaturity, and the constraint under which it labors is compounded as well: as long as imperialist domination endures, the immaturity of the proletariat will endure with it, and its immaturity in turn reduces the proletariat's chances of leading the anti-imperialist revolution to victory. Thus the proletariat of underdevelopment can neither overcome its immaturity nor renounce, despite this handicap, its mission of initiating the industrial revolution abandoned by the bourgeoisie.

The contradiction between the vastness of the task facing the proletariat and the frailty of its means constitutes the objective background of the Leninist dictum of the leading role of the party. Even under mature capitalism Marxism recognized that the proletariat was incapable of achieving class consciousness through its own means. To develop class consciousness is the task of the revolutionary intelligentsia, and indeed, a material demonstration of this shift of roles is Marx's theory itself. Under imperialism, the inability of the proletariat to acquire class consciousness is compounded by its inability to assume the leading role in the industrial revolution as prescribed by history. For all practical purposes this role then passes to the revolutionary intelligentsia, now embodied not in a theory, but in an organization, specifically a Leninist party. The price the proletariat has to pay for its compound inability to accomplish its historical mission was the surrender of these two essential functions: the forging of its class consciousness and the building of its organization were accomplished essentially independent of its own ranks. Itself the functional surrogate of the bourgeoisie in the industrial revolution, the proletariat now found itself in turn replaced by the party in the leadership of the anticipatory revolution. The substitution of the proletariat by the party largely preceded Stalinism; indeed it was all but fore-ordained, given the objective contradiction in underdeveloped countries between the potential role of the proletariat and its real possibilities of fulfilling that role.

For Leninism this anticipation of the qualities of the proletariat as a historical subject was a decisive precondition for the revolutionary anticipation of history. In Leninist strategy, the party was but a temporary compromise, but in its surrogate role it became a cardinal institution, fixed and unchanging, of the Stalinist social order.

In provoking a conflict of a higher order between the particular conflicts of the epoch, antinomic necessity in effect reverses the direction ordinarily taken by the dialectic: instead of raising contradiction to the level of conflict, it suppresses conflict to the level of contradiction. In its sporadic violence and fitful development, the diffuse conflict, reeling darkly onward, inevitably dissipated immense social energies and, thus sapped, risked becoming historically sterile. Leninist strategy was able to collect this immense energy and channel it in a prescribed direction. This strategy, indeed, played a crucial role, not only because of its inherent virtues, but also because of the particular constellation of events of the time. Because of the relative formlessness and infirmity of the principal social factors, the diffuse conflict was poorly suited as a generator of spontaneous mass actions capable of turning the tide of events. Consequently, for that conflict to be transformed into a revolution, and above all a victorious one, the constructive virtues of subjective factors, theory, strategy, and organization were necessary to an unprecedented degree. The fate of the revolution, steered by antinomic necessity, thus acquired dramatic qualities of a particular force, to be played out in the sphere of politics.

The following is a summary comparison between the two models of objective necessity: univocal and antinomic.

Univocal necessity	Antinomic necessity
1. Prime source: the linkage between two factors as inseparable as they are fundamental, namely the forces of production and the relations of production	1. Prime source: the intermeshing of this linkage with the web of relations linking the world economy, dominated by imperialism, to the national economies of the periphery, the result being an intermeshing of higher order between these two intricate networks of relations.
2. The roles of the two terms are not interchangeable.	2. The roles of the two linkages are not interchangeable but they are inter-

penetrable; the center cannot itself survive without the periphery, upon which it encroaches continuously.

3. The linkage is unidimensional: it is intrinsic to the system.

3. The links are multidimensional: univocal for the world system, and conflictual for its two subsystems, i.e., the center and periphery, as well as for each country taken separately.

4. The essential content of the linkage has one dimension: temporal, a before-and-after relation. The forces of production invariably evolve more rapidly than the relations of production.

4. The links extend over three dimensions: temporal, spatial, and atemporal; spatial and temporal in that the historical lag is compounded by the geographical separation between center and periphery, the internal necessity of each in opposition to the external necessity represented by the other; and atemporal in that the illegitimate past of the periphery nourishes the illegitimate present of this center. The consequence is an inertia of fundamental structures, and the historical dimension of inertia becomes entrenched in timelessness.

5. The unidirectional lag between the forces and relations of production generates a social structure that tends to polarize in a social conflict, itself tending to dichotomize.

5. The unidirectional disparity between center and periphery brings together two dissimilar structures into a third and global one, the prime function of which is continuously to reproduce this heterogeneity over time. Diffracted through these composite and separate structures, antinomic necessity is reflected in the life of men in a conflict that nfluctuates—now mounting, now abating, now fitful, now unfolding unreined, now of two, now of many terms—depending on the era and on the level on which it is played out. A contradictory necessity produces an ill-defined conflict; a plurivocal necessity entails no single, necessary solution but only a range of objectively possible solutions. Immanence is supplanted by contingency.

The relationship between possibility
and necessity

Leninist theory is the conscious understanding of the transformation of capitalism into imperialism, and of the possibility of breaking out of the circle into which this transformation encloses underdevelopment. Leninist strategy is a project for making this possibility a reality.

As an analysis of the new relations between possibility and necessity, Leninism is fundamentally valid. It has three distinguishing features: an adequate theory of imperialism; a strategy, borne out historically by the anticipatory revolution; and its theoretical incognizance of the society born of such a revolution.

Leninism was most fully in its element on the question of revolution, although it displayed some serious shortcomings nonetheless. It was strongest in amplifying on the possibility of expanding the contradictory nature of the revolution from anti-imperialism to anticapitalism. It was weakest in its confusion between anticapitalism, which was possible, and socialism, which was only a desideratum of the revolution, and in its hedging analysis of the anticipatory nature of the revolution and its practical consequences.

Leninism proposed or, more accurately, suggested the idea that antinomic necessity created two major possibilities for fulfilling the necessity of industrialization: either through capitalism or through its negation. The implication is that the abolition of capitalist relations of production is not a derivative necessity contained in the necessity of industrialization, but an objective possibility in its own right, with its foundations rooted in economic and social structures deformed by imperialist domination. To choose between these two possibilities was beyond the capacity of the spontaneous forces of revolution; a strategy for employing these forces was needed. And because that strategy—itself a product of a valid theory—was called upon to make this choice, to pursue and carry through one of these possibilities, the Russian revolution may truly be considered a revolution of the possible, or, if you will, a strategic revolution, and as such it marked the beginning of a new era in the history of mankind.

Leninist strategy had two points of attack: the social conflict, and historical time. It endeavored to work the diffuse social conflict into a polarization opposing the worker–peasant alliance to the alliance of imperialism, feudalism, and the bourgeoisie, and to force the successive stages of history's spontaneous flow into the mold of simultaneity: abolition of feudalism, abolition of capitalism, and transition to socialism—all in one stroke. This strategy worked selectively on antinomic necessity, urging the possibilities bred by it toward a social conflict whose outcome would bear a maximum of historical probability.

There was a certain authenticity to this quickening of history's pace. It served two ends: to repair the backwardness imposed by history, and to lift society out of the leaden stagnation imposed by imperialism. But the logic of revolution was deflected by the revolution's very achievements. The revolution was victorious, and capitalist relations of production were indeed eliminated, not, however, by the advancement of industrialization but deliberately, beforehand, to make that advancement possible. Capitalist relations were abolished not because the forces of production had reached a particular level, but in spite of the level they had reached, i.e., before they had become universal, before the bourgeoisie had accomplished its progressive historical mission of industrialization. All these foreshortenings of a presumed natural sequence of events gave the Russian revolution its anticipatory nature.

But anticipation did not avoid antinomy: on the one hand, the aim of the proletariat was to eliminate the bourgeoisie before it became the dominant class, but on the other the proletariat found itself with the role of dominant class conferred upon it before it itself had coalesced not only into a class "for itself," but also a class "in itself." Indeed the historical circumstances that conferred upon the working class the possibility of playing the leading role in the revolution failed to give it the means to accomplish this role. But it was not its anticapitalism, but its workerism, that risked reducing Leninist strategy to a utopian exercise. To combat this tendency, Leninism relied on three levers capable of temporarily compensating for the weakness of the proletariat: the avantgarde party, the peasant alliance, and support of the international proletariat. These three factors, it was hoped, would enable the proletariat to fulfill a role beyond its capacities, but essentially only one—the party—consolidated the anticipations of the strategy. The defeat of the revolutions abroad and the debilitating vacillations of the peasantry left the party completely alone to bear the full weight of its crushing commitments. Its imposed solitude was a foretokening of the monolithism that the party itself was later to impose upon society.

These levers required favorable circumstances, which Lenin described as follows:

> Russia has not achieved the level of development of productive forces necessary to establish socialism. Yes, but what if a singular set of circumstances had situated its evolution at the margin of the nascent revolutions and the revolutions already under way in the East? And what if this situation, an absolute dead end, by unleashing the forces of the workers and peasants, should offer us the possibility of proceeding to the creation of the essential preconditions of civilization in another way than all the other states of Western Europe had done?

The first contingency motivating anticipation is that of "singular circumstances," i.e., chance, and the second that of revolutions in other countries. The keynote was the perception of a *possibility* (my emphasis) whose premises remained theoretically undefined, although its material implication could already be discerned: industrialization on a basis wholly other than that on which it was begun in Western countries.

For Lenin, the proletariat held the key. Under the right circumstances, the proletariat would seize political power and, thus armed, would establish new socialist relations of production that would not only make possible but indeed require the accelerated development of the productive forces. But such a possibility entailed an inversion of the fundamental relation between the forces and the relations of production. Imperialism had severely undermined this relation, and anticipatory revolution had reversed it with the intention of reestablishing it on another basis. Contrary to Marx's model, it was no longer the development of productive forces that forced a commensurate transformation in the relations of production; rather the establishment of new relations of production by noneconomic measures would permit, or even compel, the development of the productive forces. In effect, Leninism placed its trust in the possibility of reversing for a time the order of historical cause and effect to enable history to resume its natural course, which imperialism had held in check. This tack distinguished Leninism from Marxism, but it did not signify a departure. Marx was sensitive to the caprices of historical chance and proved himself a supple interpreter of its determinism, showing how history was receptive to unanticipated possibilities favorable to the progress of revolution occurring *à l'improviste*. For Marx the prevailing of the possible over the necessary was a contingency of a secondary order, whereas Lenin made it the basis of social revolution.

The shift from the necessary to the possible is relative inasmuch as it does not entail substitution of the former by the latter. What it does require is sufficient subjective control over necessity to deliver it of one of its possibilities at the expense of the others it may contain. One objective possibility had to be played off against the others, which meant that, while accepting the necessity of industrialization, its internal mechanism (the causal relation between the forces and relations of production) would be modified to render contrary possibilities, themselves antinomic, inoperative: namely, reproduction of underdevelopment and capitalist industrialization.

In social terms, the main aim of this strategy was to unleash a bourgeois revolution so as then to eliminate the bourgeoisie, which represented one of the possible issues of antinomic necessity. These dislocations, reversals of roles, successive substitutions, and inversions of relations held to be natural—all these things taken together are what is entailed by the concept of a relative shift from the necessary to the possible.

Directed toward smashing the obstacles preventing escape from underdevelopment, this shift nonetheless tends at the same time to sap the sources fueling history's movement, slackening its pace. The preemption of the necessary by the possible in the short term buttresses the possibility of anticipation, but over the long term nourishes the probability of stagnation. The incompatibility of the possibilities it contains enables antinomic necessity to survive on the strength of anticipatory possibility. The achievement of anticipation substantially reduces the chances that possibilities contrary to it will be realized, but at the same time new possibilities are engendered, giving antinomic necessity a new physiognomy; thus, rather than disappearing, antinomic necessity is merely transformed.

Anticipation reveals its limitations through its strategy. As a possibility it must remain but partially realized, for while the revolution can modify contrary possibilities it cannot annul them or prevent the unforeseen emergence of others. The victorious anticipatory revolution would remain incomplete. Burdened with the problems handed down from the past, there were two possibilities open to postrevolutionary society: either it would succumb under the heel of a new necessity or, by virtue of the subjective factor, it would succeed in prolonging the dominance of the possible over the necessary. With the shift from the necessary to the possible, the subjective factor assumed a preeminent role which the possibility of anticipation merely perpetuated, quite independent of the theoretical and strategic capacities of the historical agents that embodied it. On the other hand, it was those agents that would decide whether postrevolutionary society would bow to a new necessity or explore new possibilities.

The objective preeminence of the subjective factor assumed the fraudulent form of the "personality cult" common, despite notable variations, to all known versions of Stalinism. From this perspective, the genesis—I emphasize, *the genesis* of Stalinism, and not its continued existence—is the spontaneous product of the conflict between the objective impossibility of an immediate transition to socialism, and the subjective rejection of the restoration of capitalist relations of production, as the state of productive forces required. Stalinism arose as an empirical attempt to find a practical solution to the vital problem that Leninism had left unresolved: what was there, if anything, of a positive nature in anticapitalist relations of production based on undeveloped productive forces?

By leaving a problem of this magnitude unresolved, Leninism lost its doctrinal unity: a plausible theory of anticipatory revolution and an effective strategy for carrying it through, but an incoherent, fragmentary, essentially ideological vision of postrevolutionary society. Heir to this incoherence, Stalinism proceeded solemnly to enshrine it, first abandoning and then banishing a theory forever inaccessible to it. Stalinism gave the name Marxism-Leninism to its aggressive empiricism; it is probably neither the one nor the other, but to both it owes the theoretical lacuna out of which it arose. In reality, what Stalinism developed was not the discoveries of Marxism or Leninism, but their limitations.

*   *   *

To sum up, the foregoing sketch of my theoretical project and the concepts on which it is based was undertaken to aid the reader in making his way through the following analysis of the Russian revolution and its contribution, if any, to the rise of Stalinism. An exhaustive analysis of the actual events in terms of each of the concepts proposed would be a laborious undertaking. Concepts may be changed, events remain the same. To avoid tiresome repetition, I have decided to center the analysis on a traditional concept, namely, the "character of the revolution," which, however, I interpret in a way that is not so traditional. It seemed to me that the category of "character" is the nodal point at which all the categories used in this analysis mesh.

Further, in view of the variety of meanings given to the term "the Russian revolution," it might not be irrelevant to specify that I shall be using that term to mean essentially the events that took place in Russia between February and October 1917.

Finally, because my access to the professional literature published in recent years has been extremely limited and uncertain, with few exceptions I have not referred to this literature. In the case of classic authors or those ranked as such, and Soviet documents, I studied them in Romanian translations which it did not seem useful to cite here.

I. METHODOLOGICAL QUESTIONS

Stalinism would have been impossible without the revolution of 1917. This is merely an affirmation of fact. It does not resolve the problem, but rather first poses it: is Stalinism merely the temporal successor of the revolution, or is it its natural consequence, and hence its historical continuation? The most attractive hypothesis is that certain defining traits of the revolution are, in variously modified forms, programmed in the genetic code of Stalinism. In exploring this hypothesis we shall be studying not the revolution itself but rather one of its principal traits in the prospect that it might have some bearing on the emergence of Stalinist society.

Stalinism did not follow directly upon the revolution; between the two there was an intermediate period, different from either, that lasted more than a decade. Did the society of that period serve as the filter, active or passive, through which the features of the revolution were passed on to Stalinism, or was it the sole historical source of Stalinism? Was Stalinism the indirect and belated product of the revolution, or was it the direct and immediate product of this intermediate society? Was it a phenomenon in which the traits of both the revolution and this intermediate society were blended together? Or did it represent pure historical discontinuity, a total break with all that came before it? Finally—and it seems that this is the most plausible hypothesis—continuity and discontinuity might be intermingled in Stalinism, and if so we must distinguish between that which is but a carry-over of the old, and that which is totally new.

The following pages will therefore not be dealing with the revolution, except insofar as it is a historical source of Stalinism. This approach can neither ignore events nor submerge itself in a mere recitation of them; it requires a critical rereading not only of the specialized literature, but also of real events. The first aim of this critical rereading is to determine just what was, precisely, the character of the revolution, and what was its nature.

The apologists of Stalinism and the paladins of anticommunism agree that Stalinism is the only legitimate heir of the revolution: such a rendering invests Stalinism with revolutionary legitimacy and gives a counterrevolutionary legitimacy to anticommunism. Over time, such views have become an enormous obstacle to the study of the revolution and its character, the primary effect of which has been to close the door on vital source material.

The question of sources is by no means a mere technical matter, or a matter of records and documents. It bears directly on one of Stalinism's organic traits: its antihistorical bedevilment. It admits the past only insofar as that past can be adduced to demonstrate the progress of mankind toward Stalinism. The future becomes illusory, drained of substance by an insuperable present, arrived before its time. Reduced to the role of justifying indefinitely a perpetually flawed present, history implicitly rids itself of any real future. Becoming is replaced by unending repetition. Eviscerated of its substance, history itself becomes atemporal. Perpetual movement gives way to perpetual immobility. Where a real future is barred to the imagination, a real past must be suppressed here and now. In Orwell's *1984*, reshaping the past to conform to the needs of the present became a special profession. The everlastingness of Stalinism is based on the suppression of history. It is not Stalinism that perdures; it is history that loses the quality of duration. The present becomes perpetual, and past and future, from being its conditions, become its sustaining forces. To repeat itself, the present must disavow its past and the future, which, if left to an autonomous existence, would signify its negation. A relationship, poetic in form, is established between past, present, and future: they "rhyme," they strike the same chord. History becomes a poetaster's work.

The ideologization of real history is the transmuted expression of an essential trait of Stalinist reality: its reduction to homeostatic existence. Stalinism is the institutionalized rejection of history; it in fact immobilized the dynamic potential in the historical transition from one social formation to another. The noisome quality of Stalinism derives less from the fact that it came into being than the fact that it continues to endure. Indeed, its perdurance is but the obverse of its organic incapacity for change. It can endure only by remaining inert. Stalinism's reworking of history is undertaken to make of it the ultimate reason, the *telos* of all that has gone before: thus the Russian revolution of 1917 broke out solely in order ultimately to triumph in Stalinist society. This transparent teleology of history is matched by the enigmatic opacity of its written records. Since 1927–28, studies of the revolution have all drawn sustenance from these murky archives. The one major exception is Trotsky's doing; he succeeded in taking a considerable portion of his own archives with him into exile. There, untrammelled by the burden of Stalin's constraints, he drew on those records to write his expansive *History of the Russian Revolution* at Prinkipo, between 1930 and 1932, about which Isaac Deutscher said in 1967: "Since no other history worthy of the name has up to now seen the light of day in the Soviet Union, Trotsky's work is still, in the fifth decade after the October revolution, its only complete history." Indeed, this work has served as my primary source in writing the present book [quotations are taken from the Max Eastman translation]. My choice has no political implications, and was guided not by Trotsky's vision, but by his documented material.

But, returning to the character of the Russian revolution, what above all mars the discussion of this theme is, I would say, excessive rigidity in defining and applying the standards used for assessing it. The first thing that results from this is a persistent confusion between the subjectively defined ends of the revolution, and the objective changes it effected. The consequence is a veritable mania for relating these changes not to the real society that they had, in fact, transformed, but to ends attributed to the revolution by its leaders. Thus a hierarchy of standards has spontaneously evolved, in violation of all logic: rather than the strategy of revolutionaries being judged in terms of the revolution's real achievements, the real achievements of the revolution came to be judged in terms of the strategy of the revolutionaries.

Lenin's frequent references to the character of the revolution cover a wide range of interpretations. For example, he refers variously to the bourgeois-democratic character of the revolution, to its bourgeois and its democratic character independently, its socialist or proletarian character, and even its dual character. In his draft platform for the proletarian party, written in April 1917, he said: "The chief feature distinguishing our revolution, its distinctive feature, calling most imperiously for profound reflection, is its *dualism of power.*" Later on in the same draft he wrote: "Another extremely important distinctive feature of the Russian revolution is that the Petrograd Soviet *voluntarily* handed state power over to the bourgeoisie and its provisional government." On other occasions Lenin also speaks of the international European character of the revolution, of "revolution in the broad sense" and "revolution in the strict sense," or political revolution as an alternative to socialist revolution. "The Russian political revolution will be the prologue of the European socialist revolution." Fernando Claudin observes: "[Lenin] too thought that the destiny of the Russian revolution depended on its quality of being a prologue."

This abundance of phrases is not due solely to the complexity of the phenomenon they are meant to describe; the very meaning of the concept "character of the revolution" may well be doubtful. The confusion noted earlier between strategic ends and practical consequences is compounded by a diachronic approach, often strained beyond its capacity. The continuity of the revolution runs the risk of being wasted in discontinuity. The distinctions drawn between the various "characters" of the revolution seem to distinguish between different stages, and even between different revolutions. Thus, for example, Hélène Carrère d'Encausse refers to "three revolutions with divergent ends: a peasant revolution, a workers' revolution, and a national revolution." Three different criteria—ends, class content, and level (political, as regards the national aspect)—are combined to designate, in a manner that must inevitably be incoherent, three characters which in their turn break down the Russian revolution into three distinct revolutions.

Charles Bettelheim takes a different approach. Proceeding from the Leninist idea of the dual nature of the revolution, this French Marxist regards the latter as "both a proletarian revolution and a democratic, essentially peasant, revolution. The proletarian revolution is paralleled by the *leading* role played by the proletariat in this party. The democratic revolution is paralleled by the determining role played by the peasantry.'' Thus the analysis steps imperceptibly from a revolution with a dual character to two distinct revolutions. He ascribes an essentially political character, i.e., democratic, to the revolution, defined exclusively by its social content, i.e., the peasant class. And to the revolution defined by its social and political content together, i.e., the proletariat and the party, he ascribes an exclusively social character, i.e., proletarian. The character of the revolution seems totally independent of its content. But if the revolution is to have one content or the other, the different classes cannot fulfill the same role; their roles must differ—a leading role in one case, a determining role in the other. It is not sufficiently clear why the leading class should not also be the determining class, or vice versa.

Not all Marxists share the view that the character of the revolution derives from the respective roles played by the different classes. For example, as regards the bourgeois revolution in Western Europe, Isaac Deutscher notes that ''capitalists, entrepreneurs, merchants, and bankers were not conspicuous among the leaders of the Puritans or the Ironsides, in the Jacobin Club or at the head of the crowds that stormed the Bastille and invaded the Tuilleries; rather the lower middle classes, the urban poor, the plebians, and the *sans culottes* made up the big insurgent batallions.''

This disjunction between the social forces that effectively make the revolution and those that reap its fruits is quite applicable to the Russian revolution, as is evident in its most decisive moments, i.e., the two insurrections. Between these two moments the social and political basis of the coalition between the bourgeoisie and the feudal class collapsed under the blows of the peasant movement. Still, the revolution cannot be defined as a peasant revolution because it did not make the peasantry into the dominant class. Nor can it be defined as a bourgeois revolution because all the major social movements of which it was a synthesis were directed against the bourgeoisie. Finally, it cannot be defined as a socialist revolution because it did not establish socialism, either immediately or over the long term.

Although the bourgeoisie formally held state power during the revolution, that did not automatically make it a bourgeois revolution. First, this power was only partial, because it was shared with the soviet (dual power); and second, it was ineffective because it was for all practical purposes disregarded by the masses. The bourgeoisie failed in its attempt to subordinate the revolution to its own interests, and in the end was itself eliminated by it so as to abolish the property of the nobility and end Russia's participation in the imperialist war.

It is not the purpose here to cast doubt on the received interpretation of the 1917 revolution as at once worker and peasant, national and international, political and social, etc. Nevertheless, one might venture to suggest that not every feature of a revolution must necessarily represent one of its characters. An informative classification of all these features would need appropriate criteria. Applied to the Russian revolution such a classification might employ the following categories:

(a) *character*—comprising the deepest and most enduring changes effected by the revolution and so expressing the objective historical functions it performed to fulfill the necessity that produced it.

(b) *content*—indicating the dynamic intermeshing between the course of the revolution on the one hand and the participation of diverse social forces on the other.

(c) *level*—denoting the social locus where the various phases of the revolution are played out with the most energy and effectiveness.

(d) *dimension*—expressing the geopolitical compass of the revolution, defined by the dual, external and internal, aspects of the necessity that gave it birth.

(e) *nature*—synthesizing the most productive links between the preceding categories at a high level of generalization. Each of these five categories includes a range of defining attributes; i.e.,

Category   Attributes

Category	Attributes
Character	anti-autocratic, anti-imperialist, antifeudal, anticapitalist
Content	proletariat, peasantry, bourgeoisie, feudal nobility, autocracy, army, Bolshevik party
Level	social, economic, political
Dimension	national, international
Nature	strategic, anticipatory, antinomic.

A few more details may be useful for the sake of further clarification.

(a) The list is not exhaustive; it contains only those attributes that can inform our problem. Thus, for example, "dimension" is not only national or international, but can also be worldwide, European, regional or even local (e.g., the crucial position of the capital of Petrograd in the revolution); the class "content" does not distinguish between the bourgeoisie and the petty bourgeoisie, although this distinction was at certain moments quite important; the basic criterion for including an attribute in our list was whether it played a role in shaping the irreversible consequences of the revolution.

(b) The heterogenous composition of class "content" is evident, inasmuch as it lumps together four totally distinct categories of social forces; the social classes had three types of organization: state, military, and political, as their vehicles. But this "taxonomic" heterogeneity is merely a reflection of the real situation: the outcome of the crucial episodes of the revolution, and especially the two insurrections, was decided by social forces that were not social classes. In February the decisive role was played by the army, in October by the Bolshevik Party. The epicenter of the diffuse social conflict had shifted to a point beyond the strictly drawn limits of class structure.

This approach is clearly unacceptable to traditional Marxism, for which every social force is in the last instance but the expression of class interests. Here, the theoretical reflection of reality is infinitely more linear than reality itself. Let us take the February 1917 insurrection as an example. The decisive role in the overthrow of the autocracy was played by the army. On the plane of direct action, the conflict did not oppose two classes, but two social forces whose relations were being veritably turned upside down. The prime instrument of autocratic rule became the prime instrument of its abolishment. It is not easy to descry the direct projection of relations of class in these relations between institutions: an army of peasants undertakes a historical task toward the which the civilian peasantry remains totally passive. It was not the bourgeoisie, but the peasants in uniform, who overthrew the autocracy; it was not the peasantry but the bourgeoisie that profited thereby, and indeed, its first impulse was to save this institution on the ruins of which its own power rested. The inconsistency displayed by the bourgeoisie was not merely in its behavior, but was rather a product of its antinomic interests. The Russian bourgeoisie was pursuing the unrealizable historical goal of bringing an anachronistic society into the modern era. The proletariat alone had a solid anti-autocratic interest and, moreover, a concept of it. On the other hand, the army's behavior certainly cannot be attributed to the proletariat's influence. A similar phenomenon occurred in the 17th century in England when the army, the principal support of Parliament, itself became an effectively autonomous social force. Class struggle may be the principal, but it is not the only driving force of history, neither constantly nor directly determining its flow.

These functional shiftings were due to structural peculiarities that were much more accentuated in Russia than elsewhere. The relative lack of structure to the conflict, and thus to relations between the classes, was due to the lack of structure within the social classes themselves. They were not clearly demarcated; their basic interests, which should have given each of them an internal cohesion, sometimes converged and sometimes diverged reciprocally, so that consciousness of these interests necessarily remained vague and blurred. The result was an incoherence of action, where at certain moments one class might be substituted by another or even by a social force (not a social class) that happened to be more cohesive.

As they become consolidated, major institutions tend to shake off the determining class influences that had prompted their birth. Church and monarchy, the army and police, often themselves end up subjugating the classes of which they had originally been the instrument. These institutions then become social forces in their own right, enjoying a broad range of autonomy, and carrying considerable weight within the totality of social relations. Class relations are not only filtered, they are also modified and even held in leash by the intervention of these social forces. The interplay between class relations and the social institutions supposed to serve as their expression will range from one of concordance to separation, subordination and even substitution. In Russia, the catastrophic organization of class relations had marked this interplay profoundly. While serving as the guarantor of the privileges of the possessing classes, the autocracy set itself above them, assuming sovereign control over two functions: that of social arbiter, and that of supreme commander of the military forces. With the professional armed forces as its sole instrument, the autocracy would respond to the spontaneous violence of periodic peasant revolts with an organized violence of its own to restore former class relations in full. Thanks to this mechanism of social control, it became the historical habit of the privileged classes to protest against the abuses of the autocracy while at the same time encharging itself (especially in times of alert) with the task of defending the system that safeguarded their property. Hence the double game they played in February 1917, sacrificing a Tsar to save the monarchy.

Class struggle is therefore the principal but not the sole driving force of history, a point amply demonstrated not only by the Russian revolution, but also by other events of commensurate scale from the Crusades to the events of May 1968 in France or the overthrow of the Shah in Iran.

This mobility within the hierarchy of social forces played an especially important role in the Russian revolution: in October 1917, for instance, a political party, extremely capable, but in the minority, became the functional surrogate of a heroic but immature working class. After ten years of shifting fortunes, this role of substitution would finally stabilize in a social organization in which a social force, not itself a social class, assumed the role of dominant class.

The heterogeneity of the category "content" in our conception thus does no more than reflect the actual complexity of the social relations that gave form to a revolution that went far beyond the sphere, narrowly defined, of relations between social classes.

(c) The category "character" comprises four attributes, alike in their negativity but differing in their lastingness. Each of these in turn assumed a predominant and hence determining role in one or another of the diverse phases of the revolution. The one exception is the revolution's anti-imperialist character, which, being oriented to processes taking place beyond the country's borders, remained important throughout. In February the revolution was invested with all these characters simultaneously, although it was defined by its anti-autocratic character, which, however, having achieved its purpose, died away. With the autocracy gone, feudalism, of course, lost its political custodian, but did not with that disappear as an economic and social phenomenon. At this point the revolution experienced the first cleavage between its political level and its economic and social levels. But even at the political plane, the task of protecting feudalism shifted from the deposed autocracy to the shoulders of the bourgeoisie, now vaunting the panoply of state power. This explains why in October the revolution was unable to realize its antifeudal character, while its antibourgeois character was effectively fulfilled. Unlike the feudal nobility, which disappeared as a social class, the bourgeoisie lost its political power but retained its property and hence the basis for its continued social existence. At this point the revolution produced the second cleavage between its political and its economic and social levels, and as a consequence its dominant character became antibourgeois, not anticapitalist.

In our conception, the category "character" excludes the "palace revolution" planned in February, but never realized, by some of the bureaucratic aristocracy, nor does it include the proletarian and socialist characters, inasmuch as they too remained unrealized.

Our five categories, like the diverse attributes defining them, have a number of points of articulation. Thus the antifeudal character of the revolution is articulated with a content dominated by the peasantry, which accomplished its revolutionary task on the economic and social planes but did not move on to the political plane. Until October, the peasant movement had been steadily undermining the property foundations of the feudal order without attacking directly the power of the government defending it and without undertaking to establish its own power.

The conception outlined in the foregoing represents primarily a set of analytical tools. In the following I shall be drawing selectively upon them as the needs of my topic, which is not the Russian revolution but the historical paths linking it to Stalinism, may require.

II. THE ANTIFEUDAL CHARACTER OF THE REVOLUTION

Hypotheses

In the discussion of the antifeudal character of the revolution I shall be examining a number of hypotheses, namely:

(1) The most profound of the direct socioeconomic effects of the Russian revolution was the abolition of feudalism;

(2) One secondary effect of the antifeudal movement was the erosion of the power of the bourgeoisie entrusted with the defense of feudalism;

(3) This secondary effect was the main premise of the October insurrection and the establishment of the new power;

(4) The Bolshevik party, which had neither determined, inspired, organized, nor led this movement, was, however, the only one to foresee, support, and in the end bring it to its fulfillment, thereby transforming a peasant war against feudalism into a proletarian victory over the bourgeoisie;

(5) The price of this transformation was that peasant demands remained but partially fulfilled, as evidenced by the ambiguous structure imposed upon postfeudal agrarian property;

(6) The concordance between Bolshevik strategy and the spontaneous peasant movement came to an end with the land decree promulgated by the insurrectionary power;

(7) Agrarian property was left in a suspended state, obstructing the succession of the old, now abolished, feudal order by a well defined and thus viable postfeudal order. In this respect, the antifeudal character of the revolution remained only partially fulfilled;

(8) This fact, together with the ambiguous agrarian property relations, and differences in orientation between the peasantry, which was spontaneously capitalist, and the Bolshevik party, which was consciously anticapitalist—differences which tended toward opposition—were conditions that altogether broadly favored the emergence of Stalinism.

Definition

The historical necessity that the Russian revolution of 1917 was called upon to fulfill was that of industrialization, or, more precisely, the elimination of the obstacles barring its way. Isaac Deutscher identified these obstacles as "the heavy residuum of feudalism, the underdevelopment and weakness of the bourgeoisie, the rigidity of the autocracy, the archaic system of government and, last but not least, Russia's economic dependence on foreign capital." To simplify, we can say that the principal obstacles to the industrialization of Russia were imperialism, feudalism, and the national bourgeoisie. In proportion as it succeeded in eliminating any one of these obstacles, the revolution may be said to have assumed that character. A character is predominant as long as social conflict is concentrated on the obstacle that the character is bent on eliminating.

To say that the Russian revolution had an antifeudal character is to say that it effectively fulfilled the historical mission of abolishing feudal property, feudal social relations of production, and the feudal nobility as a social class.

This character moved into the forefront of the revolution with the transformation of local peasant revolts into a veritable peasant war up and down the country. The antifeudal character was the expression of the most profound changes wrought in Russian society by the revolution between February and October 1917. The weight of these events was underscored by Lenin, who in September 1917 wrote: "In the face of a fact of such scope as the peasant uprisings, all other political symptoms, even if they should be in opposition to this ripening of the general crisis of the nation, would be utterly unimportant."

Implications of this definition

In Western Europe the abolition of feudalism had been necessary to the industrializing mission of the bourgeoisie; for this reason, the revolutions there were bourgeois in character. In Russia, neither the liquidation of feudalism nor industrialization were the work of the bourgeoisie which, on the contrary, obstructed both. The abolition of feudalism by the peasants—who to accomplish this task were obliged to crush the resistance of the bourgeoisie—did not produce a bourgeois type of society. Despite frequent assertions to the contrary, therefore, the Russian revolution was not a bourgeois revolution.

The revolution destroyed the autocracy, abolished feudalism, overthrew the political power of the bourgeoisie, and established a decidedly antibourgeois power; these were the changes wrought by the revolution in Russian society. And none of these changes, however real they were, had anything to do with socialism.

The historical decisions of the new regime consecrated the victory of the two popular movements: the one against the imperialist war, the other against feudalism. Likewise, none of these decisions was socialist in character.

Despite frequent claims to the contrary, the Russian revolution was not a socialist revolution.

Consequently, Stalinism was not a deformation of the socialist society created by the revolution, as Trotsky's followers would often have it. In terms of the historical functions that it actually fulfilled, the revolution that stood at the beginnings of Stalinism was not socialist, and Stalinism is even less so.

Russian feudalism

The virtues and limitations of the movement that gave the 1917 revolution its antifeudal character cannot be viewed in isolation from the grand tradition of peasant uprisings in Russia, nor on that account from the singularities of Russian feudalism which, indeed, have occupied generations of historians. These singularities were essentially two: its belated birth, and its lack of autonomy—and so its sluggish inertia. The social relations Russian feudalism represented in 1917 had been shaped by Tsar Alexander II's emancipation of the serfs in 1861 after Russia's defeat in the Crimean War. The tremendous belatedness of this act, which came four centuries after its English counterpart, was matched only by the grim restraint with which it was effected. The landlords themselves were entrusted with the redistribution of the seigneurial lands put up for sale. Thus the peasants had been generously granted the right to purchase the most barren of all lands for fabulous sums to be paid off in forty-nine years, during which time they were to remain for all practical purposes bound to the village. Other vital resources—pasturage, forests, etc.—remained at the disposal of the large landowners. Modest though it may have been, the emancipation created rumblings among the rural nobility. In the half century that passed down to the revolution, the gravity of the situation was magnified further by two trends: overpopulation, and the spread of market relations which clashed with the low productivity of the still primitive level of rural technology.

Some authors (e.g. Jenkins) are of the opinion that in this period in Russia a market economy was combined with a subsistence agriculture having rentier relations as its principal mechanism. According to James Scott, this type of economy is an association between subsistence and disaster. The crux of such an association, he continues, was "that level of income below which nothing is saved." This pendulation between subsistence and disaster was perpetuated in Russia by feudalism but did not disappear with it: after October 1917, it was to show up again in the "procurement crisis." This balancing act at the brink of famine, which postrevolutionary Russia was never able to overcome, played a crucial role in the advent of Stalinism.

By the turn of the century the autocracy had become an anachronism, agrarian structures were outmoded, and capitalism was timidly feeling its way; it had become clear that Russian society was incapable of integrating all of these facets, compounded by imperialist affinities, into a viable system. And it was this general incapacity that led to the first Russian revolution of 1905.

The peasant revolts of 1905 acquired an unprecedented scope. After having crushed them, the autocracy redoubled its repression with a whole series of new reforms encouraging a capitalist type of development that but added fuel to the process of differentiation taking place amongst the peasantry. Incapable even of subsisting under these conditions, those who lost out in the process began to leave the villages. The migration swelled the ranks of the urban proletariat with a mass of backward elements, while at the same time consolidating the links between the city and the countryside. The countryside was plunged into a veritable turmoil of conflicting tendencies, becoming a theater of subdued conflict marked by intermittent outbursts of violence. The old village communities opposed the individual peasants, poor peasants opposed the rich peasants, all these together were opposed to the large property owners and finally the vast majority of the rural population was opposed to the autocratic bureaucracy. "All this," wrote Trotsky "created an intolerable confusion in agrarian relations to which partial legislative measures were of no avail."

Land distribution remained severely disproportionate at its two extremes: at the time, 30,000 noble families possessed the same amount of land area as 10 million peasant families. The minuscule size of peasant plots made any significant growth in productivity impossible. "The backwardness of prerevolutionary Russia," observes Ernest Mandel, "derived especially from the rural economy which had been carved up into 25 million peasant enterprises."

Such were, in their broad contours, the principal coordinates of Russian feudalism on the eve of the 1917 revolution, shaping its relations not only with the peasantry, but also with the autocracy, the bourgeoisie, and the proletariat.

The feudal nobility and the autocracy

More than anywhere else, feudal relations of production in Russia were based on the direct exercise of noneconomic constraint. But the dispersion of feudal property was compounded by the centralization of the principal instrument of this constraint, namely the army, which was wholly under the control of the autocracy. Peasant revolts took place with almost measured regularity and, indeed, became a cog in the normal functioning of society. Given these circumstances, the autocracy, with its monopoly over the military, became the regulator, by means of repression, of the dominant social relations. During the frequent outbursts of violent clashes, these relations were not defended by the feudal class, which benefited from them, but by the autocracy, which had the means to do so.

The economic cost of these means increased as their social importance grew, reaching fantastic levels. The autocracy built up a vast bureaucratic apparatus which effectively split the feudal nobility into a land-owning nobility and a court nobility, with interests that did not always coincide. To fulfill its role of defender of the status quo, the autocracy cut out for itself a broad autonomy vis-à-vis the social relations of which it should have been the expression. Russian feudal society was thus dominated not by the feudal class, but by a military-political institution with a total monopoly of state power. This reversal of relations of determination between socioeconomic structures, on the one hand, and political and military structures on the other, would later be reflected, albeit in different forms, in the power structure established in October 1917 and by Stalinism later on.

The autocracy permitted the feudal nobility to retain its economic privileges, but prohibited it the direct exercise of authority in public life. Their interests were identical yet divergent at one and the same time. The inevitable clashes, generally subdued, broke out into the open in February 1917, almost one hundred years after the first eruption (the Decembrists' conspiracy) in 1825. The autocracy collapsed under the explosive impact that saw the coalescence of popular exasperation, its own anachronistic existence, the progressive debilitation of those very classes who should have been its support and whom it had itself cultivated, and finally Russia's incorporation, fraught with contradictions, into the world imperialist system. Though itself under the imperialist yoke of the advanced countries, autocratic Russia sought to impose at any price its own authority on countries even more backward or weaker than itself. Lacking the economic premises, this imperialism of underdevelopment had military resources alone at its command. The beginning of the 20th century found Russia prostrate, sapped by wars that had been as hapless as they were frequent. The institution that had suffered most, of course, was the army. Bled dry by losses of monumental proportions, demoralized by a chain of defeats, it was obliged to parcel out its forces between foreign wars and internal wars, each fuelling the other. With the army dissipated and adrift, the autocracy's monopoly over the military was no longer anything other than an illusion, and the autocracy, deprived of its defenses, became the first target of popular discontent. Under the blows of the revolution, this rotten system of surrogate authority fell like a row of dominoes: the autocracy could not survive the collapse of the army, the feudal nobility the collapse of the autocracy, nor the bourgeoisie the collapse of the feudal nobility. The strict and perennial separation between the exercise of the rights of property and the application of extra-economic constraints had made the feudal nobility deeply dependent on the autocracy. This class, and later the bourgeoisie, had through force of historical habit become infinitely better bred to obedience than to autonomy, to passivity rather than to initiative, the product of the peculiar bent of Russian culture to despairing resignation, called the "Slavic soul." One result of this perennial inertia was the utterly stupefying inability of the possessing classes to translate the advantageous economic odds in 1917 into political cash, and it was this incapacity that was later to be a crucial factor in determining the course of the revolution and, later on, its epilogue.

The feudal nobility and the bourgeoisie

In modern societies the bourgeoisie had emerged by destroying feudal social relations, thereby touching off an unprecedented expansion in productive forces.

In the course of carrying out this dual "modernizing" mission the bourgeoisie as a class gradually became committed to the status quo, making the safeguarding of its dominant position in society a condition for every further step forward. The Russian bourgeoisie, born much later, and then under the double yoke of imperialism and autocracy, diverged from this pattern: without having even accomplished its modernizing mission it had already become a reactionary class. Thus it was not on this real bourgeoisie that the Petrograd Soviet undertook to confer power in 1917, but on its abstraction. Conversely, it was not this abstraction, but the real bourgeoisie which, befuddled by reaction, would play a decisive role in transforming a potential bourgeois revolution into what in fact it became an anti-imperialist, antifeudal, and antibourgeois revolution. To the extent that it had a hand in the development of the national industry, the bourgeoisie had perforce to be antifeudal and anti-imperialist. But insofar as it benefited directly from its subservience to imperialism and its cooperation with the feudal nobility, the bourgeoisie was inclined to be pro-imperialist and profeudal.

The objective ambiguity in the interests of the bourgeoisie created a subjective ambiguity in agrarian policy. All the parties participating in the provisional government had reform programs for agriculture, yet the government adopted no reform whatsoever, and consistently opposed the confiscation of the large estates by the peasantry. Thus the bourgeoisie in power, legitimated by its would-be antifeudalism, in actual fact became the defender of the feudal nobility against the peasantry.

So long as the peasants maintained, events to the contrary, their belief in this legitimacy, they accorded their suffrage en masse to the parties that backed the provisional government, in particular, the Social Revolutionaries (SRs). But as the peasants began to lose patience and set about confiscating the lands of the nobility, the profeudal inclinations of the bourgeoisie assumed the character of a definite strategic option. Whereas the ties with the peasantry had in the main been politically motivated, solidarity with the aristocracy was rooted basically in a broad community of economic interests. The four millions in bank loans that had been advanced to the large estate owners was of minor importance compared to the threat the abolishment of feudal property posed to private property in general, and especially private ownership of the means of production. Based on very fundamental considerations, this strategic decision put the bourgeoisie on a political course at cross-purposes with its historical mission, and placed its shaky regime at the mercy of the natural forces of the revolution. Once it had opted for this inflexible and hapless path, the days of the Russian bourgeoisie were numbered, and no more than eight months separated its assumption of power from its utter and everlasting ruin.

To conduct its war against feudalism, the peasantry had to smash the power defending it. This indirectly antibourgeois aspect of the peasant movement became direct and explicit in the October insurrection, and a social movement, antifeudal in character, culminated therefore in the establishment of a political regime that was antibourgeois.

The peasant movement and the proletariat

The countryside remained virtually a passive witness to the fall of the autocracy. The Petrograd proletariat, on the other hand, played a crucial role in transforming the "palace revolution" into a revolt against the autocracy, thus destroying the principal pillar of the feudal nobility's support. In the two months that followed, the peasantry did nothing to translate the collapse of the autocracy into the end of feudalism as well. On the other hand, the proletariat, much more cohesive than the peasantry, continued its struggle and created a social and political environment without which the antifeudal movement would have found it difficult to acquire the momentum and breadth it did.

The antifeudal character of the revolution posed no problems for the proletariat. First, there was no interest, real or imagined, that could have tempered its elementary hostility to feudalism. Second, every blow aimed at the authority of the provisional government, which it ceaselessly assailed, could only be to its advantage. Third, for obvious reasons, its actions could not normally be focused as directly on the feudal nobility as could those of the peasantry. Concentrated in a few industrial centers, with a heterogeneous composition made worse by the war, and a long way still to go toward social and political maturity, the Russian proletariat was unable to play either a leading or even a determining role in the antifeudal movement, the most deepgoing of the revolution. Nevertheless it did serve as an energizing force, which fanned out as the struggle against the feudal nobility approached its climax.

The peasant movement against the feudal nobility and the proletarian movement against the bourgeoisie perforce converged in their common revolutionary project at the same time as they closed ranks in the general movement against the imperialist war, thus effectively cementing a worker–peasant alliance. The longer-term convergence of interests, however, had to await its *a posteriori* proof in the aftermath of the October insurrection.

The peasant movement and the Bolshevik party

Of the social factors that faced off in the revolution, the Bolshevik party was the only one with a strategy based on a sound analysis, while the peasant movement was the furthest from possessing such an instrument. Yet it was not the Bolshevik party but the peasant movement that had overturned the structures of Russian society from top to bottom. Leninist strategy counted on (without making it an absolute) the possibility of a peasant revolt that would be countered by the combined forces of the bourgeoisie, the petty bourgeoisie and the feudal nobility. Driven by its wrath alone, the peasantry spontaneously followed Bolshevik strategy without, however, knowing anything of it. Long impregnable to the influence of the party, the peasantry nevertheless behaved as if it were acting under its leadership. Effectively, however, the appearance of leadership was created by the felicitous meeting of paths between an anticipatory strategy and a social movement that gave the truth to that strategy without itself being alive to the fact. The Bolshevik party gave its unconditional support to the revolutionary peasant movement for most of the period. It was the only party to do so, but in view of its meager means, this support was marked out much more by its constancy than by its effectiveness. The peasantry—the social category least capable of acting autonomously—did so nonetheless, practically without so much as a thought to the SRs, who offered it slogans in return for passivity, or to the Bolsheviks, who offered it a strategy in return for its readiness to join battle. This accord in mutual detachment is by no means a mere abstraction. The Bolshevik party gave the actions of the peasantry a political expression which the peasantry itself was unable to achieve down to the very end. In turn, in its spontaneity the peasantry not only confirmed Bolshevik strategy, it also gave it its substance, transforming it from a prophetic exercise into a fervid historical reality. In vacating its antifeudal interests, the bourgeoisie effectively abandoned the peasantry—to Bolshevik strategy in the first instance, and ultimately to their effective leadership. Having neither instigated nor led the revolutionary peasant movement against the feudal nobility, the Bolshevik party was able, through its strategy and the collapse of the movement's adversaries, to steer it toward its epilogue.

The antifeudal movement of the peasantry

The peasant movement was slow to pick up momentum, but once fully in motion it swiftly spread, assuming increasingly radical forms as it did so. From a peaceable refusal to pay land rents, by summer it had grown into a generalized state of violence. There were more rural conflicts in the seven weeks preceding the October insurrection than during the entire previous six months. "In reality," wrote Trotsky, "the Russian muzhik was completing a business entered upon many centuries before the Bolsheviks appeared in the world. He was fulfilling his progressive historic task with the only means at his disposal. With revolutionary barbarism he was wiping out the barbarism of the middle ages."

Thus the antifeudal movement was transformed into a peasant war and the conflict, initially diffuse, came to center on a dominant dichotomy, which, however, was apparent rather than real: although the peasantry struck its blows at the landowners, it was the bourgeoisie that mounted the principal resistance to it. There were occasional clashes among the peasants over the parcelling out of the estates of the nobility, and attacks on rich peasants, but these incidents remained marginal; the movement was able to direct its essential forces against the feudal lords. Thus by virtue of its steadfastness of direction, its scale, and its geographical synchronicity, it was the peasant movement which in the end gave the Russian revolution its predominantly antifeudal character. Not only did this character dominate the countryside, its reverberations convulsed the army, reduced the authority of the provisional government to an empty fiction, and set the stage for the October insurrection. The crucial role of the antifeudal movement was mirrored in events themselves: the peasant war had for all practical purposes expunged feudal property from the face of the earth, independently of the October insurrection, but without the peasant war it is highly unlikely that the October insurrection would have been able to smash the power of the bourgeoisie. In a sense the October insurrection was the principal political consequence of an apolitical movement led by the Russian peasantry against the feudal nobility. The possibility of the insurrection, and its triumph, rested not simply with the movement, but with the apolitical nature of that movement.

All political forces did their utmost to divert this movement from the antifeudal course it had clearly taken—with one exception, the Bolshevik party, which had long lacked effective ties with the countryside. Circumstances had gotten out of control, and everything was possible, from the best to the worst. "We must be prepared for the possibility of seeing a peasantry united with the bourgeoisie," declared Lenin in April just after his return, to the great consternation of the old Bolsheviks. Trotsky commented: "While admitting the possibility that the peasantry, as a caste, might act as a revolutionary factor, in April Lenin nonetheless prepared for the worst, namely a resistant bloc consisting of noble property owners, the bourgeoisie, and broad layers of the peasantry." This risk was enhanced by the apolitical nature of the peasant movement, manifested in its dismissal of the soviets and its partiality toward the SRs, who supported the profeudal policy of the provisional government.

Unlike the workers and soldiers, the peasants were not drawn to the soviets, preferring instead their former communal organizations. Many historians of the Russian revolution maintain that the antifeudal movement had only imposed new functions on the old *obshchina*, on which feudal and autocratic domination in the countryside had based itself over the centuries. "Indeed," wrote Bettelheim, "between February and October 1917 the actions of the peasant masses almost invariably took place independently of the Soviets." Another author, Oskar Anweiler, underscores the peasants' position with regard to the provisional government's decision to convene the first All-Russian Congress of Soviets of Peasant Deputies to provide "a counterweight to the radicalization of the city soviets" (Bettelheim). Even the few rural soviets that did exist at this date (May 1917) were opposed to participation in this congress. The congress convened nevertheless with 1,100 delegates (more than half of whom declared themselves SRs, compared with 14 Bolsheviks; this, however, did not prevent Lenin from speaking)—an institution attuned to peasant interests, to which the peasants had not so much as given a thought. The peasant movement's aloofness to the soviet is brought out graphically by the fact that the Second Congress, which ratified the land decree, convened workers' and soldiers' soviets only; the peasant soviets were absent.

The apoliticism of the peasant movement showed up as well in the utter discordance between the peasants' electoral behavior and their practical actions. All the while the Socialist Revolutionary agrarian policy met with their increasingly firm opposition, the peasants continued to give the SRs their vote. Thus a diffuse conflict produced correspondingly confused effects: the SRs retained their votes in the countryside, but saw their influence wane. The peasants believed they were attacking the feudal nobility but not the bourgeoisie, while the bourgeoisie attacked the peasantry but not the feudal nobility. The ambiguity of the conflict was heightened by an ambiguity of interests. The discordance in behavior reflected an absence of policy in the case of the peasantry, while in the case of the bourgeoisie and the SRs it was an actual policy. The government and the parties backing it inundated the countryside with a deluge of agrarian programs and institutions centering on the expropriation of seigneurial lands, which they continued in practice to defend. For their part, the peasants continued destroying that property while maintaining a show of political fidelity to its defenders. The political contact between the two classes gradually lost all relation to their actual activity. This dual discordancy was in fact the reflection of both the relative lack of structure to the social conflict and the internal ambiguity of the bourgeoisie and the peasantry whose relations were inverted. The bourgeoisie was able to pursue its aim only by feigning another aim; the peasants could pursue theirs only by effectively pursuing another; the peasantry could abolish the feudal nobility—which was indeed its aim—only by smashing the power of the bourgeoisie, which in fact was not its aim. The decisive class struggles were played out through a series of substitutions, and indeed were to end in the same way. "History," commented Trotsky, "knows how to make use of accidents." The peasantry believed it was eliminating the nobility, when all the while it was smashing the bourgeoisie without being aware that it was doing so. The victory of the peasantry first acquired concrete substance in the Bolshevik seizure of power. This device whereby an actual result comes to be substituted for the goal originally pursued was the same process that later would substitute Stalinism for socialism.

Finally, the supreme manifestation of the apoliticism of the peasant movement was its utter indifference to the positive consequences of its negative action. By destroying the old order, the movement created the objective necessity of an alternative order, yet subjectively it had no idea what order this was to be. This inability to translate historical negation into affirmation was responsible for the discordance between the significance of the movement and the significance of its victory. Apoliticism makes no distinctions and the peasantry was as indifferent to the political order that had defended the feudal nobility as it would later be to that which replaced it. It was therefore quite normal that it should play the key role in smashing the old order, but vacate that role in the establishment of the new.

Connections between the antifeudal and the antibourgeois characters of the revolution

If the actions of the peasant movement were apolitical, the consequences of these actions were not. The principal political consequences of this apolitical movement were the actual hostility to it provoked within the provisional government and its supporting parties, its spontaneous accord with Bolshevik strategy and tactics, and finally its general convergence with the revolutionary movements of workers and soldiers. This discordance between action and consequences created a historical space favorable to a political movement directed against the political shield of the feudal nobility, namely the bourgeoisie. Although it did not rule out other possibilities, Bolshevik strategy had banked first and foremost on the transformation of peasant revolt into a peasant war. Only with such an escalation of violence would it be possible to reduce the formlessness of the social conflict and coax it into its most productive form, namely that of two antagonistic forces pitted against one another. Such a course would not have eliminated the original formlessness of the conflict, but it would have given it a transitory form in which the forces squaring off would quickly develop into a direct confrontation between peasantry, feudal nobility and the bourgeoisie—i.e., three factors bringing the conflict to an issue favorable to a fourth factor, namely the Bolshevik party.

Once again substitution of social factors was matched by a substitution of ends. Because of its apoliticism, the peasant insurrection was able to achieve its final goal only by means of another insurrection, pursuing another end. Thus the end of the first insurrection became the means of the second. Yet it was the exploits in the first insurrection which alone made the second one possible. One of the novelties of the Russian revolution in fact lies in this intersection of the two insurrections which enabled the revolution's antifeudal character to be fully realized in its antibourgeois character.

On the other hand, the conditioning of the anticapitalist character of the revolution by its antifeudal character would, after October, become the conditioning of a society prepared to "storm the heavens" by a peasant mass engaged merely in an onslaught on the land.

Other connections

To recapitulate, the principal bearer of the antifeudal character of the revolution, i.e., the peasant movement, interacted with the other features of the revolution in the following manner:

As regards *content*, it objectively converged in its actions with the proletariat, the soldiers, and the Bolshevik party, against the nobility and the bourgeoisie.

As regards its *level*, it destroyed the property of the nobility and hence the class that benefited from that property without giving thought to the state power protecting it; in other words, the peasant movement acted at the social and economic levels but not at the political level.

As regards its other characters, the anti-autocratic character of the revolution was not directly articulated with its antifeudal character; the link that did exist was indirect, owing to the interdependence between the autocracy and the feudal nobility. For this reason, the antifeudal character did not become predominant directly following the fall of the autocracy, but only several months afterward. On the other hand, the predominance of the antifeudal character reached its peak only to yield that position to the antibourgeois character of the revolution.

Whether it did so deliberately or not, the antifeudal movement destroyed structures on which imperialist domination had been based, thereby establishing the principal articulation between the antifeudal character and the anti-imperialist character of the revolution.

As regards the *nature* of the revolution, the antifeudal character of the revolution was linked to each of the traits forming this category. Intermingling with the other characters, it gave the revolution its contradictory quality; by destroying one order without preparing the way for an alternative one, it participated in its negativity; it contributed to the incomplete nature of the revolution by its inability to provide the necessary political complement to the economic and social transformations that had taken place; its objective convergence with Lenin's predictions invested it implicitly with strategic force; finally, as an indispensable condition enabling the antibourgeois character to come to predominate, it constituted an important ingredient in the anticipatory nature of the revolution.

The antifeudal movement and the October insurrection

The connection between the antifeudal and the antibourgeois characters of the revolution was the pivotal point of the revolution. The two characters were not of equal status. The first became predominant largely independently of the latter, while the latter became predominant only by virtue of the former having been achieved, and of its limitations. This is presumably what Trotsky had in mind when he said that the bedrock of the revolution was the agrarian question.

The violent abolition of feudal property by peasant revolts is common to all great antifeudal revolutions; these revolts are rooted in historical necessity. But if anticapitalist social forces harness them to their advantage, this partakes of the possible, not the necessary. It was the realization of this possibility that gave the Russian revolution its principal distinctive characteristics. Unlike the French revolution, in the Russian revolution the dominant position vacated by the peasantry passed not to the bourgeoisie but to a political party which—far ahead of its time—expressed the organic anticapitalism of the proletariat.

The October insurrection transformed the necessarily antifeudal character of the revolution, making it predominantly antibourgeois, at least potentially; the insurrection then transformed this potential into a reality.

The political indifference of the peasant movement put it extremely at risk. "The peasant movement," stresses Bettelheim, "did not itself pose the problem of power; however, it unfolded unevenly, locally, thus laying itself open to repression 'blow by blow.' In this situation, then, if the provisional government remained in power there was a risk that the peasantry, and thus the revolution, would thereby be defeated." At this point the revolution assumed a common destiny with the peasant movement, which, though able to act, could not neutralize the risks assailing it. That the antibourgeois October insurrection should lead to the predominance of the anticapitalist character of the revolution belonged to the realm of the possible, but as a measure to safeguard the revolution's antifeudal character, October was necessary. As the revolution unfolded, and thus as the original necessity approached its fulfillment, the possible itself became more and more necessary. The October insurrection fed on the antinomy between the social efficacy of the peasant movement and its political sterility.

The peasantry could not be a class "for itself"; hence its violent struggles required some substitute to be found for it. "A scheme of things characteristic of backward countries is for one class to undertake to find a solution to questions that are in another class's interests," wrote Trotsky. In modern times, it has been the bourgeoisie that has benefited from the antifeudal victories of the peasantry. Rather than extracting their advantage from these victories, the Russian bourgeoisie attempted to obstruct them. This, together with the conditions generated by imperialism, the Bolsheviks recast into strategy. The gist of this strategy was that the Russian proletariat would be able to contend with this crippled bourgeoisie for the spoils of the peasants' victory over the feudal nobility.

The following points of intersection are discernible between the antifeudal movement of the peasantry and Bolshevik strategy.

(1) The basic similitude between the forecasts of this strategy and how the movement actually developed;

(2) The Bolsheviks' unconditional support (albeit of minor importance for most of the time in question) for the peasantry;

(3) The ability of the peasant movement to establish the social preconditions for political transformations from which it itself was incapable of benefiting;

(4) The possibility of a prolongation of the spontaneous antifeudal peasant movement by the Bolshevik party's deliberate antibourgeois undertakings, as carried through in the October insurrection.

The antibourgeois October insurrection capped off the peasant war with the establishment of a nonpeasant power. But no sooner was it established, than this power distinguished itself by historical acts intended in the first instance to satisfy the peasantry. Fragile as it was, it was able to deal the death blow to feudal property on the strength of the socioeconomic upheavals caused by the antifeudal movement of the peasantry. However, it was unable to proceed in the same way with capitalist property, since as yet the equivalent foundations did not exist for it. The antibourgeois power established in October was thus a faithful reflection of the sweeping away of the socioeconomic structures of feudalism, although not of those of capitalism. This means that, instead of being the product of economic and social conditions, as Marx's theory has it, this regime obliged itself to bring about these conditions. No political power in the modern era has over the long term assumed tasks of this scale, which were still ill-defined yet at the same time overwhelming.

Stalinism represents the mutilation suffered by the revolutionary political power under the immense burden of such tasks, a burden it had assumed without being prepared to carry them out. In this respect Stalinism may be considered the belated effect of the discordance between the basic structures of society.

The land

The Bolshevik party's substitution of the peasantry revealed its limits from the start: it was effective for the seizure of power, but not for establishing the postfeudal order. These limits were clear enough in the Second Congress of Soviets and in the historic land decree. Substitution was at work in the very composition of the congress, on which Shapiro commented: ''It did not represent the peasants in the villages, but only the workers and the peasants in uniform.'' Thus was enshrined the peasants' victory over feudalism—with no peasants in attendance. The nonpeasant congress had up to a point acted in accord with the historical interests of the peasantry, crossing the threshold separating representation from substitution. The next threshold, separating substitution from subordination, would be crossed twelve years later. The land decree was the point on which the antifeudal works of the congress, in its ephemeral existence as the agency of the new power, were focused. From the Bolshevik standpoint the decree was to serve a dual function: a social function, which consisted in legalizing the demise of the feudal nobility, and a political function, which consisted in establishing the peasantry as the pedestal of the new power after it had smashed the foundations of the old. ''We will gain the trust of the peasants,'' declared Lenin in his report on the decree, ''only by a decree which will abolish landed property.'' The momentousness of this goal accounts for the discrepancy between the agrarian program the Bolshevik party put forth in opposition, and that present in implicit form in the decree, also clearly the work of the Bolsheviks.

The Socialist Revolutionaries had built their popularity in the countryside by demanding socialization of the land since 1903. The Bolsheviks themselves at the time considered this demand utopian. ''No socialist,'' objected Lenin, ''can tell us revolutionary socialists that the abolition of private ownership of the land right now would satisfy the proletariat, since the millions of ruined peasants are at present not in a condition to exploit the land even if they had it.'' Indeed, given the primitive level of the productive forces in Russian agriculture, any egalitarian redistribution of the land by revolution would rapidly revert to nonegalitarian re-redistribution through commerce. For a medieval agriculture, socialization of the land could only open the way straight to capitalism, and this the Bolsheviks hoped to avoid. They were caught between two opposing constraints: to avoid capitalist development in agriculture, and at the same time to avoid open conflict with the peasants who were heading in this direction spontaneously. This contradiction was behind the seesawing in agrarian policy; the measures adopted, of which the October decree was one example, created serious doubts as to whether the Bolsheviks even had an agrarian program of their own to speak of. To mention some of the resting points in these hesitant gropings over the course of fourteen months, for instance: in April 1917 the party called for nationalization of the land; the decree in October of the same year did not mention the term nationalization; three months later, in January 1918, the "Law on the socialization of the land" was promulgated, which acknowledged the deficiencies of the October decree, but made no notable changes in the effect of ownership of the land; four months passed and in June 1918 a new decree created Poor Peasants Committees, charged with redistributing land, livestock, and farm equipment, this time at the expense of the "kulaks." The waverings were considerable. There is no alternative to capitalist development of agriculture discernible in these measures, nor did the Bolsheviks gain the peasants' trust, although, to be sure, the worst was avoided.

The October decree, which was supposed to resolve once and for all the perennial question of feudal lands, extended its prescriptions to apply to all forms of land ownership. The decree proclaimed the immediate expropriation without indemnity of lands held by the large landowners and the clergy, an area of 150 million hectares, and cancelation of the land debt, which amounted to 1.5 billion rubles in the accounts of the peasant bank alone, to which were added the private debts, tenant debentures, and sums owed for acquisition of the lands of the nobility—about 700 million gold rubles all told.

The expropriation of feudal possessions was spelled out in infinitely clearer terms than their appropriation. Article 2 of the decree provided that the lands and the inventory of the large landowners "should be placed . . . under the *control*" (my emphasis) of the local land committees and soviets of peasant deputies. The terms socialization, nationalization, or *étatisation* were replaced by the thoroughly vague right of "control." The vagueness of this right was compounded by the equally vague description of those who were to benefit from it, defined not as social categories but as institutions, and moreover not one but two, neither with roots in the life of the countryside, or any administrative competence or experience, and with their respective prerogatives in no way delimited. It was decreed that the two institutions were to ensure that the confiscation of the large holdings would proceed in an orderly fashion, determine which lands and other assets were to be subject to confiscation, and finally to maintain "the most rigorous revolutionary surveillance" over them. Clearly the exercise of these responsibilities is not the same as the exercise of the right of ownership, even if an optimum form were to be found for it. The old form of ownership was effectively abolished but no new one put in its place. In the terms of the decree, the possessions expropriated from the feudal nobility were to be appropriated by no one. Property in general followed feudal property into historical oblivion. The suspension of property was rooted not only in the provisions of the decree, but also in the fact that the decree itself proclaimed that this suspension was to be temporary, leaving the agrarian question to be finally resolved in the future constituent assembly—which, however, was dissolved by the Bolsheviks themselves before it had the opportunity even to address the question.

The vagueness of the regulations adopted in October was made even worse by the fact that the five articles of the decree itself were complemented by the seven articles of the "model decree."

In addition to the provisions concerning feudal property, the decree proclaimed all land to be "national patrimony," thereby transforming a large number of peasants from owners into users of the land. Article 5 notwithstanding (which protected the possessions of peasants and Cossacks against confiscation), the last act in the life of feudal property proved to be the first act in the disappearance of peasant property. This historical process, which began in October 1917, would continue without pause with but a few variations up to its conclusion twelve years later. "The land decree," observed Hélène Carrère de Encausse, "introduced the contrary principle of property to the countryside." Thus the suspension of property was extended from former feudal possessions to include agriculture in its totality. Later extended even further from agriculture to the whole of the economy, this situation, which I call "a property vacuum," was to become the principal economic source of Stalinism.

The 242 delegates to the first Congress of Peasant Deputies each brought a notebook containing the wishes of their electors as regards the future organization of agriculture. A summary of them, edited by a group of Socialist Revolutionaries and published in *Izvestiia* on August 19, where it was dubbed the "model decree," was incorporated in the land decree "as a general guideline for the great agrarian reforms." Unlike Article 5 of the decree, which exempted peasant and Cossack holdings from confiscation, the first article of the "model" stipulates: "The private right to ownership of the land is abrogated forever. . . . All lands, those of the state, those of the court, those of the crown, those of the churches, . . . those owned privately, those of the *obshchina*, and those of the peasants and so forth are hereby expropriated without indemnity, becoming the possession of all the people and available for the use of all those who work it."

Thus the same regulation established both nonconfiscation and the expropriation of peasant lands. In his report on the decree Lenin gives political reasons for this incongruity, saying: "As a democratic government, we cannot disregard a decision of the broad masses of the people, even if we do not agree with it."

The official *History of the Communist Party of the Soviet Union* published during the Khrushchev era brings out this ambiguity: "in addition to the demand for the abolition of private property in land and the confiscation of the landlord estates without compensation, the instructions called for an equalitarian use of land, a point with which the Bolshevik Party did not agree." Trotsky's commentary on this same point is more incisive. "Whereas the collated instructions say that all the land, that of both the landlords and the peasants, 'is converted into national property,' the basic decree does not commit itself at all as to the new form of property in the land. Even a none too pedantic jurist would be horrified at the fact that the nationalization of the land, a new social principle of world-historic importance, is inaugurated in the form of a list of instructions adjoined to a basic law. But there was no editorial slovenliness here. Lenin wanted as little as possible to tie that hands of the party and the soviet power *a priori* in a still unexplored historical realm.'' Trotsky continues: ''. . . If the distribution of the land would strengthen the socialist government politically, it was then wholly justified as an immediate measure. . . . The decree together with the instructions meant that the dictatorship of the proletariat assumed an obligation not only to take an attentive attitude toward the interests of the land laborer, but also to be patient of his illusions as a petty proprietor.''

This indecision over a fundamental problem was to last longer than any revolution could afford to permit. It would plunge postrevolutionary society into an endemic crisis of subsistence, bring about an irreversible breach of cooperation between workers and peasants, and accustom society to the ineffectiveness of legal regulations. But above all, it would permanently alter the bedrock of economic and social structures: the organization of property. Stalinism would be the problem's ultimate resolution.

Incomplete realization

That the antifeudal insurrection of the peasantry ended in an antibourgeois insurrection of the party of the working class was a *quid pro quo* that left history at loose ends, with antinomic effect: the feudal organization of agriculture was abolished, but there existed no postfeudal organization to replace it. Hence the antifeudal character of the revolution was incompletely achieved. The October insurrection resolved the major problem of feudalism, but in the process created another major problem that it left unresolved, namely, that of the historical continuity between antifeudalism and anticapitalism. In the presumed natural order of things, antifeudal revolutions give rise to capitalist societies. In the order of things imposed by imperialism, an antifeudal revolution can lead directly to a postcapitalist society. It is this perturbation of the natural scheme of things which makes for the possibility of anticipation. Bolshevik strategy outlined this possibility, but did not define the structures of a society that negated capitalism before capitalism had even had a chance to mature. The first product of this historical quandary was the suspension of agrarian property.

Underdevelopment, imposed and sustained by imperialism, was followed by a premature curtailment of capitalist development. Between the antifeudal revolution and postcapitalist society there is a natural break, which was forcibly bridged over to reestablish a continuity of spurious quality. The transformation of historical discontinuity into historical continuity reflected the negative and incomplete nature of the revolution. The feudal order was not replaced by a demonstrably superior postfeudal order, but by economic and social disorder which became paralyzing through its persistence. The failure of the revolution to bear positive fruits put the results of its negative work in jeopardy. As a negation of a negation, it entailed the risk of never being able to return to the *status quo ante*.

Capitalist development of agriculture presupposed competition, the fruits of which must necessarily fall to a minority. If that development could be checked, then the interests of the great majority of the peasantry would be safeguarded. The Bolshevik party had counted on the convergence of those interests with its own agrarian policy, the gist of which, however, escaped that majority. The long-term interest of the peasantry, namely to forestall the ruin otherwise in store for them, was counterbalanced by the more immediate interest of tempting fortune, on the hope of ending up among the lucky minority. But the new regime appeared intent on abolishing not merely the minority already profiting from this competition (insofar as it had begun to function) but competition itself. A process of internal stratification was already taking place among the peasantry, and the Bolsheviks were gambling on this objective fact in their bid to win over the poor peasants so as thereby to stifle tendencies toward capitalist development. But notwithstanding the inequality in their initial positions, all peasant layers vied with one another on an equal footing in the zeal with which they entered the fray of competition, even if the end result could only be a graver inequality than had existed at the outset. As regards long-term interests, the poor peasants were the one social factor in principle capable of forging a continuity in the countryside between antifeudalism and anticapitalism. Their immediate interests—their illusions, as Trotsky called them—obstructed this possibility. The poor peasants showed little spirit for combatting capitalist development in the countryside, and the price paid for this general lack of fire and lack of resolve in the anticapitalist struggle in the countryside was the repression of the kulaks by the center; Stalinism had taken its first steps.

An entire series of objective discontinuities had to be overcome for a continuity to be forged between antifeudalism and anticapitalism. For the political changes that had come about to be matched by changes in the socioeconomic order as well, a historical motor force was necessary.But that force failed to materialize. The poor peasants did not rise up spontaneously against capitalism as they had against the feudal order; for this they had first to be mobilized by the Bolshevik party. Their interest in expropriating the rich peasants went no further than an interest in enriching themselves.

Nor did this discordancy leave Bolshevik strategy unaffected; both its functions and its potential suffered. As an instrument for the conquest of power, the function of Bolshevik strategy was to harness the revolutionary currents that were making their way independently of it; once that end was achieved, its function was to suppress or even replace these movements. As for its potential, as the functions of Bolshevik strategy became objectively more complex, its ability to adapt to the new conditions began to meet limits of a subjective nature. Leninist strategy had shown its capacity to anticipate the destruction of a social order based on private ownership of the means of production; it had less affirmative to say about how to construct a new social order without that basis. It was not then to be wondered that the Bolsheviks should experience difficulties in transforming political structures that were antibourgeois into socioeconomic structures that were anticapitalist. Leninism was a strategy for the conquest, not the exercise of power. The power thus established bore the markings of having been based on a strategy yet having none for the future. Later Stalinism would make

use of this antinomy to effect a categorical transmutation: the anticipatory necessity of a strategy was replaced after October by the category of the possible, which
later permitted the emergence of the infallible leader.

Based on a property vacuum, with relations of production confused and
infirm, agriculture, now of its feudal chains, seemed able to unharness itself from
capitalism only at the expense of forgoing capitalist productivity as well. A
premature anticapitalism, reduced to negative constraint, created a state of
underproductivity throughout the whole of agriculture.

The first anticapitalist measures of the October insurrection were directed
against the one social force that had made it possible: the peasants. The prime
subject of the victory over feudalism became the prime object of its anticapitalist
restraints, and the principal mainstay in the struggle against feudalism became the
principal obstacle in the struggle against capitalism. Once the anticapitalist character of the revolution had achieved its ascendancy, the objective role of the
peasantry changed and the question of a worker-peasant alliance was placed on
the order of the day.

The alliance with the peasantry

For Lenin, an alliance with the peasantry was a favorable but not indispensable
condition for an anticipatory revolution. Just after his return, during the April
1917 conference, he declared, to the astonishment of the "Old Bolsheviks," that
it was "not admissible at the present time for the proletarian party to place its
hopes in a community of interests with the peasantry." In Trotsky's view, this
declaration "shows among other things how far Lenin was from the theory,
which his epigones were later to attribute to him, of a perpetual harmony of
interests between the proletariat and the peasantry." An alliance necessarily
presupposes a community of interests, but a community of interests is not necessarily expressed in an alliance. An alliance translates an objective community of
interests into a common strategy. An alliance is thus an agreement arrived at
jointly, spelling out mutual obligations in the pursuit of a common end; it is
therefore an eminently political act. Before October the peasantry and the proletariat were linked by their common interests in abolishing feudalism. But neither
had been able to translate this vital interest into a strategy; though they acted in
parallel, their actions were never able to attain the form of an overall political
agreement taking in the whole. Not that the workers and peasants were on equal
footings on the political plane; workers were infinitely more sensitive to the
political aspect of the social conflict and, moreover, were represented by an
extremely capable party, indeed the one party that possessed a valid strategy for
revolution.

Nonetheless the proletarian class was not identical with the Bolshevik
party. As for the peasantry, there was no party that truly represented its interests,
and its organic apoliticism made it totally unsuited for an alliance in the proper
sense. Commenting on the period before October, Bettelheim says: "There are
manifold reasons why the activity of the peasant masses remained confined to

direct actions focused on the land, and not oriented toward an *organized alliance* with the proletariat in the cities.'' But Bettelheim sees the phenomenon, not its causes. The term ''organized alliance'' implies the possibility of an ''unorganized alliance,'' which would be a contradiction in terms. Actually workers and peasants engaged in a mutual aid of sorts in pursuing the same end, but the upshot of this was not an alliance but a spontaneous convergence of their actions. That same end was the abolition of feudalism, by virtue not of a political accord, but an objective meeting of vital interests. The prime reason this convergence of interests did not become an alliance in the proper sense was the low level of politicization, but above all the historical imperviousness of the peasantry to matters political.

The direct transition from an insurrection against the feudal order to a victorious antibourgeois insurrection brought about a profound but contradictory transformation in relations between the proletariat and the peasantry. The first change was in the enhanced role of the Bolshevik party, from that of mediator of these relations to their regulator. In relations with the peasantry, the Bolshevik party no longer merely represented the proletariat, but replaced it. The peasant question was a key aspect of a process that altered the nature of the ties between class and party. In practical terms, peasants were less served by an alliance directly with the workers than by an alliance with the party. This reshuffling of social factors marked also a change in substance. With state power in their hands and a high degree of political ability, the Bolshevik party offered the peasantry not cooperation, but leadership. However, such unilateral relations of leadership and subordination are incompatible with the terms of an alliance. On the other hand, this leadership was necessary under the circumstances, for it marked the only chance of steering a part of the peasantry in a direction that would put it in advance of its time, i.e., toward the abolition of capitalism in agriculture even before it had firmly struck roots. The Bolshevik party, which had not led the peasantry in its victorious war against the feudal nobility, which it had waged and won almost entirely on its own terms, was obliged to lead it in a war against agrarian capitalism to which the peasantry was by no means eager to commit itself.

The central problem was that of cooperation between the party and the rural populace. The peasants' first hope was that the new circumstances would enable them to enlarge their holdings. But for that to happen it was first necessary for these circumstances to endure. Thus the proletariat and peasantry alike were interested in keeping power under Bolshevik control since the Bolsheviks, unlike the Socialist Revolutionaries when they were in power, had demonstrated in deeds their determination to put an end both to the war and to feudalism. Thus the peasantry had differing short-term and long-term interests. Their immediate interests led them to give their support to Bolshevik power, although this was at variance with their interest in the development of capitalism over the long term. By the fact alone of having to assume an attitude toward the Bolshevik party, therefore, the peasantry had, if unconsciously, crossed the threshold into politics. The dichotomy between its procapitalist and anticapitalist interests was complemented by the discordancy between its political aspirations and what it aspired to economically.

The antifeudal struggle had brought the party, the proletariat, and the peasantry together as it unfolded, but once it had achieved its end, its tendency was to sunder them anew. The new economic conditions plunged the peasantry into a capitalist competition rejected by the Bolshevik party, which chose instead to place its reliance on political power. But the limits of that power soon became evident: it might attempt with political means alone to counteract the effects of these economic conditions, but political means alone were not sufficient to change the conditions themselves. To refashion socioeconomic structures through the instruments of politics alone proved an extremely difficult undertaking. The mere wielding of power was not enough; a strategy designed to this end was also needed. The Bolshevik party had the power; it did not have the strategy.

The October insurrection strengthened the links between the Bolshevik party and the peasantry, while at the same time introducing the seeds for a later crisis in them. When it came, that crisis embraced the whole: the Soviet regime, the party itself, and the entire economy from top to bottom. The crisis was later to demonstrate its perennial nature in becoming the single most important molder of the new social structures. In this way a distinct social order gradually emerged which would make of this crisis the norm of its existence. That social order was Stalinism.

From antifeudal revolution to the emergence of Stalinism

To achieve its antifeudal character the Russian revolution had to become predominantly anticapitalist in character. Generally speaking, this continuity between the two characters, by nature separate, contained the historical germs of what would later become the Stalinist distortion of the revolution. The antifeudal character of the revolution was incompletely achieved because its continuity with the anticapitalist character was able to find no positive issue at the economic and social levels, and hence remained at the political level. Conversely, the discontinuity of the revolution at the social and economic levels was itself due to the fact that social and economic structures continued intact. The revolution did not effect any positive innovations at these latter two levels comparable to that which it achieved at the political level (where it established an anticapitalist power).

The break in the revolution at the social and economic levels showed up in various forms. In the first place, the peasantry, which had thrown itself into the task of dragging Russian society out of its feudal backwardness, did not plunge with the same zeal into the process of restoration on a—premature—anticapitalist basis. With the achievement of the antifeudal character of the revolution this work of historical negation ground to a halt. The transformation of political power, for its part, was less a necessary product than a possible consequence of the revolution's antifeudal character. To define its own natural determining factors and carry the revolution to positive fruition at the economic and social levels as well, power needed a viable strategy fashioned specifically to this end. To bring the socioeconomic achievements of the revolution up to a level with what it had achieved politically entailed a whole series of conditions, ranging from an adequate strategy to concrete constructive works, both economic and social. Further, if this series of conditions was to have issue, it had to be complete: none of its three terms could be lacking. Stalinism violated this imperative: it attempted to effect a positive program of social and economic change and to ensure continuity between antifeudalism and anticapitalism without having a suitable strategy for this. The result of this attempt was an anticapitalism which, in industrializing, carried society not onward toward socialism, but into an unending process of autoreproduction of its initial condition. The manner in which the Russian revolution fulfilled its antifeudal function established the premises on which Stalinism was later to build. The most important of these were at the level of the economy, power, and the relations between power and the peasantry.

The land decree gave Stalinism a historical model for the economy, the principal elements of which were:

(1) political regulation of the fundamental economic relation—property;

(2) the substitution of an efficacious form of property by a form lacking real definition;

(3) a legal consecration of this undefined form of property, which gravely eroded the foundations of both the economy and the law.

The Stalinist economy is not identical to this model. It replaced the mechanisms of self-interest with the mechanisms of force, and filled the lacuna left by the absence of a strategy with the pervasive presence of a providential leader, while for the undefined form of property it substituted the illusory form specific to Stalinism. Law over property thus deteriorated from imprecision to dissimulation, which would in the end result in its generalized impotence. A law that is unable to secure property is unable to secure anything at all, the freedoms and the lives of society's members inclusive. The decomposition of the law is important for our discussion primarily insofar as it revealed one of the principal intercepts between power and the economy. In every modern revolution the edifices of the law are smashed under the impact of revolutionary violence, and every postrevolutionary society intent on attaining stability reestablishes the law and its functions. These twin processes were arrested by Stalinism half way. In the order established by Stalinism, the exercise of violence outside the law, which is a fundamental instrument of revolutionary change, remains to become the basic instrument for maintaining stability and preventing change. Initially a crucial manifestation of the liberty of the revolutionary masses, it became the expression of the monopoly of power. Power, with its effective monopoly over the function of ownership, also secured for itself a monopoly on the instruments of extraeconomic and extralegal constraint, with the only function yet left to the law being that of ratifying their application. Unlike the precarious legality of the power installed in October, the extralegality of Stalinism was an indispensable auxiliary to the form of property specific to it, and thus one of Stalinism's inherent traits. The forms of this extralegality fluctuated over the course of time from extreme brutality to considerable discretion, but although these fluctuations have been of tremendous consequence practically, they cannot be said in any essential way to have modified the extralegality of power that has been the hallmark of Stalinist society from its genesis down to our own day.

Stalinism's principal reaccommodations to power were:

(1) The property vacuum was transformed into an illegal but real state monopoly over all the social means of production. To adapt to this new function, power had to modify the very substance of its structures and its prerogatives, which became practically unlimited;

(2) The inversion of the relations of determination between political structures and socioeconomic structures, initially a transitory effect of the phenomenon of anticipation imperfectly fulfilled, was not only stabilized by Stalinism but ultimately enabled Stalinist power to become the universal regulator of all social activity;

(3) Power, in this capacity of universal regulator of all social activity, tended spontaneously in two directions in its unfolding:

(a) It tended to place itself above society, and so to destroy all those mechanisms society has for keeping it in check;

(b) It tended to develop an energy greater than that of the whole of society.

These tendencies operated through:

(a) the creation of mechanisms obstructing any social activity not required by power;

(b) the maximal exploitation of all available means of power, and especially of the monopoly over the legal and extralegal (but legalizable) use of violence, which however was not the same as mass repression, the latter being merely one of the most primitive and barbarous of its possible manifestations.

The metamorphosis of Stalinist power in these directions was in great measure the effect of its relations with the peasantry, which were characterized by:

(1) Peasant reservations with regard to anticapitalist development in the countryside: the peasants tended to resist integration into the economic process, while their labor remained underproductive. Both these factors contributed to the famous "procurement crisis";

(2) the about-face of the Bolshevik party: after having supported the concentration of the forces of the whole of the peasantry against feudalism, it now endeavored to divide them by inciting the poor peasants against the rich. These shiftings and turnings would ultimately culminate in the subjugation of the whole of the peasantry, its vitality extinguished by Stalinism;

(3) The antifeudal revolution launched from below by the peasantry had ended in the abolition of the property of the landed nobility; later a veritable antipeasant revolution was launched from above by the power monopoly and the result was the abolition of small peasant property in all its forms;

(4) An illusory agrarian property, institutionalized in the form of collectivization, provided the basis for confiscation of the agrarian product, institutionalized in the form of forced contracts with the state. Instead of developing toward capitalism, agriculture became the principal economic accessory of anticapitalist industrialization;

(5) The forced transformation of the economic structures of the countryside amounted in essence to universal expropriation. The general trend was in this direction from the very beginning:

(a) The 1917 decree barred private ownership of the land; collectivization prohibited its private use;

(b) The class struggles in the pre-Stalinist period affected the rich peasants; collectivization affected all strata of the peasantry;

(6) The forced transformation of the social structures of the countryside amounted in essence to the creation of an undifferentiated peasantry. The surest way to prevent capitalist development of small peasant farming was to suppress it. The countryside, where social stratification verged on atomization, became the social locus of a homogeneous populace whose social cohesion rested with the fact that all had been expropriated. With this metamorphosis, the objective sources of conflicts among the peasantry were reduced to nil, but the objective premises were created for a conflict that would oppose the whole of the peasantry to the expropriating power;

(7) With time, the economic and social transformations imposed upon agriculture acquired definition of their own: anticapitalism, repressive but lasting, and irreversably antiproductive (regardless of the technological level of farm machinery);

(8) These structural changes having been imposed on the immense majority of the populace, they then served as a launching pad for industrial "take-off"; thus did the Stalinist power monopoly provide the first dramatic demonstration of its efficiency as an expeditious extrasocial and extra-economic regulator of all social relations, the relations of production inclusive. Be that as it may, this achievement, of decisive importance for the establishment of the Stalinist social order, cannot be separated from the manner in which the 1917 revolution had fulfilled its antifeudal function.

III. THE ANTIBOURGEOIS CHARACTER OF THE REVOLUTION

Hypotheses

In this discussion of the antibourgeois character of the Russian revolution, the principal hypotheses I shall be examining are:

(a) Contrary to the widely accepted (especially by Marxist authors) view, the October 1917 insurrection did not mark the passage of a bourgeois into a socialist or proletarian revolution; the transition was rather from a predominantly antifeudal revolution to one that was predominantly antibourgeois in character;

(b) The anticipatory and unfinished nature of the revolution was most intensely in evidence in the predominance of the antibourgeois character. With both of these antinomic features present in it, the antibourgeois character reproduced with a particular fidelity the antinomies present in the original necessity of the revolution;

(c) The antibourgeois character of the revolution had indeed gained ascendancy, yet only as an intermediate stage during which the anticapitalist character bided for a moment in the face of the possibility of itself becoming dominant. The revolution thus remained unfinished;

(d) The October insurrection marked both the triumph and the finale of Leninist strategy. The triumph, insofar as it established an antibourgeois power before its historical time had arrived, on which basis a society emerged for whose functioning a conscious strategy became an objective necessity; the finale, by virtue of its subjective incapacity to meet this objective necessity;

(e) The inability to develop a strategy was fraudulently requited by the capacity for producing infallible leaders. The providential leader was the institution supposed to provide a subjective response, albeit a fraudulent one, to the objective need for a strategy. The personality cult was not exclusively of Stalin's making, nor was it exclusively his own. It is found in different forms in each of his successors, including those who made their mark attacking him, for its true

source lies not in human intentions but in the contradiction between the functional needs of this society and the means it had to fulfill those needs—or, more concisely, in the discrepancy between objective tasks and the subjective capacities of the historical actors to fulfill them. The embodiment of an illusory strategy in a real person was not the product of personal excesses, although it could well give rise to them;

(f) The inability of the Russian bourgeoisie to assume the role of ruling class was a decisive factor in the victory of the antibourgeois insurrection;

(g) The premature senility of the Russian bourgeoisie was not matched by the early maturation of the Russian proletariat. It, like the bourgeoisie, was unable to transform itself into the ruling class of Russian society at but the wink of an eye. Although it displayed an astonishing militancy, in most cases its challenge was addressed more to the immediate functions of capitalist relations of production than to their general existence, and it was for this same reason that the proletariat did not play a decisive role in preparing and carrying through the antibourgeois insurrection, although its role was nonetheless considerable.

(h) When therefore the social conflict polarized, it did not oppose the two social classes, the proletariat and the bourgeoisie, but rather two political institutions, the Bolshevik party and the Provisional Government;

(i) The effective role of the Bolshevik party in the October insurrection was to replace, rather than to lead, the proletariat;

(j) The substitution of the class by the party, already a fact in the seizure of power, became the determining factor in the exercise of that power;

(k) The first function conferred by history on this power was to adapt the economic and social structures to its own nature; in other words, to transform the antibourgeois character assumed by the revolution in October into an anti-capitalist character imprinted in the new society;

(l) For the first time in history, the role of ruling class was assumed by a ruling party. Class structure lost its relevance, and class struggle ceased to be the prime driving force of history in this society;

(m) The rule of one class presupposes the existence of other classes. The rule of one party is strengthened by the disappearance of others. To make itself as invulnerable and functional as possible, power pruned its structure down to its simplest equation: "monolithism" is not properly a structure;

(n) The "destructuring" of power was accompanied by a parallel phenomenon in the economy. Like the socialization of the land, socialization of the industrial means of production was impeded by the underdevelopment of the productive forces, the producers inclusive. Society had the capacity to expropriate the means of production, yet without effect, as it had not the capacity to re-appropriate them on another basis. The property vacuum extended from agriculture to the whole of industry;

(o) The underdevelopment of the productive forces impeded the abolition of capitalist relations of production, while the continued existence of these relations impeded the development of the productive forces. Entrapped in this vicious circle, society was unable to hurdle the obstacle separating the antibourgeois from the anticapitalist character of the revolution: the former was merely an unfinished form of the latter, and the economy and power became disjunctive;

(p) Postrevolutionary society attempted unsuccessfully to synchronize the economy and power; Stalinism succeeded where that society had failed by extending the substitutive functions of power. The working class, substituted by the party in the seizure and exercise of power, would also be substituted in the exercise of the functions of property;

(r) Prohibited to capitalists and to individual peasants and workers, proprietorship over the means of production would be assigned effectively, if illicitly, by power, and on these foundations Stalinism would accomplish a spectacular industrialization that was *anticapitalist* and *antisocialist* at one and the same time;

(s) In Stalinism monopoly of power and monopoly over property merge. This merger, which imperialism had used to effect the triumph of private property, was used by Stalinism to eliminate it;

(t) In effecting the transition from the antibourgeois to the anticapitalist character of the revolution in this manner, power changed its function; henceforth it became the universal regulator of all economic, social and cultural activity;

(u) To fulfill this function, the tendency of the proprietary power was to place itself above all social control, and so above society itself. The exercise of this function by power modified not only its structure, but also society's.

Similarities

The two different characters of the revolution may be discussed separately, but the social factors and the events that made up the revolution remain of course the same. What changes, depending on the emphasis, is primarily the hierarchy of factors and the significance of events. Now that we have discussed the antifeudal character of the revolution, a discussion of its antibourgeois character, using the same approach, should give a different perspective on the same social factors and the same events.

Definition

The antibourgeois character of the revolution was determined as much by the specific function it fulfilled as by the limits placed on its achievement. Its function was that of overthrowing the state power of the bourgeoisie and establishing an anticapitalist state power in its place. The limit was that, while the revolution succeeded in radically divesting the bourgeoisie of its political privileges, it did not abolish its economic privileges. The revolution shied from crossing this threshold after October, and the character that thereby came to predominate was anticapitalist in only a partial sense. Because of its duration, the difficulty in going beyond it, and its subsequent effects, I shall use the special term "antibourgeois character" to designate this semi anticapitalism. Conceptually it is meant to express the intermingling of two real processes: first, the crumbling of the political power of the bourgeoisie under the impact of the popular movements, leading ultimately to the advent of a power that was not only antibourgeois, but also anticapitalist; the second process was that of a reduction, but not the elimination of the economic positions of the bourgeoisie, i.e., the material basis upon which political power rested. The dominance of the antibourgeois character was a reflection of the deterioration in the social relations of control, as evidenced by the disjunction between political and economic relations. On the one hand there was a new political power that had no economic underpinnings, and on the other there was an economic power that had no political power. In politics and the economy different social forces held sway.

The limit to the antibourgeois character of the revolution also placed limits on its anticipatory and strategic nature. In remaining but half achieved, this character also demonstrated in a most evident fashion the unfinished nature of the revolution.

Theoretically, the Russian revolution of 1917 could have been antifeudal yet not necessarily anti-imperialist, or vice versa. It could also have been antifeudal and anti-imperialist, yet not necessarily antibourgeois. But to be antibourgeois without having first been antifeudal and anti-imperialist was impossible. What this means is that the effects of the other characters of the revolution were borne in a special way by its antibourgeois character. Representing as it did a specific synthesis of the other characters of the revolution, the antibourgeois character was to have the most direct influence on post-revolutionary society and later on its detour into Stalinism.

In the preceding section this connection was dealt with in terms of the revolution's antifeudal character. There the emphasis was on the dissimilitude between the organic apoliticism of the peasant movement and the eminently political activity of the Bolshevik party. Here I shall examine this connection from an opposite point of view, centering on the relation between historical backwardness and political anticipation. Indeed, from an antibourgeois perspective, this relation constitutes the very substance of the interdependence between the antifeudal and antibourgeois characters of the revolution. That interdependence is one of genetic, yet antinomic necessity: the two characters of the revolution mutually determined and negated one another. Each character was the battlement upon which the other was achieved, and yet an obstacle to its continuation. The tardy achievement of the antifeudal character made possible, and was itself made possible by, the anticipatory achievement of the antibourgeois character of the revolution. Yet at the same time, the tardy achievement of the antifeudal character obstructed the transformation of the antibourgeois character into an anticapitalist character, and the anticipatory achievement of the antibourgeois character impeded the transformation of the victory over feudalism into the development of individual peasant farming. Each of these two characters enabled the other to be achieved, at least partially, but did not permit its development.

The anticipatory nature of the revolution directly affected only its antibourgeois character; its impact on the antifeudal character was only indirect, mediated by the latter. But even on the antibourgeois character the anticipatory nature of the Russian revolution imposed its antinomies: the antibourgeois insurrection was itself an act that was antinomic in two respects: it was tardy with regard to feudalism, and anticipatory with regard to capitalism. Delay and anticipation are interlinked in a way that is both linear and inverse, where the equality of the terms is but apparent. Mutual determination was an expression of reciprocity, not parity. If the antifeudal character was conditioned by the antibourgeois character, this was so only in its achievement, not as it was gaining ascendancy. The inverse determination, i.e., of the antibourgeois character by the antifeudal character, affected both its achievement and its ascendancy, both occurring in the same historical act. The antifeudal movement was an indispensable precondition for the antibourgeois insurrection, which in return provided that movement with a possible issue. The delay had to be made up, and the epilogue to that was to render anticipation possible. Thus the category of the possible served as a necessary condition for the achievement of the necessary. Indeed, the echo of necessity may be heard in the only possible act that would enable such a necessity to be fulfilled. The antibourgeois character of the revolution became dominant, as but one possibility, seemingly, among others relative to the existence of an immature capitalism, but a necessity relative to a feudalism that had survived long past its time.

The historical necessity embodied in the overthrow of bourgeois power was that of an immediate and total abolition of feudalism, not of capitalism, and the antibourgeois insurrection heralded the same in its public proclamations. Necessity remains necessity whether supported by adventitious possibility or not. The possible is fueled by necessity only insofar as necessity is served by it. When the possible takes leave of the necessary to embark totally on the path toward its own realization it soon finds itself sapped of much of its force and its historical productivity enfeebled. This ontological inequality in the alliance between these two qualities was likewise reflected in an intrinsic inequality in Lenin's strategy. Lenin's definition of the aim of an antibourgeois insurrection was more solidly concatenated with antifeudal premises than with an anticapitalist perspective. Here too Lenin's strategy remained true to reality. The anticipatory, antibourgeois character of that strategy proved more efficacious for breaking with the past than for forging links with the future; in turn its predicate, borne out subsequently by events, was more a reflection of the realities of the past on which it rested than a foretaste of a real future.

The anticapitalist movement remained solid and socially productive so long as it served the antifeudal movement, but as soon as it presumed to make its own way it became hesitant and its social productivity ebbed visibly. The possible gains no sustenance from solitude. The permanent reduction of the anticapitalist character of the revolution to an antibourgeois character was a reflection of a reduction of the power of the possible to effect transformations on its own once it has severed its links with necessity. A strategy specializing in incisive solutions was replaced by recourses to compromises more tailored to the exigencies of the moment, which the New Economic Policy was later to institutionalize and Stalinism to abolish.

Predominance

The antifeudal character of the revolution became predominant before its final achievement. Its antibourgeois character became predominant *only after* its achievement, i.e., after the installation of an anticapitalist power. In the latter case, its predominance was subsumed by its achievement. The achievement of the antibourgeois character of the revolution was not the effect of its predominance; indeed the contrary was rather the case: it became in effect predominant by virtue of being achieved—a simultaneity of sorts, which takes up in another form the discontinuity as well as the anticipatory nature of the revolutionary process. Seen from a broader perspective, the same phenomenon brings out another aspect of this discontinuity: one character (antibourgeois) of the revolution was achieved by virtue of another's (antifeudal) being predominant.

The antibourgeois character of the revolution was by no means snuffed out upon its achievement; it merely ceased to be predominant. Nonetheless it experienced a dynamic of its own before being achieved; largely in eclipse as long as the anti-autocratic character was in ascendancy, it became manifest when the antifeudal character assumed predominance, until finally becoming predominant itself with its achievement in October. This dynamic traced an ascending curve, which was the product of an interaction between the overall continuity of the revolution, its tendency to radicalize, and the exhaustion of those characters that had previously been predominant. The anti-autocratic character and antifeudal character were spent as soon as they were achieved. They could go no further. At this point the revolution had either to stop or to continue by assuming an antibourgeois character that would be more than just predominant: it would be exclusive. Thus those traits deriving from its predominance were added to the specific traits of the antibourgeois character of the revolution.

Sources. The revolution's antifeudal character had become predominant by virtue of a social conflict dominated specifically by the clash between the peasantry and the feudal lords. Initially, the predominance of the antibourgeois character did not derive from the social conflict setting off the proletariat against the bourgeoisie, but rather from the antibourgeois implications of the antifeudal movement. Whereas the antifeudal character of the revolution owed its predominance principally to an intensification of a conflict specific to it, the antibourgeois character derived its predominance principally from the escalation of a conflict not specific to itself.

Social factors. The antifeudal movement was not only dominated, it was also incorporated by the peasantry. The proletariat was undaunted in its opposition to the bourgeoisie, but this opposition also encompassed a social movement that extended far beyond the proletariat and in which, moreover, the latter did not even play the leading role. The overthrow of bourgeois power was in the first instance the indirect work of the peasant movement, and the direct work of the Bolshevik party. The reference is, of course, not to the zeal, but to the effectiveness of each of these factors in the antibourgeois movement. The fervor of the proletariat far surpassed its effectiveness. This is why after October the proletariat spontaneously took up the cause of an immediate transformation of the revolution's antibourgeois character into an anticapitalist character. But meeting with the disapproval of the Bolshevik party and the indifference of the peasantry, this action would soon dissolve in its own ineffectuality. Thus the predominance of the antibourgeois character derived neither from the predominance of a conflict specific to it nor from the predominance of a social factor even presumed to be specific.

Ends. The plurality of factors involved in the antibourgeois struggle was translated into a plurality of ends pursued, with the exception of the question of the war. The peasantry's aim in the achievement of the antibourgeois character of the revolution was the total abolition of feudalism, the aim of the proletariat was the immediate elimination of capitalist relations of production, while the Bolshevik party had set its sights on the establishment of an antibourgeois power. The first was less than what was objectively possible, the second went beyond that limit, while the third of these aims was the only one that corresponded in any measure to the objectively possible, and incorporated in its own way the first of these. Thus it was only the most specific of these three goals, that pursued by the proletariat, which ultimately proved beyond reach.

Forms. The antibourgeois, unlike the antifeudal, character of the revolution generally asserted itself in forms other than direct use of revolutionary violence. The most common of these were the political and propaganda campaigns of the Bolshevik party, and strikes and demonstrations by the workers. The proletariat combatted capitalism, which it wanted to abolish at once, using means which at best could only have weakened it. The forms of the workers' struggle were unsuited to its ends, and especially after October, this discrepancy would be manifested in the "wildcat nationalizations," equally unproductive, to which I will return later on. The actual events of the conflict, which was to bring the antibourgeois character of the revolution to a position of ascendancy, did not reach the intensity that had marked the struggle abolishing feudalism.

Effects. The movement against the feudal nobility had destroyed this class without going so far as to install a specifically antifeudal power. The movement against the bourgeoisie did not annihilate this class, yet had established an antibourgeois power. This discrepancy between premise and conclusion was due essentially to the decisive role of the Bolshevik party in the immediate events that marked the achievement of the antibourgeois character of the revolution, i.e., the October insurrection. Seen retrospectively, one can say that the antibourgeois character of the revolution combined with the ascendancy of the Bolshevik party, and the effect was a triple transformation:

—of a secondary effect of the antifeudal movement into the predominant function of the revolution;

—of workers' actions to restrict the economic power of the bourgeoisie to actions by the Bolshevik party, supported by the proletariat, aimed at overthrowing the political power of the bourgeoisie and establishing an antibourgeois power;

—of the shortlived anticapitalist character of the revolution into the achievement of its antibourgeois character.

Despite its unequaled historical consequences, the predominance of the antibourgeois character of the Russian revolution was less decisive in its concrete effects than the predominance of its antifeudal character. It seems that the power of any character of the revolution to effect transformations diminished the more profoundly anticipatory it was in its nature.

Summing up, one can say that the antibourgeois character of the revolution, derived from a conflict nonspecific to it and dominated by factors likewise nonspecific, was concentrated on the least specific of ends and assumed relatively diluted forms. Consistent with this, its first effects were nonspecific, while its later effects, though specific, were but partial.

The structure of the conflict

As I have shown in the Introduction, univocal necessity tends to manifest itself in social conflicts having a dichotomous structure, while antinomic necessity engenders conflicts that are less concentrated and in structure rather fluid. In conflicts of this latter type space is created for the emergence of objective anticipatory possibilities, in which category the anticipated achievement of the antibourgeois character of the Russian revolution may be included. This explains the tendency for revolutionary energies to seek concrete forms that cut across the lines of social conflict so that ultimately in the Russian revolution the antibourgeois character came to predominate. The outcome of any conflict depends on a series of general factors such as, for example, necessity, possibility, the momentary combination of circumstances, chance, and the historical actors. The presence of these factors is constant throughout history; what varies is their hierarchy, and that in turn is determined by the relationship between necessity and possibility. The more direct the impact of necessity, the less receptive will be the conflict to the autonomous action of the other factors. Conversely, the more the conflict is conditioned by the possible, the less independent it will be of the autonomous action of these other factors.

Consider one historical example in illustration. In September Lenin proposed to the Bolshevik Central Committee the immediate organization of an insurrection against the Provisional Government. There was only one voice in favor of this proposal, his own. Lenin's response was to resign. There was nothing in his general behavior that would lend credence to the hypothesis that in resorting to this extreme step he had been guided by personal reasons. It would seem more likely that it was an expression not of the Bolshevik leader's excessive sensitivity, but of the extreme fragility of the positive combination of circumstances which existed at that moment. The revolutionary fervor of the masses receded drastically after the repressions of July, although the attempted military putsch in August brought about an impressive rebound. However, it was impossible to say how durable this recovery might be. Apart from the objective forces at play, any revolution will depend on broad hesitant social groupings, subject to unforeseeable shifts in mood. It is effectively a tautology to say that stable social forces are basically less sensitive to adventitious changes and that shifting contingencies are therefore in the main the reflection of the waverings of unstable social groupings. The less solidly a conflict is structured, the stronger will be the influence of these groupings, and hence of momentary circumstances, on the ultimate course of events.

Conjuncture, the circumstances of the moment, is an objective factor inasmuch as it is itself contingent on objective factors: necessity or possibility, on the one hand, and chance, on the other. Conjuncture occupies a place between these two extremes. Insofar as social instability is one of its ingredients, it is essentially transitory and irreversible, and thus very difficult to control. To take advantage of it requires, if not foresight, at least the ability to size up a situation quickly and correctly to evaluate the tendencies implicit in it. The extent to which historical actors do or do not possess the qualities requisite to this end is primarily a function of chance. Thus the respective roles played by conjuncture, the historical actors and chance are all determined by the fluidity of the conflict. Lenin's reaction in September was in a sense the expression of all these contingencies. Antinomic necessity made for a weakly structured social conflict that was but a reflection of the weakly structured society from which it has arisen. So was prerevolutionary society, and so indeed is every backward society under imperialist domination. The intermingling of stagnation and a halting modernization had produced a situation in which different types of social relations, normally separated by centuries of history, existed side by side. The classes and institutions of the old order coexisted with the classes and institutions typical of modern societies. The anachronism of the former and the immaturity of the latter, plus their mutual incompatibility, compounded by the shocks between internal and external contradictions, rendered impotent the self-transforming forces within society. Its basic structures lacked cohesion, were severely dysfunctional, and showed a marked tendency toward disintegration. No wonder then that the social conflict that emerged on this basis was weakly structured, diffuse and prone to dissipate or change its course abruptly. This general lack of consistency in social relations transformed class relations into relations of power, a transformation that has outlived its time, for it may be found in autocratic society, postrevolutionary society, and of course in Stalinist society.

One of the symptoms of the lack of structure to the social conflict was the number and the constellation of factors involved directly in its resolution. These facets varied from one episode of the conflict to another. For example, the antifeudal character achieved its ascendancy as a result of the direct confrontation between the peasantry, the Provisional Government and the landed nobility. The predominance of the antibourgeois character was rooted in a different combination of forces that embraced the proletariat, the bourgeoisie, the Provisional Government, the peasantry, and the Bolshevik party. Outwardly, the structure of the conflict seemed both more diffuse and more heterogeneous: more diffuse, because the number of factors involved grew perceptibly, and more heterogeneous, because social classes intermingled with political institutions and a social category that was itself stratified, and because one of the decisive factors was involved only indirectly in the specific conflict. Existing specifically to give political expression to the interests of two antagonistic classes, the two institutions, the Bolshevik party and the Provisional Government, secured for themselves sufficient autonomy to decide the outcome of the conflict in a direct confrontation. This autonomy had accrued to them less on the strength of their own virtues than by dint of the particular conditions pointing up the antagonism between the two principal classes. The first of these conditions, the conflict between proletariat and bourgeoisie, was shaped to a substantial degree by the broader, deeper and more radical conflict between the peasantry and the feudal landlords. The second condition, the squaring off of the proletariat with the bourgeoisie, was merely a conflict between two underdeveloped classes, and hence itself bore the marks of underdevelopment.

In influencing the conflict, these conditions also implicitly influenced the coordinates of how in the best of cases it would be resolved. The fact that both classes were underdeveloped meant that, even though the proletariat should emerge victorious, this alone would not be enough to ensure its ability to govern society, an ability that the bourgeoisie had demonstrated itself to be lacking. The social antagonism between the two underdeveloped classes was therefore transformed into a political conflict between two institutions, rather than being expressed in it. The antibourgeois character of the revolution came to predominate not as a direct effect of the antagonism between the working class and the capitalist class, but because of the direct clash between the Bolshevik party and the Provisional Government. The historical division of labor here is obvious to the eye. Rather than the conflict being raised from the social level to the political level by the same forces, there were different alliances of forces corresponding to the different levels. Thus proliferation of the factors involved in the revolution did not have a simple additive effect, but rather formed the precondition for a functional division. This was but a compensation for the limited ability of the basic factors to fulfill their historical roles. The incomplete fulfillment of their respective roles by the proletariat and the bourgeoisie meant that the antagonism between them would likewise remain but imperfectly resolved, i.e., the achievement of the anticapitalist character of the revolution would remain incomplete.

But a proliferation of factors has other effects. It dissipates the energy with which they fuel or oppose one another, magnifies their lack of cohesion, and broadens the range of possibilities engendered or favored by the conflict. In such a fragmented universe, with instability its dominant feature, it is only the deliberate pursuit of a real possibility that will enable one factor to assume ascendancy over the others and in the end determine the conflict, its resolution, and its consequences.

The bourgeoisie: economic positions

The bourgeoisie of course occupies a central position among the factors in the antibourgeois character of the revolution. Its behavior was to a large extent molded by the predicament of its existence, which Trotsky described as follows: "A class that had emerged in good time to muster millions, but too late to assume the leadership of the nation. Bearded old gaffers, muzhiks, and enriched shopkeepers piled up money without giving much thought to their special role." The belatedness of industrialization was aggravated by its slow pace and by its being embodied in structures handed down from the past. Social production, dragged fitfully and erratically into the modern era, reproduced and utilized the vestigial forms of primitive economy rather than abolishing them.

The territory of Russia resembled a sea dotted with isolated atolls of industry. Despite a certain adaptability to the old structures, the economic and social structures of these islands of industry differed profoundly from those existing in the country at large. The two 1917 insurrections took place in one— and moreover the same one—of these insular micro-societies, St. Petersburg, which was unique in many respects and utterly unlike the rest of Russian society. There were fateful limitations on the extent to which these two types of society could be forged into one. Together they formed not a functional society but an aggregation of disjointed elements—a syncretic society. Carried over into postrevolutionary society, this syncretism, this generator of social entropy, would be transformed by Stalinism into a social order in itself.

Another trait peculiar to Russian industry was the fact that its centers were dominated by foreign capital. "One of the reasons for the social instability of the Russian bourgeoisie," writes Trotsky, "was that its strongest element consisted of foreigners who did not even live in Russia." The capital that did remain in the hands of the national bourgeoisie in Russia was for the most part under the yoke of imperialism. The handicaps the bourgeoisie had carried from its very birth were aggravated by its involvement in the war, which further reinforced its dual dependence on international imperialism and on national imperialism, i.e., on the autocracy. Its already benign opposition to the autocracy was dampened further by the war orders that came its way. The Tsarist government created a special Conference of Industrialists to stimulate war production. The Unions of the *zemstvos* and cities and the war industries committees functioned in the same vein. The state Duma found itself more and more playing the role of intermediary between the monarchy and the bourgeoisie, and the latter obtained favors sometimes exceeding, in a single transaction, the total value of invested capital. But by virtue of the same circumstances that had made it possible to begin with, this prosperity, far from consolidating the bourgeoisie, merely made it more vulnerable.

The bourgeoisie: political positions

The dual economic dependence of the bourgeoisie was one of the principal obstacles to its affirmation as a political class: "The lack of any genuine political initiative on the part of the bourgeoisie with regard to Tsarism, which denied it almost all political rights, was also due to its economic dependence on the latter," writes Bettelheim. The political behavior of the bourgeoisie was far from coherent. To the ignorant, to the indifferent, to those who had placed their reliance on the goodwill of the autocracy, was added a liberal current, the mouthpiece of which was the constitutional democratic party, the Kadets. The object of this party was to bring Russia peacefully into the modern era while avoiding any revolutionary convulsions. Sensitive to populist traditions, this liberalism preferred after 1905 to adopt—to a point—Marxist rhetoric. However, far from betraying its true identity, this terminological radicalism was rather the reflection of a lack of political identity—a problem it shared with the most advanced layer of this class. The Russian bourgeoisie was unable to overcome its historical dilemma, and vacillated between an intolerant autocracy and an intolerable revolution. The effect of this protracted balancing act was to render it unable to embark upon any coherent action that would have enabled it to fulfill its civilizing historical mission.

For Russian liberalism, revolution was unacceptable as a remedy against Tsarism, but once the Tsar was overthrown, revolution became totally superfluous. Undesirable generally, from this point of view the revolution had exhausted its role by February in any case. The Kadet party was utterly captivated by the events it was witnessing, and did not notice that history had thrust it into the eye of the most awe-inspiring revolutionary maelstrom of the modern era.

One of the most eloquent manifestations of the political blindness of the Kadet party was that of its leader, Professor Miliukov, Minister of Foreign Affairs of the first Provisional Government, who sent a confidential memorandum to the Western Allies in April 1917 reaffirming the fidelity of the new cabinet to the treaties signed by the Tsarist government. The disclosure of this memorandum provoked an explosion of popular outrage which literally swept away Prince Lvov's first cabinet. This example merely illustrates the direction in which the Kadets were leaning generally, which was to oppose the vital demands of the population and put an end to the war and to feudalism.

Once in power, the bourgeoisie used it in an attempt to divert or throttle the social forces at work in the revolution—a futile effort, and a task too vast for its meager means; it was the bourgeoisie that would crumble upon impact with those same forces.

Trotsky stresses "the political weakness of the Russian bourgeoisie" to explain the "ease with which we broke our bourgeoisie." The remark is revealing: it suggests that by reason of its failings the bourgeoisie served in the last instance as a positive factor in the revolution's achievement of its antibourgeois character. The bourgeoisie had its proper contribution to make to the historical confirmation of Lenin's strategy, and hence to anticipatory revolution—its elimination as a class. Its exercise of power keenly demonstrated to what extent the bourgeoisie had declined before even having achieved maturity. Bound more to the autocracy than to democracy, more to feudalism than to free enterprise, more to war than to commerce, and more to international imperialism than to its own native land, the Russian bourgeoisie, stricken by a precocious senility, had itself provided one of the most important objective grounds for its early elimination.

Plekhanov derided "the utterly false idea that it was possible to accomplish a bourgeois revolution without a bourgeoisie." The Bolshevik party believed it could demonstrate the contrary but it did not; in reality, instead of accomplishing a bourgeois revolution without the bourgeoisie, it substituted an antibourgeois revolution for it.

The fate of the Russian bourgeoisie, essentially identical with that of the Kadet party, was in the last instance but the fate of the Provisional Government.

The socialist parties and the Provisional Government

The popular revolution gave birth to an unpopular government, thanks to the leaders of the socialist parties—the Mensheviks and the SRs—who made up the majority in the executive committee of the Petrograd Soviet, the author of the uprising. At the time, these parties had a considerable influence. The Mensheviks, with their outstanding leader, Martov, had continued to share a common program with the Bolsheviks since before the split of 1903. They had the firmest roots among the workers.

The SR leadership, very popular in the countryside and among the intellectuals, included some well-known militants from the struggle against the autocracy—people who had passed long years in prison or in exile, such as Tsereteli, Cheidze, Spiridonova, and others.

Marxists and revolutionaries, these people believed that the abolition of the autocracy and of feudalism should be the cause if not the effect of capitalist development in Russia. The development of capitalism was merely the development of productive forces, and hence the objective basis indispensable for the later transition to socialism.

Russia's economic backwardness was complemented by the theoretical backwardness of its prominent socialists, who had remained within the classical Marxist theory of capitalism, with its axiom of unequivocal necessity. Faithful to the text, they did not perceive that a fundamental historical mutation had occurred in the present era: namely, the emergence of international imperialism. They therefore continued to impute to the Russian bourgeoisie an industrializing mission of which it, under the heel of imperialism and autocracy, had already demonstrated itself incapable. The *quid pro quo* of the Commedia dell'Arte descended into history: the soviet handed over power to a class that it mistook for another.

In this view, Russia was on the verge of entering a sagely ordained period in its history in which an antifeudal revolution had necessarily to assume a bourgeois character. If, therefore, a bourgeois government were established, it could not do otherwise than consciously to adapt the character of the power *in situ* to the necessary character of the revolution. The shakiness of this argument did not detract from the reality of the undertaking. This gift horse of power, without precedent in the history of modern revolutions, notably reduced the possibility of the antifeudal revolution being transformed into an anticapitalist revolution before its time.

The Mensheviks and SRs were much less deluded about the proletariat than about the bourgeoisie. It was their opinion that the objective backwardness of the proletariat would render it unable to govern society even if by a fluke of history it were given the chance. Marxist revolutionaries had a duty, therefore, to avoid just such an anticipation as had been made the central aim of Bolshevik strategy. The Bolsheviks were able to pursue their strategy only by demonstrating an uncompromising opposition to the bourgeois government and the political parties that had carried it to power. To the socialist parties, confident in the bourgeoisie and mistrustful of the proletariat, the Bolshevik party opposed its mistrust of the former and confidence in the latter, despite its underdeveloped state. At the theoretical level, one could say that the Bolsheviks opposed their own overestimation of the capacities of the proletariat to the socialists' overestimation of the capacities of the bourgeoisie. History would corroborate in different ways the mistrust of both, and at the same time puncture the excessive confidence tendered in either case.

There are quite a number of scholars who hold that the premature overthrow of the Provisional Government was the point where the revolution took its decisive turn toward Stalinism. But this view does not square well with the historical facts. The October insurrection merely wrested from the bourgeoisie the last vestiges of a power which by that time it had already almost completely lost. It is difficult to determine to what extent power was seized by the Bolsheviks or lost by the bourgeoisie. By the time the insurrection took place the bourgeoisie had already accumulated an impressive record of historical ineptitude. It had failed in its attempt to arrest the revolution, at the time certainly not the design of the proletariat, which on the contrary was resolved to continue it. Bourgeois power had taken eight months to disintegrate and expire, but antibourgeois power took more than ten years to degenerate into Stalinism. During the eight months it remained in power, the bourgeoisie was unable to come up, even in outline, with one plausible alternative to the political course that led ultimately to its downfall, whereas during the ten years it lasted, antibourgeois power generated several plausible alternatives to the course causing it to deviate toward Stalinism. The exercise of bourgeois power amounted in practical terms to a coalition of the bourgeoisie, the feudal nobility and imperialism; the exercise of antibourgeois power was not necessarily consonant with its linear evolution into Stalinism. These facts considered, we may say that the possibility of a stable bourgeois government entailed the necessity of its fall, while the possibility of its early overthrow entailed but the possibility, no more, of Stalinism.

The strategy of the socialists was actually based on two propositions: one relating to the bourgeoisie, the other to the proletariat. They were not of equal force. Confidence in the beneficial effects of bourgeois power was an infinitely less sound proposition upon which to base a strategy than were doubts with regard to the possibility a premature proletarian power coming into being. Thus socialist strategy proved valid at the point where Bolshevik strategy ceased being so.

The mistakes of the socialists are traditionally attributed to the influence of the petty bourgeoisie. However, this diagnosis tends rather to invert the real relationship: the petty bourgeoisie influenced the development of these ideas less than it was itself seduced by them. The most important point where socialist strategy converged with the aspirations of the petty bourgeoisie was their mutual aversion to the revolution taking a radical turn that would pose a direct challenge to private property.

Strictly speaking, the transfer of power in February was the logical conclusion of a correct line of reasoning based on a false premise. To say this is to explain, of course, not to justify, but even that can no longer be done in the case of the socialists' later behavior. For soon after February it became evident that the bourgeoisie, whose mission it was to destroy feudalism, in fact had become its principal defender; thus, in continuing to defend the bourgeoisie the socialists were defending the *de facto* guardians of feudalism. Worse yet, the socialists did not merely support this reactionary policy; they assumed direct responsibility for it. Such a development can in any event no longer be attributed to doctrinal models; at fault was rather the petty bourgeoisie's leanings toward the bourgeoisie.

The Provisional Government was not the expression, but a distortion of class relations. What it actually expressed was an ill-omened break between social relations and political relations. A consequence of the social conflict's relative lack of structure, this break found support in the most weakly structured social layer, the petty bourgeoisie. It was because of the pressures from this latter group especially that between February and October the antibourgeois character of the revolution would remain effectively concealed by the bourgeois and the petty-bourgeois character of the government. Once its mystifying function was exposed, the power of the government, already shaky, was rapidly reduced to a fiction.

In February the socialist parties were still insisting on the right to control the government to which they had given birth. Shortly afterwards they agreed to be part of a coalition government prefatory to the formation of an exclusively socialist government sometime in the future. In its composition at least, the government was moving steadily toward the left. Schapiro explains this drift of the socialist parties as follows: "Their leaders eventually entered the government and thereafter progressively drove it further to the left." But this leftward movement was only apparent. The real movement was in the contrary direction. The government had managed to change its overall composition, but had modified not one bit its basic positions on the two vital questions: land and the war. The recastings therefore did not signify a shift of the government to the left but the drift of the non-Bolshevik left toward the fundamental positions of the government. While the masses were becoming more and more resolute in affirming their demands, the government's inertia in turn propelled it more and more to the right.

The socialist parties changed roles when they entered government. Initially they tolerated the bourgeois government they had installed while keeping their distance from its policies. Later, when they joined the government, they implicitly associated themselves with these policies as well. In the end, those who had once been its guardians became the most active protagonists of a policy the ultimate aim of which was to prevent the radicalization of the revolution. Such was the itinerary of the political suicide of the left-wing parties. Upon assuming a direct hand in government the socialists acknowledged in practice the inability of the bourgeoisie to lead postautocratic society. Thus it was that in practice they abrogated the theoretical arguments they had invoked in support of the transfer of power in February. The identification of the socialist parties with the pro-imperialist and profeudal policies of the bourgeoisie had one other effect: the Bolshevik party became the only credible left-wing political organization existing in Russia at that moment. The socialist parties had assigned a historical role to the bourgeoisie which it then proved incapable of fulfilling. Thus the failure of the bourgeoisie was also a failure of the socialist parties and, by implication, of political pluralism. Impervious to the real course of events, the Mensheviks and SRs forced the Bolshevik party into that triumphant solitude that was to be the first source of Stalinist monolithism.

For both social and political reasons the socialist parties pursued a strategy at cross purposes with the revolutionary movement of the masses. As for the Bolshevik party, it had no need to adapt its strategy to the direction of the movement; the movement itself had spontaneously taken the direction this strategy had foreseen.

The Provisional Government

In February, the most active forces of the revolution—the workers, soldiers, and the ordinary people of Petrograd—smashed the old political power and entrusted the new power to the municipal Soviet. But instead of assuming that power itself, the Petrograd Soviet thereupon handed it over in their name to the party of the liberal bourgeoisie. Thus Russian democracy was the product of a profoundly antidemocratic act; an act by representatives against those they represented. The transfer of power in February was a violation of trust. Although itself limited, the political position thus acquired by the bourgeoisie was severely out of proportion to its economic strength. The disproportion was to reappear in October, although of course in very different forms. But the likeness goes no further, for the bourgeoisie still possessed considerable economic power whereas the proletariat had none (not to speak of the Bolshevik party). Further, whereas the bourgeois government was established in opposition to the popular movements, the Bolshevik government was their product, albeit an indirect one. Finally, the liberal bourgeoisie acquired state power through conferral, while the Bolshevik party acquired it through struggle.

A genetic antinomy. The first structures transformed by a revolution are the structures of power. In February, the forces of revolution only half resolved this problem: it was they who brought down the autocracy, but it was not they who installed the Provisional Government. Trotsky defined this discontinuity as "a contradiction between the character of the revolution and the character of the government that emerged from it." This point would seem to be essential for the discussion of the character of the revolution. A power which is not imposed *by*, but *on*, the revolution, can confer upon it its character in only one way: by stifling it. As the facts will show, when the Russian bourgeoisie accepted political power, it had already exhausted most of its potential for change.

In prerevolutionary Russian society, where capitalist relations of production were still a long way from being the general case throughout the country, the bourgeoisie was even further from being the ruling class. When it formed the government that status became a possibility. The socialists thus invested the bourgeoisie with a historical function in which it would ultimately fail. The bourgeoisie did not attempt to impose its own class character on the revolution; it endeavored only to arrest it, if it could not force it to retreat. Europe and the world would look different today if the Russian revolution had restricted its objective to abolishing the autocracy. Commenting on the experiences of Austria and Germany, Isaac Deutscher wrote: "If Russia had become similarly arrested in the February Revolution and produced in 1917 or 1918 a Russian variety of the Weimar Republic, what reason is there to assume that we should have remembered the Russian Revolution today?" He concludes: "The February Revolution of 1917 holds its place in history only as the prelude of October."

Action. But instead of being arrested, the revolution bit by bit achieved its antifeudal and antibourgeois characters. The bourgeoisie failed in its bid to become the ruling class of society, and the failure was to an appreciable measure due to its own actions, whether in terms of government program, effective strategy, or political tactic.

No sooner was it formed than Prince Lvov's first cabinet published on March 6 a declaration setting forth its program. The issue of the war was skirted, although there was no lack of assurances of loyalty to the Western Allies. A solution to the problem of the property of the landed nobility was promised, although left indefinite and without dates. The most important project in domestic policy was to convoke a Constituent Assembly within a time likewise left indefinite. The Tsar had already announced his abdication some days before, but the new government's program contained not even the slightest allusion to the future form of the state in Russia.

As is evident from what the Provisional Government actually accomplished, its strategy consisted in continuing the war, equivocating about peasant demands, and snuffing out the revolutionary *élan* of the masses.

The Provisional Government was remarkably inept in implementing this project in defeatism. Its chronic disjointedness is amply illustrated by the progression from the democracy of March to the repressions of July, from the "peace appeal" to the offensive in Galicia, from systematic equivocation on real problems to endemic proliferations of fictitious institutions, from the remanding of all burning issues to the Constituent Assembly to the steadfast refusal to organize the assembly's election, from the promotion of Kornilov to the rank of Commander in Chief to the tolerance, to the point of complicity, of his preparations for a military putsch, etc.

General features. All these factors together rendered the power of the bourgeoisie unstable and but partial.

The ministerial composition of the Provisional Government changed with a frequency reminiscent of French politics in the years leading up to World War II. Formed in early March, the government had its first shake-up on May 6, in the aftermath of demonstrations provoked by Miliukov's note. The socialists began their government career, which was later to end in utter defeat. On July 24 they formed the majority in a government which after Kornilov's putsch would assume the name of Directory, soon replaced by the name "Committee of Public Safety." "Every new transformation in the government," observed Trotsky, ''was made in the name of a strong power, and each new ministerial cabinet began in a major key only to fall prostrate a few days later until finally a stroke from without was all that lacked for it to crumble. The mass movement was causing continual tremors; beyond misleading appearances, each change in the government was in a direction counter to the mass movement.'' The instability of the Provisional Government was the expression of the nonviability of bourgeois power. That experience was to play a role later when a power that was stable became immutable.

The limited power of the Provisional Government is habitually confused with ''dual power,'' to which we shall return later. But first a few comments on the articulation between political relations and social relations and the monopoly on the legal exercise of violence.

The establishment of a bourgeois government was justified neither by the economic and social positions of this class, nor by the revolutionary skirmish of which it was the distorted outgrowth. State power became estranged from its natural social premises. What ensued was a relative autonomy of policy, which paved the way to the equally autonomous final conflict that saw the Bolshevik party in armed uprising against the government. The relative autonomy of bourgeois state power was an expression not of its independence from social structures but of its isolation from them. Later on, preventing its own independence of social relations from developing into an isolation from them would be one of the crucial problems of the power installed in October.

The isolation of bourgeois power meant essentially that it was impotent to control the society it was presumed to be governing. The conditions and instruments for this were simply lacking. For example, the existing structures barred it from access to an essential function of any government: monopoly over the legal exercise of violence.

The Provisional Government shared decision-making powers with the soviet, while its monopoly on the use of violence was restricted by the revolutionary movement of the masses (first and foremost the peasants). The first of these limitations, dubbed dual power and resting on agreement, was less undermining of its authority than the second, which it was forced resignedly to accept. The utter indifference of the mass movement to legal constraints demonstrated that revolution was gaining in momentum, not losing, inasmuch as an identifying trait of every revolution is the erosion of a government's monopoly on the use of violence. Consensus secured by legal and material means falls to pieces and the use of violence becomes democratized. Revolution smashes the legal edifice of society, which had become obsolete, and through the instrument of mass violence lays the foundation for another.

In Russia this process was accelerated by a sequence of special circumstances. First the class that acquired the legal monopoly on the use of violence had not itself participated in the extralegal violence that had abolished the previous monopoly. The new monopoly it tried to establish did not represent the legalization of an extralegal violence in which this class had earlier participated. The lack of continuity meant a lack of legitimacy.

Consequently the monopoly enjoyed by the Provisional Government remained formal and the instruments that might have made it effective remained elusive. First among these instruments was the army. The army eluded the control of the Provisional Government, and the flaw became flagrantly manifest on several occasions—for example, the offensive ordered by Kerensky in June, Kornilov's putsch, and the attempt to evacuate the Petrograd garrison. The Provisional Government made this deplorable state of affairs even worse by its utter inability to comprehend it; nor was it aware of its own impotence or the overwhelming strength of the revolutionary current. Blindly groping its way in this explosive situation, it of course achieved just the contrary of what it set out to do. Not only did its policies fail to check the spread of extralegal violence, it became one of the principal stimulators of that violence. Thus it contributed to the transformation of peasant uprisings into a peasant war.

The compound inability of the Provisional Government on two fronts, namely to use legitimate violence itself and to block its extralegal use by the masses, culminated quite naturally in its not very violent disappearance in October.

A balance sheet. "The experience of the Provisional Government," wrote Bettelheim, "demonstrated the inability of the bourgeoisie and the petty bourgeoisie to lead Russia out of the dead end situation in which it had fallen." This experience also demonstrated something of even greater moment: the inability of the Russian bourgeoisie to become the ruling class of a postfeudal Russia and to lead the country down the path of industrialization. Bourgeois power collapsed under the same signs that marked its advent, namely its political ineptitude and historical sterility. Thus in October it found itself shorn of the political power which in February had been conferred upon it, having shown itself as incapable of defending that power as of exercising it.

The soviets

The historical importance of the soviets certainly does not lie in the fact that the anti-autocratic revolution had conferred upon them a power which they, instead of exercising it, had transferred to the bourgeoisie, nor in the fact that in October they had assumed supreme power only to hold it for one night, albeit employing that power in a way that was to convulse the history of Russia and of the world. To fully grasp their historical importance a number of other facts must be added to these to complete the picture. The struggle against the autocracy in 1905 was structured around the soviets. In 1917 the soviets shared the new power with the bourgeoisie whom they had supported and opposed at the same time. It was in the soviets that the Bolsheviks had set up the military committee, which led the direct preparations for the October insurrection. It was the soviets that formed, even before October, the effective structure of the future antibourgeois power, a structure that was formalized immediately after victory. In Lenin's vision the soviets were to be the cornerstone of a democratic system; history, however, transformed that system into its opposite, and the soviet movement was ultimately appropriated and institutionalized by Stalinism. Together these facts justify the view that the historical importance of the soviets lies first and foremost in the fact that they seem just as perennial as they are functionally misbegotten.

The vast array of facts such as these and the multitude of roles, often contradictory, performed by the soviets, makes the determination of their overriding function extremely difficult. At first sight, the soviets present a functional picture dominated by a lack of coherence and by antinomy, which suggests the hypothesis that what we are a witness to in this spontaneity is a mechanism operating at the very foundations of society: the antinomic necessity which ruled society at large was reflected in the antinomy dominating the soviets.

The high points of the existence of the soviets were the two insurrections, in each of which they played a different role. In February, a local soviet, formerly nonexistent, was invested with a power that it rejected by a revolutionary movement that it had not led. In October the Congress of Soviets, formally constituted, arrogated to itself the supreme power of the state, which it had been denied and which it then proceeded to employ in compliance with an antibourgeois movement that the soviets had not led. Having played a minor role in the affirmation of the antifeudal character of the revolution, the soviets played an irreplaceable role in affirming its antibourgeois character. As it was manifested, this role was fashioned out of a multitude of waverings and contradictions.

In February, while the masses were sealing the demise of the autocracy in the streets of Petrograd, in one of its several palaces, a group of left-wing militants proclaimed themselves the executive committee of a soviet that did not exist and so could not elect them. The legitimacy of this committee was based on the prestige the soviets had acquired in 1905, on the prestige of the militants who had created it, and above all on the trust the popular movement immediately placed in it. Prevented by this movement from installing another Tsar in the place of the one they had dethroned, the authors of this palace coup had created unawares a power vacuum which only the soviet, on the strength of its legitimacy, was able to fill. Thus did a frail and tottering local institution assume a nation's supreme prerogative: the exercise of state power. Its use of this prerogative was totally unheard of: the soviet declared itself incapable of exercising power, yet capable of bestowing it. The antinomies in its behavior joined ranks with the antinomies of its birth, of its formation, and of its structures.

The workers and soldiers very quickly began to form their own soviets. The peasant soviet was not created until May, by a government initiative with a view to checking the influence of the former. The Mensheviks considered the soviets a class organization of the proletariat and in this were seconded by the SRs. In reality, in each and every one of the soviets the workers were buried under the masses of soldiers, the vast majority of peasant origin, and the masses of the rural and urban petty bourgeoisie. The class character of the soviets was restricted because they remained closed to the bourgeoisie and the aristocracy. The diffuse structure of the soviets had three principal hallmarks: class heterogeneity, a vacillating political leaning, and territorial dispersion. After February the Petrograd Soviet, the Executive Committee of Workers' and Soldiers' Soviets, and the Executive Committee of the Peasant Soviets were often in disagreement among themselves on various problems. Moreover, the control of these three supreme soviet bodies over the local soviets, which were primarily receptive to immediate influences, was largely illusory.

This lack of intrinsic structures became steadily more accentuated under the impact of events, reaching its culmination in July in a veritable mitosis. After the new ministerial reshuffling, the individuals who in February had personified the soviets were now intermingled with the government. The actual soviets, representative of the population, took their leave of those who had represented the soviets in their persons, but were now part of the same government that they, the soviets, opposed. The soviets objectively rallied to Bolshevik positions, and had to endure repressive measures from a government formed by the very people who had formed the Petrograd Soviet in February. "The July turning point," wrote Trotsky, "affected the soviets much more directly than the party or the trade unions." For the soviets "could only abide on the basis of a revolutionary situation and when it disappeared they disappeared with it." History introduced a crucial modification to this observation: the soviets did not disappear with the revolutionary situation, they changed their function.

The soviets responded to the repressive measures of the Provisional Government in the antinomic fashion consistent with the times. While the already established soviets curtailed their activities substantially, the formation of new soviets in the countryside acquired new impetus.

This contradictory turning in the course of events was abruptly brought to a halt by the shock of the military putsch, which provoked a general upswing in revolutionary energy. The result was that by the end of August there were 600 soviets counting 23 million voices. This proliferation was consolidated by an impressive rise of militancy. Swept along by events, the Petrograd Soviet now created its own military arm, known as the Revolutionary Military Committee. Henceforth no government order concerning troop movements could be executed unless countersigned by this committee. The breaking of the government's monopoly on the exercise of violence—in the event, its exclusive command over the army—acquired an institutional form for the first time. In a few weeks the military arm of the soviet would become the famous military committee, the principal organizer of the October insurrection. Thus within a short time the monopoly on the use of violence would be transformed from a fiction in the hands of the government into an effective power in the hands of the opposition.

The contradictory behavior of the soviets explains the contradictory functions attributed to them by the contending political forces. The Mensheviks and the SRs, while still dominating the soviets, retained the same conception of their role as they had had in February: the soviets not only had to refrain from aiming for power, they had actively to avoid it. The argument, as Anweiler puts it, was that "the soviets were class organizations that grouped only a part of the population." Power to the soviets, therefore, would entail the risk that "other social categories—the bourgeoisie foremost, but also a part of the peasantry—would break with the revolution, and the proletariat, the lifeblood of soviet power, would find itself isolated." The justification offered for wanting to reduce the role of the soviets to nil—the proletarian class character—was clearly an illusion. The socialists believed that with the formation of the Provisional Government the revolution had accomplished the historical tasks of Russian society at the present stage, and that this being the case the soviets had completed their mission as well. Moreover, now in the government themselves, their desire to be rid of the soviets could only increase. The socialist government's coolness toward the soviets had two sources: one, its own general policy, and the other, the very nature of the soviets, which no central government could tolerate. By the mere fact of their existence, the soviets had an irrepressible tendency to transform the decentralization of power into fragmentation, thereby reducing any national government to, practically speaking, a formal shell. The reality of the soviets reduced the central government to mere form without substance. Later on, the converse of this proposition would be amply demonstrated by Stalinism.

It was under these conditions that Lenin came out with his historical slogan "All Power to the Soviets" in early April. Thus only one month after the event, the historical act of February was openly being contested and the soviets were being called upon to recover the power the socialists had obliged them to relinquish.

The dispute between socialists and Bolsheviks on the role of the soviets was not limited to considerations of mere tactics; it had also to do with the structures of postrevolutionary society. "No parliamentary republic—to return to such a republic would be a step backward—but rather a republic of soviets," declared Lenin. This long-term conception was soon altered under the pressure of the changing circumstances, and it became clear that the Bolsheviks, too, lacked a genuine strategy for the organization of future society.

Between April and July, the soviets leaned toward the socialists, who refused to give them power; all the while the Bolsheviks were calling for taking precisely that step. Worse than that, the soviets' responses to the repressive measures of the Provisional Government were vacillating and irresolute. Somewhat later, the Sixth Congress of the Bolshevik Party, held (semiclandestinely) between July 26 and August 3, adopted a resolution which betokened a radical revision of the April Theses. "The familiar slogan 'All Power to the Soviets' was now out of date," wrote Schapiro concerning this resolution. But no sooner was the resolution made public than the situation changed anew. The threat of a military dictatorship galvanized the soviets, and the Bolshevik party reverted to its previous position. Though Bolshevik policies were in general distinguished by a remarkable coherence, they too did not remain unaffected by the soviets' lack of steadfastness. Through all their shiftings and turnings the soviets proved their vocation: to subserve the conciliatory line of the Provisional Government at the same time as they were bending to the policy pursued by the Bolsheviks of radicalizing the revolution. Alternately supporting the revolution against the Provisional Government and the Provisional Government against the revolution, the soviets became an arena for a political battle in grand style. Each side in the battle obviously jockeyed for the best positions. The efforts of such contradictory influences were compounded by the soviets' intrinsic infirmity of purpose, and they were thus driven to the brink of disintegration. Whereas at the epicenter of the revolution the soviets followed the government, in the countryside they stood in its stead. As Trotsky remarks, the local soviets "intervened in the leadership of the army, in economic conflicts, in questions of supplies and transport, and even in judiciary matters. The soviets decreed an eight-hour day under pressure from the workers, eliminated excessively reactionary administrators, dismissed the most intolerable of the commissars of the Provisional Government, undertook arrests and requisitions, and banned hostile newspapers." Dual power became the dual power of the soviets: the rabid decentralization to which they were inclined by nature destroyed their own centralized structures. At the base they carried the decentralization of power to the brink of dissolution, while at the top every effort was made to consolidate it. The general effect was to create a power vacuum on a national scale which became, in fact, the principal contribution of the soviets to the October insurrection and hence to the achievement of the antibourgeois character of the revolution. Assuming the prerogatives of government, the central soviets intensified the specific conflict entailed by the antibourgeois character of the revolution. Thanks to a considerable extent to the substitutive role played by the soviets, the group arrested on October 26 in the Winter Palace no longer represented anything more than a few real persons forming an illusory government.

The October revolution, so reads the official history of the CPSU, was different from all other revolutions "in that the workers created their own bodies of power . . . the soviets of workers deputies." (Thus forty years after the revolution, the official history rehabilitates the old Menshevik notion of the proletarian class character of the soviets, rejected at the time by Lenin.) Trotsky in turn writes, "The soviets were created for the conquest of power." Obviously these are two totally opposing views on the historical function of the soviets. In the official ideology of the period of the thaw this function consisted in placing the exercise of power in the hands of the workers; for Trotsky it was the conquest of power. The historical function the soviets actually performed went beyond a mere synthesis of these opposing views.

Their emergence signified the institutionalization of the time-honored aspirations of the masses to democratic power. To the extent that they remained authentic, the soviets tended spontaneously to erode centralized power. This tendency was not necessarily directed toward a specific political end. It was as much a threat to the centralized power on its way out as it was to the power in the process of being constituted. Decentralization was not a deliberately pursued end; the soviets bred it spontaneously. The effect was not in the first instance concentrated on the particular political identity of centralized power, but rather on the centralization itself. Thus the soviets represented a current of change that was just as apolitical in its essence as it was political in its manifestations and consequences. This will explain why their social effect has been perennially mistaken for a political objective: a teleology is artificially imposed upon a simple cause and effect relation. Of course this is not to imply that the soviets did not also make the political choices at various junctures: but these choices did not alter their essential nature, and hence had no lasting effects. Outwardly the political impact of the soviets was one of permanent and nonselective opposition, deriving not from a program but from their nature; they alternately opposed and supported the principal contending political forces.

Always active, the soviets were not always politically effective. Their apoliticism was qualitatively different from that of the antifeudal movement; for the latter it amounted at core to a general political indifference, whereas the apoliticism of the soviets was manifested in a receptiveness to power focused less on the designs than on the structures of power. Hence the dual oscillations: of the soviets toward the principal political forces and of the latter toward the soviets, a reciprocity demonstrating that the soviets were not merely unstable unto themselves, but transmitted their instability to other social forces and thus, more broadly, to the revolution. They were the utter social embodiment of the fragile structure of the social conflict and of the antinomic necessity that governed it. Their changeable nature was also partly due to the fact that they were leaning toward the establishment of a political system which the society was not mature enough to assimilate.

The antifeudal movement destroyed the social roots of a class; the soviet movement destroyed the social foundations of a particular type of political power. The direct action of the antifeudal movement was indifferent to the power that represented the principal target of the soviets.

Their apoliticism rendered the soviets extremely unstable politically, yet also extremely influential, and this could only enhance their importance in a revolutionary situation.

This discussion aims to broaden the perspective on the function of the soviets and by implication to demonstrate the inadequacy of the paradigmatic alternative: conquest of power or exercise of power. The view I have proposed emphasizes the essential constancy of the soviets and not their shifting behavior, which was but an outward form. Accordingly, the function of the soviets consisted in neither the conquest nor the exercise of power, but in altering its structures. Even when they were the most favorably inclined toward central power their erosion of it never stopped, as they appropriated its instruments one by one. Under the specific conditions of the Russian revolution, this undermining effect of the soviets was crucial to the establishment of a new power which, belonging to antibourgeois forces, would by implication no longer belong to the soviets. If the general function of the soviets consisted in eroding all centralized power, their activity would be inimical to the exercise of any power.

From the standpoint of the contending political forces, this general function assumed, broadly speaking, two alternative forms. In the struggle for power, the function of the soviets consisted in facilitating the overthrow of the power *in stare* and placing in power those who had opposed it. Although pursuing different economic and social ends, the new power would remain (at least) as centralized as its predecessor and thus structurally (at least) just as alienated from the soviets. The most striking example of this alienation is provided by the Second Congress of Soviets. It was the sole occasion where the soviets assumed full power, which they were to exercise never again.

In the exercise of postrevolutionary power, the function of the soviets consisted in striking a benign decentralizing note as a counterweight to centralization—or supercentralization. Deprived of their autonomy, the soviets were transformed into an instrument of the status quo and hence of a centralized power that effectively represented their negation, quite independently of its political coloration. The soviets were allowed to survive at the price of a ban on their acting consistently with their nature. From a centrifugal force against centralism they were transformed into buffers against its effects and so into its legitimators.

It was on this basis that the assimilation of the soviets by Stalinism took place; their survival was due to their functional accomplishments as legitimators of supercentralization and absorbers of its consequences.

For Stalinism, a social order essentially lacking in coherence, the soviets had another use as well: they enabled Stalinism to articulate the organization of power with that of property. Indeed, through the soviets, the effective realities of power became separated from its formal representation, which so served to dissimulate the former. The socialization of property, *de jure* wholly formal and *de facto* wholly illusory, was matched by a decentralization of power, likewise wholly formal and wholly illusory. Sapped of their vital forces, the soviets survived as a shell, compounding further the divorce between real power and power *de jure*, and so contributing to the emergence of a new form of extralegality, that of a power situated above the law, in effect one of the defining traits of Stalinism.

Heir to an incomplete revolution, Stalinism performed a historical function that consisted not so much in stabilizing revolutionary gains as in consummating them. To fulfill this function Stalinism traversed the path not from revolutionary violence to the force of law, but from a diffuse violence that was beyond the law to one that was centralized. If power remains above and hence outside the law for a prolonged period it sinks into clandestinity and centralized violence. Practiced over time by this clandestine power, centralized extralegal violence was transformed into terror. Unstable as they were, the soviets came to assume a function that was merely one of the components of Stalinist terror: they enabled Stalinism to apply its monopolization of extralegal violence to the effective decentralization of totally ineffective legal prerogatives.

Dual power

Dual power is a phrase, used by Lenin in his April Theses, that has echoed across history. Worked over in the bowels of official ideology, this concept has had the fate of so many others like it: it was eviscerated of all sense by the attribution to it of so many meanings which it did not have. As Lenin understood it, and indeed underscored, dual power was subject to two limits—in time, and in the configuration of the social conflict. In time, because the soviet did not share power with the government until it became one with it. In the configuration of the social conflict, because the limitations imposed on the government by the soviet's exercise of a controlling function over it were less restrictive than those imposed on it by the general insubordination of the populace. Therefore, the most profound and hence most enduring phenomenon was not the duplication of power but its destructuration. Still, dual power had its importance, for it demonstrated to the Provisional Government its own impotence from the moment it was born. The socialists created simultaneously the Provisional Government and the mechanism that prevented it from governing. Seen in this light, the contribution of dual power to the fulfillment of the antibourgeois character of the revolution was direct and undeniable.

The soviet did not exercise control over the government in the way practiced by opposition parties in parliamentary democracies. Such opposition, the shadow cabinet of the English included, has but one aim, to bring the government down and to govern in its place. In contrast, the soviet had willingly ceded power to the Provisional Government and therefore had no intention of bringing it down. Both the transfer of power and the limits imposed on it were the fruits of accord, a formal agreement, not confrontation. With the assistance of an institution, namely, the Contact Committee, the joint exercise of the direct executive powers of the Provisional Government and the soviet was established on this basis, by virtue of negotiated contract. This agreement was nothing else than a certificate of ineptitude served upon the Provisional Government by its creators.

By diminishing executive authority, the sharing of power also implicitly reduced the obstacles to the mass revolutionary movement. It did not take long for this to become evident, and the initiators of dual power lost no time supplanting the sharing of executive power by the concentration of these powers in a coalition government. The retreat was swift in coming, measured by the days of the calendar, but too late in terms of the time that governs the historical flow of events. The united forces (at this point a reality) of the government and the soviet, the socialist parties and the Kadet party, the liberal bourgeoisie and the petty bourgeoisie, no longer sufficed to prevent the peasants from seizing feudal lands and the soldiers from abandoning a war which only those in government wished to continue. The coalition eliminated dual power and by this act showed itself more clearly than ever for what it was: the soviet and the government squabbled over the control of mechanisms that controlled nothing at all. The revolution plied its course, totally indifferent to both the soviet and the government or, for that matter, to their merger.

The direct impact of dual power on the achievement of the antibourgeois character of the revolution was less potent than its indirect effect, which primarily affected the role of the Bolshevik party. By installing a totally paralyzed bourgeois government and implicating all the parties from the Kadets to the Mensheviks in its failure, dual power had created the first premise for the collapse of all political forces. It thus largely facilitated the emergence of the Bolshevik party as the sole credible political force—a solitary position, often mistaken for leadership. If the Bolshevik party was thrust onto center stage, this was in considerable measure due to the political vacuum produced by dual power. To maintain its position, the Bolshevik party reproduced this vacuum by centralizing power beyond measure. Spontaneous monolithism, created by the revolution, would be followed by the deliberate and conscious monolithism cultivated by Stalinism.

The army

A revolution is the resolution of society's vital problems by way of violence, and the army is the social organism most specialized in the exercise of violence. A situation in which violence becomes a matter of priority, namely war or revolution, normally confers a prime role on the army. If the historical situation combines revolution with war, this role is enhanced even further. The Russian revolution serves merely to confirm this, inasmuch as aside from the proletariat the army was the one social force that had a direct and decisive hand in both insurrections. As Trotsky pointed out in commenting on these two events: "Victory in both cases was ensured by the fact that the majority of the reserve regiments went over to the workers." The special importance of the army in the revolution has been emphasized by Hélène Carrère d'Encausse who observes: "In the two revolutionary movements (i.e., of the workers and of the peasants, P.C.), it was still a force to be reckoned with, for how it stood weighed decisively on the outcome of events." The institutions of a country in a state of war and internal ferment all gravitate to the army. During the three years of war, instead of supporting these institutions, the Russian army disengaged itself from them, which only aggravated their instability. D'Encausse continues: "The army broke with all the institutions created in February." The principal generalizing mechanism for this process in the army was its insubordination. What the army gained in autonomy, the social, civil, and military hierarchy lost in efficiency. As this evolution continued, the army would continually recreate a vacuum of authority in which the autocracy, the liberal Provisional Government, the soviet (initially in its own capacity, but later as a socialist government), the army's own commander-in-chief, Kornilov (when he attempted to establish his dictatorship), the commander-in-chief who followed him (Kerensky), and its general staff tumbled and were gone, one by one. The army's attitude toward the authorities may be defined as passivity with actively hostile repercussions. "In none of its crises, in April, July, or October, was the Provisional Government able to call on the army to help it establish its authority," commented Trotsky. The term "passivity" is intended to stress the fact that the disaggregating influence of the army came less from its actions than from its refusal to act, which affected all the structures of authority that came upon the scene between February and October, without discrimination. Thus the army not only contributed to the revolution, it also helped give it its dynamic.

The picture would be incomplete if its quantitative aspect were overlooked: the number of troops reached ten millions, a high proportion of the most active male population. Its increasing autonomy, compounded by its sheer numbers, made the army one of the principal social forces involved in the revolutionary transformation of Russia.

Like the soviets, the army did not have a homogeneous class composition, although unlike them, it had a peasant majority, without the army becoming a military wing of the peasantry on that account. A proof of this is that at a certain number of crucial moments in the revolution the peasantry and the army behaved quite differently. The army was in the thick of events during the overthrow of the autocracy, as the peasantry looked on from afar. The soldiers promptly joined the soviets, while the peasants remained very wary of them. Any direct participation of the army in the antifeudal struggle was minimal, while the peasantry threw themselves into it almost to the last man. But it was the war that determined the army's conduct, and the part it would cut out for itself in the revolution. This was the first imperialist world war, in full progress, and Russia had already lost it. No longer did the principle that war is but the continuation of politics by other means apply; the war was the direct expression of imperialist politics, with Russia being both victim and protagonist at the same time. Imperialism politicized the war, and this in turn politicized the army.

The army's mixed composition was hardly a help to consistent conduct. It wavered generally, although in the last instance it was the troops who were the decisive factor in determining what position the army would take. Long periods of vacillation, punctuated by intervals of a relatively steady course, described the historical itinerary carrying the army from its chauvinist élan in July 1914 to its objective support for leaving the war in October 1917. The country's international role also underwent a reversal: Russia, the gendarme of Europe, became the forecourt of European revolution.

Moreover, the army itself changed radically along the way: the strategy guiding its course ceased to be that of its general staff, and became that of the Bolshevik party. Not that Bolshevik strategy was adopted consciously: a spontaneous alignment had rather taken place, the objective impact of which was still enormous nonetheless. It was the need to institutionalize these changes that drew the soldiers toward the soviets. Two organizations, hybrid in composition and shifting in conduct, lent one another mutual support as they progressed down the road of radicalization. At the Second Congress of Soviets it was the soldier deputies who cast the decisive votes on a range of issues from the adoption of the peace and the land decrees to the establishment of the first Bolshevik government. "In October 1917," writes Bettelheim, "the armed forces, carrying the fate of the revolution in their hands, were no longer willing to fight for the bourgeoisie."

Each time the revolution changed its dominant character, its content, i.e., the deployment of social forces within it, also changed. The part played by the army in the fulfillment of the different characters of the revolution also varied. Its most active role, of course, was in the achievement of the anti-imperialist character of the revolution, a point I shall take up later when I discuss this character specifically. At present we shall merely make some brief observations on the position of the army in the achievement of the revolution's antibourgeois and antifeudal characters. Neither the antibourgeois insurrection nor the antifeudal war was an essentially military operation; both were civilian uprisings, distinct in their social function and their scope. The interests of the army, made up mostly of peasants, were more directly linked to the antifeudal struggle than to the antibourgeois insurrection, although its direct action was decisive for the latter, not for the first. The army's position was crucial to the workers' victorious assault on the Winter Palace, but not to the peasant assault on the feudal manors. In the October insurrection, the army's participation may be described basically as passive insubordination, while in the peasant war its formal nonengagement was punctuated by instances of informal, spontaneous action. In the struggle against the bourgeoisie, passive insubordination was kindled by the most revolutionary elements into active political militancy; the peasant soldiers, on the other hand, participated in the antifeudal movement on an individual basis, as befit its apoliticism. These differences explain why the army's historical role was more productive in the antibourgeois insurrection than in the antifeudal movement. Furthermore, the more it threw itself into the transformation of society the more it was itself transformed: during the antibourgeois insurrection, its command structures collapsed totally, but this did not happen in the peasant rebellions. The army's role in the October insurrection was expanded later into a relative stable social position in the war of intervention and civil war. Relative autonomy, and hence a facility for insubordination, enabled the army to adopt all the more readily a posture of social arbitrator.

The historical lesson in the army's evolution was later not lost on Stalinism, which would crush its insubordination unconditionally by the political and even physical annihilation of those who had created it as well as its best officers. Total obedience of the new officers was ensured by the very terms of their promotion. Its autonomous flirtation with the role of social arbitrator would be converted into a totally controlled cog in the new machinery of power. The experience of World War II put this relation of total subordination to the extreme test, but that this relation was crucial to the very functioning of the Stalinist social order would be confirmed by the dismissal, in the very midst of the anti-Stalinist thaw, of Marshal Zhukov, the war's most eminent hero.

The army's depoliticization and subordination which Stalin accomplished with particular brutality explains the rather unobtrusive figure cut by the army in the political life of Stalinist societies, which until December 1981 never experienced a military coup d'état.

The role of the proletariat

An accurate delineation of the role of the proletariat is an absolute necessity for an accurate definition of the character of the revolution, and especially of the regime that was born of the antibourgeois insurrection. The hypothesis of this book is that the antibourgeois character of the Russian revolution achieved ascendancy whereas its proletarian character remained imperfectly fulfilled. The proletariat was the revolution's most constant social force and participated in the fulfillment of each of its characters. Antibourgeois to the core, its actions in this respect were as persevering as they were limited. Indeed, the proletariat's revolutionary role was in general limited by its objective underdevelopment as a productive force. This was most glaringly apparent in the fact that the radicalization of the revolution tended to outpace the radicalization of workers' struggles. The upshot was that while the proletariat looked on approvingly as the revolution resolutely steered its antibourgeois course, its actions in the expression of that approval were much less impressive; in short, the proletariat took the lead neither in the revolution nor in the antibourgeois insurrection in which it had had such a crucial hand.

The same conditions that limited the role of the proletariat in the antibourgeois insurrection were even more drastically to limit its role in the antibourgeois exercise of power: for whereas the revolution was a confirmation of proletarian interests though the proletariat was absent from the leading role reserved for it, antibourgeois power dissociated these two factors. The antibourgeois insurrection was not led by the proletariat, yet proletarian interests were served by it; antibourgeois power was not only independent of proletarian leadership, it was also independent—for a time—of proletarian interests. The perpetuation of this cleft would become the cornerstone of Stalinism, marking it as a social order that was antibourgeois and antiproletarian at one and the same time.

Whereas in every one of the various stages of the revolution its proletarian character was in evidence, the state power to which it gave birth lacked a proletarian character both in postrevolutionary society and in the Stalinist order, signifying the absence of a positive class character in the most general sense.

The birth of the proletariat. The Russian proletariat was born with industry and its growth was marked, as industry's was, by the imperialist law of unequal development. History forced it to internalize the antinomies that prevailed over its birth and its historic conditions. The historical delay in industrialization was compounded by the backwardness of the two classes directly involved in it—the bourgeoisie and the proletariat. But not only was the latter late being born, it was backward in its origins as well. In Russia, unlike the West, the proletariat was not formed from the craft guilds of the medieval cities, but from the most backward, yet at the same time most revolutionary of peasantries in Europe, a peasantry that had been oppressed for centuries by a feudal autocracy.

The Russian proletariat, when finally it was born, plunged into a precipitous and fitful development. Whereas in other countries, such as England, the industrial working class had taken centuries to form, in Russia it took but a few decades. The majority of the industrial working class still nursed ties with its origins and former state, investing workers with a dual social identity; the working class entered the twentieth century bearing the marks of a deep internal stratification. As Trotsky characterized it, "While in the metal industry, especially in Petrograd, a layer of hereditary proletarians was crystallized out, in the Urals the prevailing type was half-proletarian, half-peasant." The proletariat that participated in the two Russian revolutions was less a class fully formed than a class in formation. The war only accentuated the effects of these characteristics of its birth.

The eve of the revolution. Within the first months of the war, 40% of the total workforce had been sent to the front, with recruitment showing a clear preference for the most militant elements. They were replaced in their jobs by retired peasants and conscripted shopkeepers, and above all by women who by 1917 represented 40% of the total workforce (the February insurrection, it may be recalled, began with a demonstration in observance of International Women's Day). In 1913 the fledgling proletariat had represented 14% of the population; now the war had drained it of its life's blood, and glutted its ranks with alien elements. It was caught in a stranglehold between the threat of the front and the intolerable conditions in the factories. With military defeats and war profits providing a dismal backdrop, the mood was becoming more and more explosive.

The Russian proletariat, soon to be immersed in a revolution without precedent in history, bore very little resemblance to the working class of the *Communist Manifesto.* That proletariat was preparing to shed its chains and free the whole of society from its division into classes. The Russian proletariat, leagues removed from this model, was much too small a minority, much too heterogeneous, and much too confused to transform its common distress into a community of objective interests and a unity of subjective ends. A few advanced elements had indeed been able to rise to a political understanding of their condition and were ready to follow up that understanding in deeds. On the whole, however, on the eve of the revolution the Russian proletariat was a far cry from displaying the characteristics of a political class.

Political consciousness. To discuss the political consciousness of the proletariat is to discuss its ability to lead, first, the revolution, and then, later, society at large. Its involvement in the revolution reached its peak in the antibourgeois insurrection, which resulted in an essentially political change. The proletariat cannot be the leading force of an essentially political insurrection without itself being a political class. Where by dint of circumstances this role is thrust upon the proletariat with no regard to its ability to fulfill it, an insurrection is doomed to failure. Lenin posed this problem in his celebrated April Theses in 1917. Raising the question of why the February insurrection had ended in bourgeois, and not proletarian power, Lenin answers: "The peculiarity of the present moment in Russia consists in the transition from the first stage of the revolution, which gave power to the bourgeoisie on account of the inadequate consciousness and organization of the proletariat, to its second stage, which must give the power to the proletariat and the poor layers of the peasantry."

For the proletariat to seize power in October, the obstacles that had prevented it from doing so in February—"inadequate consciousness and organization"—had to be eliminated. We shall come back to this point later on.

The workers largely shared the general chauvinist enthusiasm of the early stages of the war. But over a period of two and a half years this mood would undergo a total transformation. Schooled in frustration, poverty, and injustice, the proletariat would in this brief lapse of time become infinitely more militant, if not infinitely more experienced politically.

The proletariat's conduct in February was paradoxical; the fury with which it smashed an anachronistic power was offset by its indifference to the power installed in its stead. For both Trotsky and Lenin, the roots of this paradox lay not in the contingencies of events or external factors but in the political immaturity of the proletariat itself. This immaturity led to an irreparable discontinuty in action: the proletariat was able to combat a power upon which history had passed sentence, but was unable to replace it.

Whereas in February the Bolsheviks had regarded this discontinuity as catastrophic, by October they had perceived that it was inevitable and hence provisionally to be tolerated. But the most important feature of this discontinuity was not how it was received, but the way it became entrenched and reproduced itself; the lasting nature of its effects points up the antinomy in the role of the Russian proletariat, called upon to assume the role of ruling class, yet effectively prohibited from acting as such. History had invested it with a twofold mission: the industrial development of the productive forces, and their socialization, for which it had neither the capacity nor the means. It could only imperfectly accomplish this mission, thereby accentuating its negative side.

In 1917 the Bolsheviks undertook to help the proletariat carry this mission to its completion. Ten years later, Stalinism drew the lesson from their failure and relieved the proletariat of any other mission than that of toiling in a state of total submission. The political consciousness of the proletariat by no means stood still, but its development could not keep pace with the complexity of the problems spewed forth by the revolution. The level of political consciousness among the proletariat was most evident in its responses to these problems: i.e., in its *actions*.

Action. The action of the proletariat in the revolution may be productively discussed in terms of its general orientation, its ends, its forms, its dynamics and its scope. Each merits separate comment.

Orientation. The peasantry channeled its energy into many streams. The blow it dealt to feudalism was punctuated by the blows dealt by some layers within its ranks to others. The February days excepted, nothing similar was to be observed in the action of the proletariat, for which the bourgeoisie had always been the prime target. The predominantly antibourgeois orientation of the workers' movement foreshadowed the ascendancy that the antibourgeois character of the revolution was later to attain.

Ends. The proletariat in general may pursue the most diverse ends in its struggle against the bourgeoisie. Some of them may be deduced beforehand from strategy, while others can only be inferred *a posteriori* from spontaneous action. The ends impelling the Russian proletariat in 1917 were of this latter kind. But it is likewise true that the spontaneous ends of the proletariat were also the ends of a strategy, not its own, which it nonetheless applied without having either developed or even assimilated it.

In February the Petrograd proletariat fought the autocracy tooth and nail with unparalleled fervor. The autocracy fell but, as the workers abruptly discovered, the war continued; the new power that had replaced the autocracy was alien and even hostile to the working class, and, far from improving, their economic situation continued to worsen. In May the Executive Committee of the Petrograd Soviet acknowledged that the situation "for numerous categories of workers bordered on chronic want." This steady slide of the living standard, already at the subsistence level, to the brink of disaster was the principal source of unrest among the workers after February. It was not a political project, but intolerable conditions that stirred the workers to spontaneous response. They rebelled against rising prices and the reduction in bread rations, demanding the legislation of a minimum wage and a shortening of the working day.

Their actions remained within the framework of trade unionist goals, as, according to Lenin, was inherent to worker spontaneity. As long as the proletariat rebuffed the leadership of the Bolshevik party, it would in the fullness of revolution carry on its struggle both untiringly and myopically. Its objective was not to abolish but to modify capitalist relations of production. The struggle was merely antibourgeois, not anticapitalist. This limit on the proletariat's struggle would likewise later be the limit on the insurrection on which it would leave its mark without having led it.

Forms. The forms and scope of workers' action were hardly independent of its ends. The principal form of the peasant struggle, intent on destroying a class, was violence. The principal forms of the antibourgeois action of the proletariat, intent not on abolishing but on moderating the class against which it struggled, were demonstrations and strikes. The peasant struggle smashed the feudal system, while the workers' struggle accommodated to the system of capitalist relations. The revolution had no proletarian equivalent to the peasant war. The achievement of the antibourgeois character of the revolution was both less radical and less violent than the achievement of its antifeudal character.

The difference between the two characters of the revolution was but a reflection of the difference between the two classes whose negation they represented. When the revolution intruded, feudalism had already been a totally retrograde vestige for centuries, whereas capitalism, historically of quite recent birth, still did not preclude hopes of progress. The peasants smashed the feudal nobility to appropriate its property, but neither the proletariat nor capitalist property were as yet sufficiently developed to make a similar appropriation meaningful in their regard.

The Red Guards. The formation of the Red Guards will perhaps illustrate best the predicament elucidated in the foregoing. The Red Guards were armed workers' detachments, the organization of which went back to the eve of the big July demonstrations; though formally attached to the soviets, in reality they were the armed force of the Bolshevik party. The weight carried by this *force de frappe* was directly dependent on its troops, its organization, its means, and ultimately the role it played in the crucial skirmishes of the revolution.

It hardly presented a picture of a redoubtable military organization, judging from testimony. In October the Red Guards were given the mission of arresting the Provisional Government, which was guarded by a battalion of women. But the operation was postponed for a rather long time, which put Second Congress of Soviets in a delicate situation: it had showed itself capable of establishing a new government before it was able effectively to dismiss the old one; it then permitted Kerensky to escape and attempt a military uprising which, however, failed.

The Khrushchev-era *History of the CPSU* estimates the size of the Red Guards at 200,000, while Schapiro and Bettelheim each estimate 20,000 for Petrograd alone, and Trotsky admits that "on the eve of the insurrection, the Red

Guards were still few in number.'' Information or interpretations concerning other aspects bring no more clarity to the question. Schapiro, for instance, seems to believe that the Red Guards made the October insurrection. "This force, which had been organized by the Bolsheviks after June . . . was the real armed might behind the Bolshevik coup d'Etat.'' Bettelheim, however, suggests the opposite: "There were few troops, and moreover the Red Guards' organization was weak.''

What the Red Guards do tell us beyond a doubt is that the Bolshevik party was resolved to resort to violence if necessary, regardless of what position the army adopted. There was, moreover, a second implication: the only social force on which the party could count without reservation was the proletariat, and, conversely, only a party of the proletariat was ready and willing to respond positively to the call.

Though in a minority, this readiness of the proletariat to act showed its propensity to radicalize. A simple political mechanism impelled the process onward: the more receptive the proletariat was to the solicitations of the Bolsheviks, the less susceptible it was to the conciliatory blandishments of the socialist parties.

Unlike the peasant movement, which was totally apolitical, the workers' movement was in the first instance prepolitical, i.e., alien, but not impermeable, to political influences. The existence of the Red Guards was not proof that the proletariat played a leading role in the revolution, but it did show its capacity to be politicized, as well as the limits of that capacity.

Radicalization at different paces. The workers' movement waxed in intensity, although at its own pace, different from that of the other major currents of the revolution. The proletarian movement had undergone a radicalization between the two insurrections that was as indubitable as it was limited, and which amounted to much more than the mere formation of the Red Guards. The soviets of workers' deputies, the trade unions, and the factory committees were consolidated and fired to action. Out of the workers' movement crystallized political structures and political orientations more adequate to the proletariat's mission. However, this does not mean that proletarian action knew an unbroken growth in intensity and effectiveness. Proletarian radicalization had not yet posed a challenge to capitalist social relations. Indeed, when they moved in October, the workers' action did not attain the level reached in July, or even in February when the Petrograd proletariat played a crucial role in the overthrow of the autocracy. "The collapse of the Romanov autocracy in March 1917 was one of the most leaderless, spontaneous, anonymous revolutions of all time,'' observes Chamberlin, describing "the strikes and bread riots that broke out in Petrograd.'' The workers also filled the front ranks of the popular demonstrations that swept away the first cabinet of Prince Lvov in May.

But their militancy reached heights never attained before or since in the July battle: it was violent to the point of seriously imperilling the government, and its failure placed the revolution in even greater danger. On the night of July 3, 30,000 workers from the Putilov factories encircled the Tauride Palace, the seat of the Soviet, demanding that it assume power. The factories of the capital responded by calling a general strike. The Petrograd workers were bent on forcing the Soviet to change a political course supported by the majority of the population. "The demonstrations lasted for four days and became seriously menacing," writes Carr. "It was freely believed that this was the beginning of a serious Bolshevik attempt to seize power, though the party leaders insisted that it was a spontaneous demonstration which they themselves failed to keep within bounds." The situation was rendered more explosive by the decision of the machinegunners and sailors to join the workers and transform the demonstration into a "show of armed force." "To speak of a show of armed force at this moment," Trotsky justly reflects, "without wanting a new revolution was impossible." Lenin comments on the July battle: "Formally speaking the most accurate description of events would be an antigovernment demonstration. But at bottom this was not an ordinary demonstration, it was something much more than a demonstration and less than a revolution." *The History of CPSU* has the following interpretation of the same events: "The party supported the revolutionary sentiments of the masses, but it was opposed to immediate action. The workers and soldiers of Petrograd were strong enough to overthrow the Provisional Government and assume State power, but they would have been unable to retain this power, for the majority of the people in the country at that time still followed the Socialist Revolutionaries and Mensheviks." Finally, there is Trotsky's conclusion: "They combined a most radical understanding of the task with illusions as to its methods. The warnings of the Bolsheviks were ineffective. The Petrograd workers and soldiers had to test the situation with their own experience. And their armed demonstration was such a test." Further: "The people imagine that with a new blow they can carry through, or correct, what they did not accomplish decisively enough before. Hence the impulse to a new revolution, a revolution without preparation, without program, without estimation of the reserves, without calculation of consequences."

The isolated attack of the Petrograd workers unleashed a repressive reaction that soon generated an atmosphere for a military putsch. The numerous interpretations presented in the foregoing must explain three observations:

(1) Proletarian militancy reached its greatest heights in July;
(2) This was not the case with the other popular currents in the revolution;
(3) The working class was more directly militant in July than in October.

The quotes above support the first point. The antifeudal movement serves as an illustration of the second. It was only "at the critical juncture in the autumn," Trotsky stresses, "that the peasantry broke . . . with the leadership of the compromisers and moved on to civil war." But at this juncture the proletariat's actions were immeasurably more thought-out than in July, and were concerned more with being prepared than with a revolutionary twist. Kerensky convoked the Conference of State in August, setting the seal on his double victory: defeat of the putsch and victory over the revolution. "The mood in the factories," writes Trotsky, "was so hostile to this State Conference that the idea of a general strike, coming from below, was adopted almost without opposition."

The pivotal point remains the third. Nothing similar to July occurred in October. The antibourgeois insurrection was supported neither by a general strike, by large local strikes, nor by workers merely taking to the streets—which would not have contributed materially to success in any case. Unlike in July, in October the streets were largely empty and encounters restrained. One of the most important proletarian actions of this period took place in the last two weeks of the month, the All-Russian Conference of Plant and Factory Committees, which adopted a resolution stating: "The workers are more interested than the owners in the regular and uninterrupted functioning of enterprises." Thus but a few days before the insurrection, the only show of proletarian resolve of national dimensions was not a call to the workers to strike, but an appeal to proprietors to resume regular activities. The eve of the antibourgeois insurrection found the peasantry immersed in an antifeudal war and the proletariat in a mood dominated by discreet caution. Its most direct contribution to the preparations for the insurrection, it may be argued, consisted in the support it gave on an increasingly massive scale to the Bolshevik party, especially in the innumerable electoral face-offs: elections to the soviets, to the municipal dumas, the trade unions, factory committees, etc. Together with the phenomenal escalation of the peasant war, these shows of confidence gave the Bolshevik party a freedom of action it had never before enjoyed. Thus in the most archetypically democratic manner and before the whole of society, it gave the Bolshevik party a mandate to act in its name in the historical scenario being readied in the wings: the antibourgeois insurrection and the constitution of antibourgeois power.

The radicalization of the proletariat was manifested in its moderation in the antibourgeois insurrection. No longer prey to being swept along by ungoverned impulses, it instead made a political choice: it passed on the responsibility for a decisive move beyond its own capacities to another highly qualified and trustworthy social force. The effect would prove irreversible. In conferring this freedom of action on the Bolshevik party the proletariat deprived itself of all freedom of action for a whole historical period. Thus the trend of the period was reversed, with the political leadership assuming increasingly more freedom of action, and the class retaining commensurately less; Stalinism would later carry this to the extreme.

If the proletariat cannot be said to have led the antibourgeois insurrection by this transfer, it did make it possible, in this sharing honors with the peasantry, the army, and in a certain sense the bourgeoisie itself.

The October insurrection was effectively antibourgeois but not proletarian in character, because the uprising was led by a force other than the proletariat. Yet that force was tied to the fundamental interests of the proletariat, though it only partly satisfied them.

Scope. In terms of Russian society as a whole, the actions of the proletariat were moderate in scope. But this only reflected the modest social weight the proletariat carried and the rather circumscribed pale of its spread. Other than in demonstrations, workers' actions were confined basically to the factories, giving the factory committees an influence rivalling that of the trade unions and the soviets. At the day-to-day practical level, economic disputes pitted the workers of a factory against its management, and not class against class.

The territorial insularity of industry was reproduced in the proletariat. The unequal share of industrial enterprises in the capital created an exceptional situation there which the war merely consolidated further. In 1917 there were 400,000 workers living in Petrograd, with 350,000 of these working in only 140 factories. The central bureaucracy, the government, and the soviet were concentrated here as well, subsisting side by side with giant factories and family upon family of working-class traditions. The capital was a society *sui generis*, profoundly different from the countryside, and it was in this setting that the two insurrections took place. At the decisive moments, the Russian proletariat participated in the revolution with its most undaunted and steeled battalion, the Petrograd workers—who, however, represented only a segment of the class. Thus the proletariat was precluded from becoming the leading force of the revolution if for no other reason than the circumscribed scope of its actions.

Just as the Petrograd proletariat did not lead the Russian proletariat in the 1917 revolution, neither did the Russian proletariat lead the popular masses, but merely stood at their head.

Immaturity. The conflict between the proletariat and the bourgeoisie was inherent in the relationship between them, and the level at which the conflict unfolded depended on the level of development of both classes. This in turn depended on the level of the development of industry. Lenin's anticipatory theory of revolution tended to dissociate the conflict between proletariat and bourgeoisie from this context. The effect was an antinomic vision in which the underdevelopment of industry had contrary implications for each of the two classes, producing a backward bourgeoisie and an advanced proletariat. The antagonism of interests of the two classes was compounded by the antagonism in their development, despite their dependence on the same overall situation.

Clearly this antinomic view subserves the idea of a potential anticipatory proletarian revolution. To support this idea, Lenin tended to exaggerate not only the development of the proletariat, but also the development of industry. As Bahro observed, "Lenin apparently overestimated the extent of capitalist development in Russia at the beginning of the 20th century, just as Marx and Engels had done for Western Europe in the middle of the 19th century." The overestimation of the development of industry served to justify an exaggeration of the revolutionary potential of the proletariat. A relatively developed industry was necessary to produce a proletariat sufficiently developed to accomplish its own revolution and establish its rule over society. Conversely, the relative underdevelopment of industry produced a bourgeoisie sufficiently underdeveloped to be incapable of defending its privileges in becoming the ruling class of Russian society.

The events of the revolution vindicated only a part of this antinomic vision. They proved that industrial backwardness made an anticipatory revolution possible, that an anticipatory revolution is a premature revolution, and that this meant a violent squaring off of two classes both substantially—although not equally—immature. The bourgeoisie lacked the strength to defend its positions, while the proletariat was too weak to appropriate them to its own purposes. The early senescence of the bourgeoisie was not paralleled by a coming of age of the proletariat. Both immature, their conflict assumed unwonted forms. A class incapable of exercising the power it held without having even conquered it, was opposed by a class incapable not only of seizing power, but even of coveting it. The anticipatory chafings of the proletariat had neither the force nor the coherence necessary to compensate for the bourgeoisie's backward sense of its own mission. From the immaturity of the two classes sprang the immaturity of their conflict.

Institutionalization. Postrevolutionary Russian society embarked upon its precipitous course toward Stalinism with a force fueled by the weakness of the proletariat. Stalinism is the alienation of the power of the working class that the class was itself incapable of wielding. Originally the product of imperialism, that inability was later made perennial by Stalinism. The proletariat did indeed participate in an antibourgeois revoution but its immaturity prevented it from anticipating antibourgeois power. Stalinism is a fruit of this immaturity, and indeed its very anatomy and survival are premised on maintaining it.

Many Marxists have tended to mistake the real role of the proletariat in the revolution, and thus the revolution's real character. On this point, the disagreements among Lenin, Trotsky, and Stalin are reduced to no more than a matter of nuances. Marxist theoreticians, intent on grafting upon the proletariat a consciousness it was unable to achieve through its own forces, have poorly withstood the temptation to regard the proletariat with condescending awe. History may have invested the proletariat with an objective emancipatory mission, but Marxists have endowed it with subjective virtues it has generally never had. Even before they discovered the providential leader, Marxists had exercised their fascination with infallibility on their vision of the proletariat. The effects of this tradition may also be discerned in the confusion surrounding the role of the Russian proletariat in the 1917 revolution.

Most of the confusion has revolved around the actual militancy of the proletariat, which is assumed as a given. Desperate resolve is mistaken for the pursuit of an end, and isolation for the mark of autonomy. At certain times the proletariat played a role that truly was decisive, but through a twofold exaggeration this has been put forth as a leading role in the revolution in general. The confusion has obscured a crucial point: the proletariat did not become the leading force in victory precisely because it had not led the field in battle.

As observed earlier on, to say that the Russian proletariat and Russian bourgeoisie were both underdeveloped does not mean that they were equal on this account. It was the bourgeoisie, not the proletariat, that was subjugated by imperialism; submissiveness to the autocracy and truckling to the feudal nobility were disastrous for the bourgeoisie, but not for the proletariat. These differences showed up with unmistakeable clarity in the revolution, when the proletariat demonstrated a historical efficacy to which the bourgeoisie did not even come close. The ultimate proof of their inequality in immaturity was provided by the epilogue of October, in which the bourgeoisie, not the proletariat, went down to defeat (the proletariat did not suffer this fate until later). What the proletariat was to lose was not the revolution but the historical fruits it ultimately bore.

For Lenin, Trotsky, and Stalin alike, the revolution demonstrated the inability of either the bourgeoisie or the proletariat to become the ruling class of Russian society. One quite wholesome current in the critique of Stalinism believes that if the proletariat did not assume that position it was not because it lacked the ability, but because it had been expropriated by the ''new class,'' whose interests are served by the Stalinist social order.

Stalinism was not the cause of the proletariat's immaturity; the converse was true: it was the immaturity of the proletariat that produced Stalinist society. What Stalinism did do was forcefully to perpetuate this immaturity, despite the fact that the class had matured objectively as a productive force. It is impossible to arrive at an understanding of the class nature of Stalinism if the role played by the proletariat in the revoution is not itself adequately understood. Yet the limitations on the proletariat did not have to do with it alone, but were the limitations of the class structure of Russian society in general.

Class structure and class relations predominated neither in the revolution nor in Stalinist society. Stalinism is not a class society, which means that, though it carried the heritage of the revolution further, the mainstay of this social order was not class structure.

The leading role. In Stalinism, class stratification was combined with a hierarchical division based on a distribution of social responsibilities that was only apparently a distribution of power. The reality was that stratification was rather vague and ineffective, whereas hierarchical division was extremely rigid and very functional. This hierarchical, one-dimensional structure produced a veritable cult of vertical organization. The Stalinist view of the world is that of a relentless movement governed by laws and leading roles, and maintained by a chronic afflatus of superlatives. Stalinism constructed a system of thematic priorities which even its critics quite often adopted. This sort of manipulation indeed took place, but it is not for this reason that the question of the leading role of the proletariat and later the Bolshevik party in the Russian revoution merits our attention. This view is offset by another underlying theme indispensable to the study of the historical articulations linking the 1917 revolution to Stalinism of the 1980s. The genetic elements in this articulation may be summed up in the following:

• First, the proletariat did not play the leading role either in the revolution or in the antibourgeois insurrection;

• Second, the victory of the antibourgeois insurrection did not result in the establishment of a dictatorship of the proletariat;

• Finally, the mainstay of Stalinist society is neither the proletariat, nor another class, nor the class structure in general.

Forty years after the revolution, the official *History of the CPSU* proclaimed: ''The working class had the leading role in the struggle of the whole people against absolutism, and against the dictatorship of the bourgeoisie. . . . The principal reason for the victory of the socialist revolution of October was the fact that it had the working class of Russia at its head.''

This perpetuation of the fiction of the leading role of the proletariat has served a legitimating function: namely that of lending plausibility to the fiction of the leading role of the proletariat in Stalinist society. The legitimacy Stalinism derives thereby is twofold: first, as the lawful continuation of the revolution and second, as the historical creation of the working class.

It is indeed easier to dispute the leading role of the Russian proletariat in the revolution than to define the role it did in fact play. Its behavior throughout the revolution was inconsequent enough that to search for any one role would be futile. For example, its direct action was crucial to the achievement of the anti-autocratic character of the revolution, but not of its antifeudal character, in which its role was substantially less important than that of the peasantry in the achievement of the revolution's antibourgeois character. The proletariat abetted the antifeudal movement by anticipating it and centering its attack, not on the feudal nobility directly, but on its main bastion, the autocracy. For its part, the peasantry dealt a fatal blow to the power of the bourgeoisie through its exercise of extralegal violence across the face of Russia, abolishing the most traditional form of private property and, by that same token, the class with which the bourgeoisie had organic links.

The Russian proletariat did not lead the revolution, and this for two reasons. First, it was beyond its objective potential to do so; and second, the very nature of the revolution made it a virtual impossibility for any one social force to fulfill this role. The antinomic necessity that reigned over the society and the revolution had been internalized to one degree or another by all social forces, and none of them had the structural homogeneity and consistency of conduct that would have enabled them to assume a leading role. Hence, although its different episodes saw now one, now the other of these forces in the vanguard, no one social force led the revolution overall and throughout. Furthermore, the relative inaccessibility of that role was not the same for each of the social forces, the main differential in this respect being the kind of social relations determining them and the degree of this determination. Determined by feudal social relations, the aristocracy and the peasantry had less possibility of assuming such a role than did the proletariat or the bourgeoisie. In turn, these two classes, entrenched in underdeveloped capitalist social relations, had less prospect of assuming a leading role than did the Bolshevik party, which was governed by these relations only indirectly. In one sense the proletariat is only a necessary social expression of capitalist social relations, and consequently the immaturity of these relations made its own immaturity to a certain extent inevitable. Ultimately, it was this general immaturity that prevented the bourgeoisie from exercising power and the working class from seizing it.

If the proletariat surpassed itself in the revolution, it did so only to the extent that it was able to shed these constraints. There was only one way for it to move on to revolution; its economic and social frustration had to be transformed into social action. Although the objective condition of the Russian proletariat did not preclude its politicization, it did set limits to it, so that its result did not consist in the transformation of the proletariat into a political class but rather in disposing it to accept the leadership of the Bolshevik party.

The Bolshevik party

History prior to 1917 had never known a revolution in which a political party played a role comparable to that played by the Bolshevik party in the Russian revolution. To have consummated an antifeudal revolution with the establishment of antibourgeois power—therein lay the originality of the Russian revolution, and this in turn was inseparable from the influence the Bolshevik party exerted on its development.

Antibourgeois power had been established by revolution before in history, but the Russian revolution was the first to incorporate that power in a political party. But this is not to imply that the Bolshevik party led the revolution: my thesis is that the Bolshevik party did not play that role but rather foresaw the revolution and brought it to its conclusion.

One of the staunchest historical links between the 1917 revolution and the emergence of Stalinism was forged around the role of the party, both that which it effectively played as well as that merely ascribed to it. To provide a clearer picture of this link it is important first to examine the main springs of the party's real role, namely its potential, its strategy of anticipatory revolution, and its relations with the working class.

Potential. To realize the potential that was latent in the revolutionary situation, an appropriate catalyst had to be found; that catalyst was the party. A well-augured match indeed, for by dint of it the party was able to steer a resolute course from an initial stage of powerlessness in the face of the circumstances of the revolution to a position of effective control over them. Yet that course was not itself smooth and free of contradiction, inasmuch as party structures did not develop commensurately with the growth in its influence. While the development of its structure was slow and sometimes even groping, the growth in its influence was one of linear acceleration. On the other hand, whereas the existence of party structures enjoyed an unbroken continuity between the two insurrections, party influence was intermittent during this period, before ascending to the heights it reached in October.

The implication is not obscure: between February and October, the Bolshevik party had fulfilled not merely one, but a succession of roles, neatly described by Carr: "The contribution of Lenin and the Bolsheviks to the overthrow of Tsarism was negligible. It is only in an external sense that they can be held responsible for the overthrow of the Provisional Government. From July 1917 its downfall had become inevitable; it was waiting only for its successor to appear. Bolshevism succeeded to a vacant throne. The crucial moments of the interval between the February and the October revolutions were Lenin's announcement at the First All-Russian Congress of Soviets in June that the Bolsheviks were willing to take power, and Lenin's decision in September that the time was ripe to take it." Absent from the first insurrection, the Bolshevik party became the organizer of the second.

While its historical stature was changing radically, organizationally the party underwent changes that were less than modest. Shortly before October—in August—the Sixth Party Congress learned from Sverdlov's report (Lenin was in hiding) that party membership was at 200,000, spread among 162 organizations. It was certainly not by force of numbers that this miniscule party would in such a short time propel this vast country along a course it had been advocating for years. The prime source of this hidden potential was quite simply the fact that the Bolshevik party had been and continued to be the one political force whose objectives were the same as those pursued by the broad popular masses. In calling for peace, land, and a government able to resolve these vital questions, the Bolshevik party naturally gained credibility in the eyes of the great currents of the revolution; namely, the workers, peasants, and soldiers, offering them a political platform adequate to their needs, and moreover as indispensable as it would have been inaccessible had the party not been there to mediate it.

Prior to the autumn, such progress was less the direct fruit of the Bolshevik party's own efforts than the indirect work of its adversaries. The first signs that the tides of popularity were beginning to turn in its favor came from the various elections, starting with those for the workers' sections of the soviets. In socially more mixed institutions developments proceeded at a less lively pace, although in the same direction. Thus, for example, in Moscow the neighborhood duma elections in June gave 375,000 votes to the SRs and 75,000 to the Bolsheviks. In September the result was almost the reverse: 54,000 votes to the SRs against 198,000 to the Bolsheviks. The collapse of the SRs was much more abrupt than were Bolshevik gains: the ratios between the results of the two elections were roughly 6.5:1 for the SRs and 1:2.5 for the Bolsheviks. All the while it was winning these electoral confrontations, in which earlier it had not even been a contending factor, the Bolshevik party was hammering out its own role and the nature of the insurrection it was preparing. It had become the leading political force in the country, and only then did it proceed to organize the insurrection which, although not the direct work of the masses, was achieved on the strength of the support they gave it, refuting the widely held idea that October had been but a naked coup d'état, nothing more.

The positive potential of the Bolshevik party rested in its strategy, the policy it fashioned to tie that strategy in with the realities of the revolution, and finally in its organizational structures and the human forces it was able to mobilize. But the party amassed this positive potential in tempered strides over the course of time, so this cannot explain the radical and abrupt transformation in its role; the cause of that transformation must be sought in the march of events, which abandoned all other political forces, spent and confounded, in its wake. Though unable to steer the course of events directly, the Bolshevik party was able to urge it on, hastening somewhat its pace, and ultimately turning it to the best account, despite the enormous difficulties plaguing it both from without and within its own ranks.

Within a period of eight months the Bolshevik party moved from a position of isolation to total domination of the political scene. No organizational structure can adapt to such a profound and rapid change without suffering the effects of such a strain, and the Bolshevik party was no exception. Moreover, the strain of events was aggravated by the party's worn condition at the outbreak of the revolution. Progressively wasted by the defeat of 1905 and the ensuing repression, and later by the wave of chauvinism that swept the country in the war's early stages, the party's edifice was in a rather rickety state in 1917. The revolutionary ebb after 1905 had weakened the party's foothold even among the working class. Its leadership had been decimated by deportation, prison, exile, and life underground. The war was only the most recent scourge, if on the positive side it provided the incentive for Lenin to develop his theory of imperialism (1916). There had just taken place a thorough rethinking of party strategy when revolution broke, thus affording its members little time to assimilate it. Indeed the internal difficulties that assailed the Bolshevik party after February derived from differing views on strategy and how to translate that strategy into political action.

Strategy. The Russian revolution was in its grand contours the historical work, direct and spontaneous, of workers, peasants, and soldiers, of the intelligentsia, and of the urban petty bourgeoisie. Its antibourgeois turn, which left its mark on postrevolutionary society, was the historical handiwork, direct and deliberate, of the Bolshevik party, and strategy was its principal tool. Once the Bolshevik party assumed control, the revolution underwent multiple changes: a change of level, because its focus was shifted to the political domain; a change in dimension, because the party's offensive against imperialism, the war, and the national bourgeoisie had profound international implications; a change in content, because a political party had placed itself at its head; a change in character, because its new and dominant function was to sweep away the political power of the bourgeoisie; and finally, a change in nature, in suffering all these modifications, but above all because strategy became the decisive element in shaping its course. To emphasize the main point, not only did its functions change, the very mechanisms of that change did so as well. The anti-autocratic or antifeudal character of the revolution achieved ascendancy spontaneously, through the direct action of the masses. The antibourgeois character did so on the basis of this spontaneous action of the masses, but through the direct action of the Bolshevik party, guided by a deliberate strategy. If the revolution changed its nature, it was because the reordering of its functions brought about a reordering as well in the forces driving it.

The revolution steered its course toward what was also the overriding aim of Bolshevik strategy, thereby itself acquiring a strategic nature. The strategy was quite specific, and the limits of its aims likewise became the boundaries of the revolution. Indeed it was because these limits had been imposed that the revolution, though strategic, was to remain unfinished. The twofold transformation in the nature of the revolution was passed on to the society born out of it. The new society bore the markings both of the imperious necessity of the strategy that sired it and the inaccessibility of that strategy's goals.

The essence of Leninist strategy was spelled out by its central objective: to achieve an—objectively possible—anticipatory, anticapitalist revolution. Anticipation itself derived its logic from specific predictive contingencies, namely:

—the collapse of the autocracy;

—its catastrophic impact on existing social structures;

—the formation, under these conditions, of an alliance between foreign imperialism and the Russian bourgeoisie and feudal nobility;

—military defeat;

—growing popular resistance to the war, in the first instance by the soldiers;

—peasant uprisings against the feudal nobility;

—the country's economic bankruptcy;

—escalation of the workers' movement against the conditions under which the proletariat lived and worked, and its rapid politicization;

—the failure of the alliance, and especially of the bourgeoisie, which was unable to come up with any plausible solutions to these problems or to defuse the great popular movements;

—ultimately, the swing of the petty bourgeoisie over to the side of the revolution;

—the isolation of the Provisional Government and the political forces sustaining it;

—the assumption by the Bolshevik party of the vanguard role in the revolution, enabling it to achieve the principal role of its strategy.

For an anticipatory antibourgeois insurrection to be achieved, these predictions had to be brought to pass. The establishment of antibourgeois power represented both the triumph of Lenin's strategy, as well as its journey's end. However masterful the achievement, Leninism proved incapable of defining its anticipatory feat correctly. The tragic flaw of Leninism was its assumption that the antibourgeois insurrection also marked an anticipatory transformation of the bourgeois revolution into a socialist revolution, and that the wielding of power by the Bolshevik party was tantamount to the dictatorship of the proletariat. But the abolition of feudalism merely meant that the bourgeoisie had been defeated politically, not destroyed socially. To be sure, Leninist strategy had defined correctly the means that would enable it under these conditions to seize power from the bourgeoisie and establish antibourgeois power in its place. But it did not define the means for transforming antibourgeois political power into an anticapitalist economic system, and so for consolidating the first step along the way to socialism.

Subjectively, the principal limitation of this strategy was that it was ignorant of the objective limits of the very revolution it had guided to victory. This vision, already distorted with regard to the revolution, became even more so with regard to postrevolutionary society. Thus did Leninism assume the qualities of paradox as a doctrine more capable of effecting profound social transformations than of grasping what in fact they actually signified; an astounding ability to foresee, offset by a gross inability to see; an approach far more sensitive to the possible than to the real: such was the dramatic turn taken by this doctrine. And thus was Leninism reduced to Marxism-Leninism, and its productive strategy to a vexed ideology, an instrument of rule beyond the grasp of the working class, belonging not to it but to a power situated beyond all classes, and hence above society itself.

The vanguard role. The official *History of the CPSU* continues to ascribe the leading role in the 1917 revolution to both the working class and the Bolshevik party at the same time. Indeed, the proletariat appears as a led leader, calling to mind the famous "transmission belt," a term Lenin used to describe the tasks of the trade unions.

Retrospective analyses of the Russian revolution undertaken by revolutionary Marxists have turned on several fundamental motifs: first, that to achieve its end the anti-imperialist revolution had also to be anticapitalist, and had therefore to be directed simultaneously against both the national and the international bourgeoisies. Secondly, such a course did not result directly from the action of the revolutionary masses, but had to have been the fruit of conscious effort by a revolutionary party. Thirdly, if the anti-imperialist revolution was to become predominantly anticapitalist, the revolutionary party had to meet at least three conditions: it had to follow Leninist strategy, which had been vindicated by history, be organized on the Bolshevik model, and seize the leading role in the revolution.

Acquiring almost doctrinal status, this interpretation has been accepted by Marxists with little modification down through the years. Here is one illustration in a version presented by an Italian Marxist on the occasion of the 50th anniversary of the Russian revolution: "The defeats suffered in a whole series of countries," declares Sirio di Giuliomario, "both before and after the Russian revolution show that the subjective factor, i.e., the revolutionary party, is a crucial element in determining the proletariat's victory in the decisive political battles and the struggle for the conquest of power." The quotation is interesting for two reasons, one theoretical, the other historical. Theoretically, because one rarely finds the identification of the subjective factor with the Leninist party expressed in such clear form, and historically, because it comes from an anti-Stalinist Marxist at a time when the Cuban experience no longer leaves any doubt about the possibility of a revolution of this kind, victorious not only without but even in opposition to such a party.

The anticapitalist path of anti-imperialist revolution was taken by Leninist parties in China and Yugoslavia, as in Russia, but independently of the party in Cuba, Benin, and Ethiopia. These revolutions, their ends similar, differed with regard to the role of the party, but not the role of the providential leader. Thus the lesson of history seems to be that the indispensable instrument for a revolution of this kind is not the party but an exceptional individual supported by an organization that could be as well a section of the army as a group of determined revolutionaries. The working class may play the decisive role, just one important role among others, or even a wholly secondary role. But these variations are confined to the phenomenal level. The essence, that which is invariable in all these cases, is the decisive role conferred by antinomic necessity on the subjective factor, which will assume now one guise, now another, depending on the case, although the most constant of these is not the party, but the providential leader. Just as the societies born of these revolutions have evolved Stalinist structures, they have also begotten Stalinist parties, quite irrespective of whether a Leninist party had or had not been present in the revolutions that had given them birth. One point should be made clear: that historical juncture in which the party is truly indispensable is not the revolution, but rather postrevolutionary society, modelled along Stalinist lines. But such a party will then be quite different from the party of the Bolsheviks in 1917.

Not all the guises gracing the subjective factor are equally favorable to the transformation of anti-imperialist revolution into anticapitalist revolution. A Leninist party, formed by hardened revolutionaries and informed by the needs of the bottom strata of the population, with a disciplined organization and a scientific strategy, has proven its superiority as an instrument for changing the course of history. To back up this claim it will suffice to compare the scope of revolutions borne by parties of this type with those in which such a party was not active. Indeed, the Russian revolution is the first in history to have demonstrated the superior potential the subjective factor is capable of developing when it assumes this form, provided it is linked to the role of a providential leader. It may plausibly be argued that, as regards its efficacy, the indispensable role of the providential leader is at least dependent upon, if not wholly determined by, the counterbalancing role of a Leninist party. Actually, the discussion of the role of the party has customarily taken place within a broader framework: i.e., the reordering of the hierarchy of social forces as the revolution changed its character, the aspect that I have called the content of the revolution. To postulate a leading role for the Bolshevik party in the Russian revolution would imply that the content of the revolution remained invariable throughout its several phases or, what is the same thing stated more succinctly, that the content of the revolution is independent of its character (the purport of which is to reconcile a changeable character with an unchanging content). A comparison of the two insurrections will help to bring out this point more clearly.

In February, when the anti-autocratic character of the revolution was dominant, its content varied: a continual reshuffling of roles took place among the different social forces, each predominating in turn. The social force that was prepared to overthrow the autocracy was not prepared to replace it, and the force that later was to declare itself prepared to take the place of the autocracy, was at the time not prepared to overthrow it. The crucial role passed successively from one social force to another at different times during the insurrection. At the level of events, the insurrection began with a conspiracy of military leaders and members of the bureaucratic hierarchy to overthrow the Tsar in order to save the autocracy. When a second social force intervened—the people of Petrograd, with the proletariat at their head—the historical sweep of the palace revolt expanded, and transformed the Tsar's abdication into the collapse of the monarchy. The third social force was rather of a symbolic nature, important not for its structure, but for what it stood for: this was the Executive Committee of the Petrograd Soviet, a self-constituted ad hoc institution to which nonetheless the prerogatives of power accrued with the support of the masses. Finally the fourth social force, brusquely propelled into the forefront of the revolution by its own adversaries, was the liberal bourgeoisie, which accepted the power handed to it by the Soviet with the intention of returning to the state of affairs *ex ante*. Between the collapse of the autocracy, itself reluctant to abandon power, and the establishment of the power of the liberal bourgeoisie, accepted only unwillingly, lay a discontinuity in the principal roles, successively assumed by the different social forces. The first of these social forces directed its assault on the personification of power, the second struck at the very essence of power, the third assumed the vacated power only to pass it on, while the fourth accepted power but was never able effectively to wield it.

In October the Bolshevik party alone covered each of these roles. It was the party that foresaw in its strategy the possibility of an anticipatory anticapitalist revolution, the party that pursued this possibility, prepared the antibourgeois insurrection, and carried it out, and finally it was the party that rang down the curtain on the bourgeoisie to assume power itself. At each of these junctures, the same social force dominated the insurrection. The limitation of this ubiquitous presence would become apparent only after victory: the change effected by a political force could not go beyond existing political structures. Thus the Bolshevik government would vainly attempt to realize what the Provisional Government before it had just as vainly attempted to avoid—i.e., to carry the changes wrought at the political level into the economic and social domains as well.

The Bolshevik party was constant in its principal role only in the antibourgeois insurrection. In neither the revolutionary events preceding the insurrection nor in the exercise of power afterward was its role the same. Sooner or later in the aftermath of victory, all anti-imperialist revolutions that are also anticapitalist create a power structure in which the party has a constant presence. In both the Russian and the Cuban models, the party role grew steadily. In Cuba, the party was absent in the revolution but not in power. The pattern was merely more nuanced in the Russian revolution: it played a role that was truly insignificant in the first insurrection, a secondary but growing role as long as the revolution was predominantly antifeudal, a crucial role in the antibourgeois insurrection, and genuinely a leading role in the exercise of power (before the advent of Stalinism). It did not lead the revolution because it did not have the means to do so, and it did not lead the antibourgeois insurrection since it was of the party's own making. What it did effectively lead, after October, was the state.

The October insurrection was a moment of social discontinuity, achieved by virtue of the continuity in political roles filled by the Bolshevik party. Only because it alone covered all these roles was the anticipatory break in the historic flow of events able to take place: a revolution of a predominantly antifeudal character gave birth to a power that was preeminently antibourgeois. The leap without any transitional stage from one character of the revolution to a revolutionary power of a different character entirely was the Bolsheviks' principal achievement in the Russian revolution. Yet what the Russian revolution achieved through the Bolsheviks, other revolutions of the same nature have achieved without a party of this sort.

The succession of disparate roles of the Bolshevik party overlapped with a dissociation between two historical processes: the deterioration of the Provisional Government and its ultimate elimination. It was indeed the Bolsheviks who eliminated and replaced the provisional government, but it was not they who had rendered it unable to defend itself: that role was accomplished by the workers', peasants', and soldiers' movements. The Bolshevik party had foreseen, encouraged, and unwaveringly supported the spontaneous movements, but had neither begotten nor led them. Thus were its creative forces concentrated not on building the premises of the antibourgeois insurrection, but on their effective exploitation.

A distinction between these processes and among the various roles played by the Bolshevik party likewise reflected a distinction between its revolutionary strategy and its tactics. Prior to October, its tactics, though tailored admirably to the party's strategic goals, did no more than promote the spontaneous developments anticipated by party strategy but occurring independently of party action. This twin concurrence, between party tactics and strategy initially, and ultimately, between these and the spontaneous mass movements, complemented by the disarray of its adversaries, was to transform within the course of a few weeks this peripheral and miniscule organization, wracked by deep internal crisis, into the party which practically alone altered fundamentally the course of the Russian revolution and of world history in general. Its true brilliance lay in the fact that it was able to establish its own power not by virtue of having led the revolution, but despite the fact that it had not.

Party and class. The Bolshevik party and the proletariat, though largely convergent in their aims, were two distinct social forces. Their mutual relations were a material factor in defining their respective roles in the revolution. Earlier these relations were examined with regard to the role of the class, but they are just as essential to a discussion of the role of the party.

The role of the Bolshevik party with regard to the proletariat during the antibourgeois insurrection often obscures the different role it in fact played in this respect during the events preceding the insurrection. In the revolution's earlier period, these relations verged on the symmetrical: proletarian militancy was at a peak at the very time when the influence of the Bolshevik party among the ranks of the working class was at its lowest ebb. The February insurrection began on the 23rd with a demonstration in honor of International Women's Day, and continued into the next day with street battles already breaking out. The ad hoc leadership of the Bolshevik party, the Russian Bureau of the Central Committee, waited until the 25th to call for a general strike. But by that time in Petrograd the general strike was already a *fait accompli*. "The general strike in Petrograd," comments Trotsky, "was already turning into an armed insurrection. The leadership looked on from on high, hesitated, procrastinated, i.e., it did not lead." In another passage the former Bolshevik leader suggests that the Bolshevik leadership did not merely hesitate in the face of the spontaneous actions of the workers but even toyed with the idea of opposing them. ". . . the fact is that the February revolution was begun from below, overcoming the resistance of its own revolutionary organizations, the initiative being taken of their own accord by the most oppressed and downtrodden part of the proletariat—the women textile workers."

Bolshevik involvement in the events of February was at a sufficiently low level that even the official *History of the CPSU* contradicts itself: "The Romanov monarchy crumbled under the blows of the popular masses, encouraged in their struggle by the Bolsheviks," it tells us, studiously avoiding mention of the byword "the leading role" and indeed, even the party's name. The revolution broke out with the spontaneous uprising of one of the most backward sections of the proletariat, uninfluenced by the Bolshevik party. Thus was the Bolshevik party caught on the sidelines, present as a mere spectator, no more, to crucial events that would serve perfectly its own ends: party strategy was accomplished by actions occurring independently of party tactic. The fall of the autocracy, which it had always celebrated, took the Bolshevik party by surprise. In February, it was passed by not only by the class, but also by events which it itself had basically foreseen.

Though all the socialist parties of Russia were alike in their unpreparedness, the political effects were different in each case. Thus in early March, when the Petrograd Soviet was formed, there were only 40 Bolsheviks among the 3,000 delegates. Three months later, at the first All-Russian Congress of Soviets, there were only 105 Bolsheviks among the 1,090 delegates. This represented a considerable growth, but it was not sufficient to relieve the marginal status in which the Bolsheviks found themselves at the outbreak of the revolution. In June as in February, the Bolsheviks were still very far from assuming a leading role. After having described the insignificance of their role in February, Trotsky continues: "The Bolsheviks did not summon the masses to the April demonstration. The Bolsheviks will not call the armed masses into the streets at the beginning of July. Only in October will the party finally fall in step and march out at the head of the masses, not for a demonstration, but for a revolution."

As the party's role in the revolution changed, so did also its relations with the proletariat. The two social forces were practically separate in February, thereafter to converge gradually; on the eve of the antibourgeois insurrection the party's influence over the class was at its peak, but victory tended to sunder them anew, although this time on a different basis. Stalinism would carry this tendency to its completion, transforming separation into subordination. Thus did the class fall under the sway of the power being wielded in its name, the party representing it becoming the party of its oppression.

The vicissitudes in the relations between party and class matched the vicissitudes in their respective roles. These changing patterns often elude the ken of even those Marxists actively involved in a critical reevaluation of Soviet historiography. Thus for Bettelheim, "In terms of the class content of the revolution of October and the state power that was born of it, what was *decisive* is the leading role of the Bolshevik party." This author observes, justly enough, that the revolution ended with the same content as the state power to which it gave birth, and that this content was imposed upon it by the party, not the proletariat. Yet this does not prevent Bettelheim paradoxically from calling it "class content," as if the Bolshevik party were a class or formed one together with the working class.

Of all the social forces of the revolution, the proletariat was the most susceptible of all to Bolshevik influence. There were two reasons for this: first, the party's concern always to be guided in its actions by the interests of the proletariat, and second, the nature of the proletariat's relations with the bourgeoisie. The objective nature of these relations contributed in a major way to the fact that the Bolshevik party converged with the proletariat in a manner different from the way it converged with any of the other revolutionary social forces. It should be clear enough, for example, that the peasantry did not destroy the feudal order so as to put itself in accord with the Bolshevik party, but that this accord flowed naturally from the peasant war, whose victory would be enshrined by the party. Nor did the soldiers oppose the war because the Bolshevik party had asked them to; rather in doing so they merely found themselves on the same side as the party, which would enshrine their victory over the war's advocates. There was the same sort of spontaneous convergence between the economic struggles of the proletariat and the general orientation of the Bolshevik party. Two factors at least made this accord deeper than the others. First, the direct and principal target of the proletariat in its economic struggle was the bourgeoisie; second, without Bolshevik leadership, the chances that the struggle would escalate beyond economic issues to become a decisive political battle were infinitesimal. Convergence was firmer in this case because it rested on more solid objective foundations. Yet though the proletariat was pitted directly against the bourgeoisie, this does not necessarily imply that it had more of a hand in its defeat. Therefore, if we may take an example, the question whether the Bolshevik party received greater support from the workers or from the soldiers in October must forever go begging.

The vision of a proletariat with the Bolshevik party at its head from first to last lives on in innumerable works on the Russian revolution. At the basis of this tendency to universalize the leading role rests a confusion between proletarian actions which the party expected to occur and those which in actual fact it guided. The coincidence between the spontaneous actions of the class, which Trotsky calls "unconscious Bolshevism" and the aims of Bolshevik strategy does not demonstrate the leading role of the party. The Bolshevik party no more led the uprising of the Petersburg workers in February than it did the peasant uprising some months later. Fundamental to the fate of the revolution, these two uprisings may have been concordant with party strategy, but they were also independent of its influence. It is here that the confusion enters the picture: a correct prediction is mistaken for the work of effective leadership.

The Bolshevik party was not the steadfast and constant leader of the proletariat. Variations over time were punctuated by the various guises dictated by its role. At its most consummate, that role saw party initiatives transformed into analogous, effective proletarian action. A less consummate form was where the party took the cue to become the organizer of actions initiated spontaneously and independently by the class. Finally, the least consummate—although for the study of Stalinism the most important—of these roles was where the party undertook actions wholly of its own making, relying not on the direct participation of the proletariat, but on its potential support, publicly acclaimed. This was the form the party's leadership took in the October insurrection. Its importance for the argument presented here is evident: party leadership of the class became the substitution of the class by the party.

Once again a comparison of the two insurrections will help to provide a clearer idea of how this tendency was manifest historically. In February the proletariat had a direct and decisive hand in the overthrow of the autocracy—but not in the establishment of the new power—independently of Bolshevik leadership. In October, this time under that leadership, the proletariat participated indirectly both in the overthrow of bourgeois power and in the establishment of an antibourgeois power or, more precisely, it participated directly in neither. Indeed, as the possibility of establishing antibourgeois power loomed closer, the proletariat backed off from undertaking any direct action contributory to this end. Gradually its role changed, and consisted no longer so much in acting as in encouraging the direct action of the party. The more accessible power became, the more evident became the proletariat's historical unpreparedness for the seizure of power.

The Bolshevik party assumed directly not only the historical mission of the proletariat, but also its practical tasks, and in so doing mustered an original solution to an unusual problem, which anticipatory revolution had ineluctibly to face. Anticipation gave a rational context to the overthrow of an immature bourgeoisie, but it could not do the same for a proletariat which, though immature, was thrust into a position of command over society, beyond its powers to fill. Instead that function was preempted by the Bolshevik party the moment it took on the practical task of an antibourgeois insurrection. Party substitution of the class thus followed from the anticipatory nature of the revolution. At the time, anticipation was necessary but provisional; under Stalinism it became both arbitrary and permanent. Though substitution, in the sense of aiding the proletariat to accomplish its mission, was indeed implied by the Bolsheviks' anticipatory strategy, how, specifically, this was to be done was never sufficiently elaborated.

According to Lenin, in February the Russian proletariat had carried out the insurrection successfully, but let power slip from its hands, because of the low level of its consciousness and organization. The eight months that followed saw considerable progress in this respect, but the proletariat was still unable to transcend its condition. With the antibourgeois insurrection in the offing, it had a chance to keep power from slipping through its hands: to wield that power for the time being through the intermediary of a competent substitute, so long as it lacked the capacity itself to do so. This substitute was the Bolshevik Party, the institutionalized consciousness of the working class. But institutionalized consciousness is a devolved consciousness, and hence its bearer was not the proletariat. Substitution separated party and class, with the party to move eventually into command. This function, namely steering the proletariat, required a party different from the one obliged temporarily to assume the proletarian mission. However, the structures improvised to enable the party to exercise its dominion assumed a permanent quality and maintained that dominion indefinitely. In this sense, Stalinism represented society's permanent adaptation to a transitory function: the division between party and class, a temporary necessity, became a permanent chasm.

The tendency toward division, concealed by the anticipatory nature of the revolution at this stage, became patent after victory. The antifeudal demands of neither the peasantry nor the soldiers required anticipatory solutions. Anticipation was relevant only to the satisfaction of the demands specifically of the workers. Thus it followed that once firmly in power the Bolsheviks were able immediately to satisfy the demands of the peasantry and soldiers, but not of the workers. Though victorious, the proletariat acquired neither power, nor property, nor emancipation from capitalist exploitation, whereas for the peasantry victory at least brought liberation from feudal servitude. With October scarcely past, the workers plunged into a veritable frenzy of expropriations, meeting resistance, however, on two fronts: from the bourgeoisie, which was to be expected, but also from the Bolshevik party, which the workers did not expect. To its bitter surprise, the proletariat discovered that the party of anticipation had become a party of procrastination, and at the expense of the class it presumed to represent.

This shift in course imposed by the constraints of history brought about a substantive change in the party's relations with the proletariat. Up until this point the proletariat may not have undertaken all the actions which according to Bolshevik strategy were to be expected of it, but in their general orientation all its actions were consonant with the goals of this strategy and thus had the party's support. Through an effective victory, foreseeable yet unforeseen, this steady convergence now entered a crisis, which persisted until postrevolutionary society, unable to resolve it, proceeded to assimilate it, and Stalinism was born.

Victory in the anticipatory revolution was premature, and necessarily so; nonetheless, because of this the proletariat was unable not only to transcend these limits, but also to acquire a consciousness of them. In turn, the Bolshevik party, which proved capable enough of leading the proletariat to power, proved incapable of guiding the class in the exercise of it.

Anticipation seemed to have placed a sanction on the social class that was the most instrumental in its achievement. Victory over its natural class enemy brought less satisfaction to the proletariat than to any other category of producers. It is therefore not surprising that after October the proletariat should spontaneously continue its militant course to transform the revolution—its antibourgeois character now achieved—into an anticapitalist revolution, proceeding from the political defeat of the bourgeoisie to its suppression as a social class. The proletariat saw the plausibility of an immediate liquidation of the bourgeoisie; it did not perceive the implausibility of itself managing the nation's economy. The Bolshevik party was aware of both, and it was this difference in consciousness that separated it from the class. Inequality in consciousness became incongruity in action.

The Bolshevik party issued the slogan of workers' control to dampen the expropriatory élan of the proletariat. The workers felt cheated by the discrepancy between the scope of their revolutionary struggle and the meager results victory had brought them. What was worse, it was no longer a hostile social force but their own institutionalized consciousness that was impeding them from balancing the accounts. Thus victory drove deeper the wedge between party and class, which the revolution had only tapped lightly. Anticipation moved from the realm of the possible to that of the necessary, expressed in the party, and negated the proletariat. Separation foretokened alienation, and for the Bolshevik government workers' control was the measure designed to avoid this danger. It empowered the proletariat to supervise an activity that it did not have the capacity to exercise itself, while as regards the bourgeoisie it placed constraints on an activity it could not prohibit. Indeed the measure was as legitimate and sound in terms of political principle as it was unsound in terms of economic practice. Politically it amounted to a ratification of the social superiority of the victorious class over the class it had defeated; economically, however, it merely placed the proletariat in a supervisory capacity over a managerial function that it felt entitled to exercise itself by virtue of its newly acquired rights of proprietorship.

From the standpoint of the Bolsheviks, clearly, workers' control was designed to deflect the proletariat from appropriating a social patrimony that it was as yet unprepared to husband, and to prevent the economic collapse of antibourgeois society. Workers' control was to give capitalist proprietorship a maximum of responsibilities with a minimum of prerogatives. At the same time, for the workers it was to have been a veritable revolutionary school of self-management. The intentions, however, optimistic as they were, were unable to mitigate appreciably the fundamental difficulty of the situation: the proletariat had defeated the bourgeoisie yet had left capitalist relations of production intact; economically, therefore, it remained dependent on the bourgeoisie. Workers' control thus represented a veritable amalgam of all that was contained potentially in the October insurrection. It was antibourgeois because it broke the political grip of the bourgeoisie and restricted its economic privileges; it was not proletarian because it had given the proletariat neither the power it had seized from the bourgeoisie, nor the means of production it had expropriated from them. The antibourgeois character of the October insurrection was thus effectively achieved; its proletarian character remained but an aspiration.

The anticipatory revolution brought victory, but a victory which had to remain incomplete for the time being. Its energy was sufficient to destroy the social domination of one class, but not to establish another in its place. Thus while it did not abolish class structures, as in Marx's model, it did alter them profoundly.

The theoretical implication of the concept of the dictatorship of the proletariat was that the end of a social structure dominated by the bourgeoisie did not imply the end of every ruling-class social structure. To this attribute of proletarian revolution, anticipatory revolution added another, which did nothing to simplify matters: the function of dominant class remained necessary, but no class, the proletariat included, was able to exercise that function. The role of dominant class was thus left vacant, and the Bolshevik party filled the vacuum. The step was a necessary one, at least for the moment, but the risk it entailed was immense: namely, substitution of the dictatorship of the proletariat by the dictatorship of the party.

Anticipation, once achieved, only aggravated the breaches it had created between party and class. The Bolshevik party had failed to find a strategy for development of postrevolutionary society to follow up its strategy for revolution. Having lost its strategic perspective, the Bolshevik party also found itself shorn of its legitimation to lead the proletariat—and precisely at a time when the convergence between party and class was entering a crisis and the party had set its sights on becoming the guiding light for the whole of society. The Bolsheviks had taken a formidable historical step in seizing power, but the price they paid was dear and even a step backward in that it brought to a halt the process of convergence between party and proletariat. From being the institutionalized consciousness of the interests of the class, the party had become the institutionalized consciousness of its limits. But if the class found itself ultimately subordinated to the party, this was no deliberate work of the latter, but rather of a fateful conflict that pitted immature social forces against one another.

Since the conflict could not be resolved through the simple workings of its objective mechanisms, intervention of the subjective factor became crucial. Thus history and its turnings did their utmost to complicate materially a role that the proletariat was totally unprepared to fill, even in its most elementary aspects. The bourgeoisie, which had lost its political power owing mainly its own weakness, was able temporarily to retain a portion of its economic power owing mainly to the weakness of the proletariat. Once again, the principle of unequal development applied: the bourgeoisie degenerated more quickly than the proletariat was able to mature.

The victory of anticipatory revolution entailed a transference of roles as well: the party took the place of the class. But though this transference of roles altered the predominant character of the revolution, it did not alter the objective backwardness of the proletariat, whose immaturity survived its victory and would later become the principal obstacle to postrevolutionary society's potential evolution toward socialism. Stalinism, far from eliminating this obstacle through industrialization, would transform it into a functional requirement of the social order. The emergence of Stalinism was no more than the adaptation of the structures of anticapitalist society to proletarian immaturity; its perpetuation was the reproduction of that immaturity by these same structures.

The subjugation of the proletariat to the party proved to be the prelude to achievements that in the short term seemed epochal enough: it permitted the maintenance of antibourgeois power, and accomplished the first anticapitalist industrialization in history on its basis. But it was unable to take, and later even prohibited, any genuine step toward socialism. In Stalinist societies, the recovery by the working class of its social, economic, and political role was and remains prerequisite to any turn in that direction.

The providential leader. In the 1917 revolution, Lenin was truly the providential leader of the Bolshevik party, which he was able to rally around himself and urge down upon the pathway to success at the same time. The significance of this observation does not stop at Lenin's merits, nor the inadequacies of the Bolshevik party: it goes further, and shows that before becoming the grotesque work of ideology, the cult of personality—i.e., the function of the providential leader— had been a real necessity of the revolution. Lenin did not create this role, but he was the historical actor capable of filling it. The origins of this essentially personal role must be sought in the impersonal premises of the Russian revolution.

The historical struggle to eliminate the effects of the unequal development of societies turns clearly on the unequal development of individuals. Antinomic necessity produces a hitch in the objective mechanisms of the historical movement. The activation of these mechanisms depends in unprecedented measure on the adequate intervention of subjective factors. It was the growing objective importance of the subjective factor that conferred a growing objective importance on the inequality among human subjects: the task of shaping men's history in conformity with elaborate human projects serves as an inexorable discriminating factor among historical actors.

It would seem necessary that we examine less an original feature of the Russian revolution than an exigency of an anticipatory revolution: asynchronous factors of an individual order become a necessity of the struggle against asynchronous aspects of the social order. This exigency is not concerned merely with inequality among individuals, but also with the inequality between individual and organization. To elaborate and direct the application of an adequate strategy in history is an elitist activity, not a democratic one. What an anticipatory revolution requires first and foremost, given inequality among individuals, is an exceptional leader. The exceptional qualities required are infinitely more accessible to a gifted individual than to the most elite of organizations. Consequently, as regards the inequality between the individual and an organization, anticipatory revolution requires the supremacy of the leader over the party. History depends on an individual. The society that is born of this dependence tends to reproduce it, and in such a society personification of strategy becomes a role whose necessity is manifested independently of individual abilities to fill that role. Anticipatory strategy creates this crucial role, which may fall to actors not sufficiently gifted to fill it. Thus, the institution of providential leader will change its foundation, which is then no longer the reality of the revolution but the fiction of an ideology. Product of a legitimate inequality among men, the institution of the providential leader becomes under such conditions the producer and the magnifier of their illegitimate inequality. The necessity of personification looks for its possibility, i.e., a person endowed with the appropriate qualities.

The institution of the providential leader emerged in the course of the revolution by dint of the embodiment of a valid strategy in an exceptional individual. These two legitimating factors were both absent in Stalinism where the institution of the providential leader, maintained by the sole act of its necessity, became illegitimate. Its loss of legitimacy was accompanied by a commensurate growth in its impact on society. Leninism was the affirmation and the satisfaction in real terms of the necessity of a providential leader during the course of the revolution. Stalinism was the exacerbation of this same necessity, and its simulated satisfaction during the course of the transition from antibourgeois society to noncapitalist society, and from underdevelopment to industrialization. The objective necessity of the role triumphed over the subjective impossibility of filling it.

The necessity of the role of providential leader expressed the broader necessity of a transfer of roles in the anticipatory revolution. Denied a historical mission that it was prepared to carry out, the proletariat found itself encharged with a second mission, namely that of the bourgeoisie. This dual mission of an insufficiently mature proletariat was assumed by the Bolshevik party by virtue of a revolutionary strategy which it proved incapable of assimilating. Under these conditions free discussion within the party seemed more to obstruct than to aid the application of the strategy by the providential leader. The transfer of roles was complete: the historical mission that had passed from the proletariat to the party now passed from the party to its leader, "The triumph of the party," writes Carr, "seemed almost exclusively due to Lenin's consistent success in stamping his personal will upon it and in leading his often reluctant colleagues in his train. The prestige of Lenin's name had been firmly established; the foundations had been laid of the ascendancy in the party of the single leader."

This dual transfer of roles is in the last analysis a product of antinomic necessity. On the one hand it created the possibility of an anticipated social change, but it also brought about a relative sterilization of the social forces intended to accomplish it. This antinomic action was translated into the specific antinomy of the Russian revolution, which combined a formidable revolutionary elan of the masses with the immaturity of the working class, on the one hand, and the failings of the Bolshevik party on the other. On account of antinomic necessity, and contrary to a classic postulate of Marxism, society seemed to be posing problems that it did not have the means to resolve. The general incapacity of social forces made necessary the exceptional capacity of a social individual. The necessity of this individual was independent of the chance on which this necessary individual, whether he appeared or did not appear, wholly depended. The independence of necessity with respect to the instrument that was to satisfy that necessity is as old as history and is at the origin of all religions. Stalinism is not a religion, in the sense that it does not project the illusory force of controlling necessity onto a being, also illusory, but onto a real individual. His exceptional powers compensate for a lack of exceptional gifts. In most ancient models, human inability is projected into the realm of the superhuman.

As for the party, Stalinism only adapted its structures to its true function, which was that of faithfully seconding the providential leader. The party at the brink of paralysis, the party of free discussion, was transformed into a party of short-term efficacy, a party of ritualized submission. The spontaneous tendency toward factionalism was transformed into the reality of a forced unity. Stalinism was the rigorous adaptation of the party and postrevolutionary society to the real effect of an absent strategy. The myth of the leading role of the Bolshevik party in the revolution fueled the myth of the infallible leader in Stalinist society. This latter myth could not be demolished as long as the first endured.

The party between the revolution and Stalinism. Stalinism selectively assimilated the experience acquired by the Bolsheviks in the revolution; namely, elements having to do with party strategy, its relations with the working class, its coherence, and the role of leader. But this was only part of a process immeasurably greater in breadth, which amounted to no less than the progressive transformations of the party's functions as it (like any other party victorious in revolution) moved from the struggle for power to its seizure and later its exercise. The functional mutations undergone by the Bolshevik party differed from what might ordinarily be expected in such a revolutionary context in a number of respects, beginning with the very nature of the conflict from which it had emerged victorious. A diffuse conflict, weakly structured, will by nature beget pseudo-solutions, which serve only to prolong the conflict in other forms. The power that emerges from a diffuse conflict tends, by way of compensation, to be highly concentrated. Indeed it was this compensatory function that inscribed the profound tendency toward monolithism and irreversibility in the genetic code of the unsteady power that emerged in October. The exercise of power placed the Bolshevik party in a contradictory situation, difficult to control. Its new functions clashed with its old structure. The party ultimately would be crushed by the weight of the social functions it had assumed but did not have the means to fulfill. Shapiro commented on this as follows: "Lenin certainly dominated the party; but he did not (as Stalin did) completely destroy it as an institution." But this interpretation seems questionable. What Stalinism destroyed, it would seem, was the real party, and not the party as an institution. On the contrary, by preserving the institution of the party along with its principal symbols, he gave plausibility to the illusion of its continuity. The persistence of the institution obscured the fact that the Bolshevik party had been demolished and replaced by an organization having essentially different functions and structures. The party's spurious continuity reflected in distorted form the effective continuity of social and political mechanisms, which after the revolution tended relentlessly toward the party's destruction and toward the emergence of a bureaucratic organization of the type embodied in the party of Stalinism.

The most astounding social function it fell to the Bolshevik party to fulfill after October was that of playing the role of dominant class, not with the aid of the proletariat, but in its stead. That being the case, the supreme virtue of the proletariat in the eyes of the party was no longer its militancy, as during the revolution, but its passivity. Obedience, rather than action, was henceforth its class role. That was the price the leading party paid to become the dominant party.

The transformations undergone by the party were in reality but the reflection of the metamorphoses experienced by power as it made its way down the tortuous and unwonted path toward belated industrialization. A force dominating the whole of society was needed: an antibourgeois monopoly of power politically, and an anticapitalist monopoly in the economic domain. Only thus did industrialization become a possibility, but neither the initiative nor leadership would come from the bourgeoisie or the proletariat, just as neither would enjoy its benefits. A direct and monopolistic control over all economic levers became an exclusive prerogative of Stalinist power, to be found with no other type of power whatsoever, not even the capitalist brand of totalitarian power, despite similarities in structures and methods that are misleading because they are outwardly so obvious. Stalinism is the only social order in which political power consists not in defending but in building an economic order of which it has become the principal controlling force. The essence of all power is constraint, and an economy controlled by political power will be likewise an economy guided by constraint. But even a monolithic power does not have sufficient means of constraint at its disposal to perform all the functions required by a monopolistic control over the economy. Hence, to economic constraint is added extra-economic coercion, and as a consequence Stalinism, in particular, was able to transform the antibourgeois structures of postrevolutionary society into the structures of an anticapitalist order. The function of class substitution assumed by political power acquired a new vitality; proprietorship, like power, would henceforth be exercised not only in the name of the proletariat, but at its expense as well. Monopoly of decision likewise became monopoly in management. An extremely cohesive power was necessary to exercise this monopoly on two fronts, if the requirements of industrialization were to be met. Under the circumstances, a cohesive power required a cohesive party, and a cohesive party required a unified leadership, the perfect model for which is leadership embodied in one person. To be effective, personal leadership must be legitimate, and personal power has sought its legitimacy in infallibility and the superhuman since time immemorial. Infallibility is inherent to the role; it is projected onto the person of the actor filling it, and withdrawn again when that role falls from his hands.

The infallibility of the role becomes the infallibility of the person, and so, ultimately, the infallibility of his decisions. A leader whose role consists in producing a steady stream of infallible decisions can hardly rely on a party of revolutionary intrepidity for his support; rather he requires an organization trained to administrative obedience, overcentralized—in a word, possessing the traits proper to every bureaucratic apparatus. To suppress politically the party of the revolution was not enough; its leaders had to be eliminated as well. Only a solitary leader can also be an infallible leader.

The absence of strategy threatened to rupture the continuity necessary to the historical process. Deprived of its original driving mechanism, that process could resume its flow only by forging a continuity of another kind, and the Stalinist institution of the infallible leader was the instrument it used to do so. Illusory though it was, this infallibility was effective—perhaps even as effective as a genuine strategy—for rescuing a society dependent on subjective initiative from stagnation, but not for steering it toward the pursuit of a deliberate end. Once set in motion, however, the process continued on its own momentum, with the institution of infallibility blurring any distinction between ends that were real and those that were utopian. Yet even the pursuit of utopian ends effects real and profound changes in society's structures, and it was the rendering of these real changes in the idiom of unreal aims that produced and maintained the legitimizing mythology of the infallible leader, which, in turn, served to nourish the mythology surrounding the role of the Bolshevik party in the revolution. Continuity in strategy, which was unattainable, was made up for by continuity in mythology, fostering the illusory image of the new bureaucratic party as the direct successor in an unbroken legacy to the revolutionary party, rather than the author of its actual destruction. Thus an adequate understanding of the real role played by the Bolshevik party in the revolution is crucial to any understanding of the role played by this new bureaucratic party in the establishment of Stalinist society.

The party's new structure and leadership adapted power to its social function, i.e., subduing the proletariat and thus the whole of society. From this moment, the division between party and class was no longer defined exclusively by differences in levels of consciousness and organization, but also—and indeed above all—in terms of the instruments of power and control over society's material goods; the party leadership possessed these instruments, the class did not. Paradoxically, victory over the bourgeoisie had reduced the proletariat from a formidable social force in the revolution to a mere productive force for industrialization. In Stalinist society its task was not to appropriate the means of production, but simply to multiply them. Leninist strategy had foreseen the possibility of an anticipatory victory over the bourgeoisie, but it had not foreseen its enfeebling consequences, among which was the temporary necessity of separating the party from the class. The cost of meeting this necessity was to render possible—yet not inevitable—the total subjugation of the class by a Stalinist type of power. Whether history would elect to realize this fateful possibility or bury it would depend on the configuration of events, the historical actors, and on chance. All these factors could influence the fate of this possibility in one direction or another, but they did not, nor could they, create it. To find the source of this possibility one must go back to the activity of the Bolshevik party during the course of the revolution; while not the determining cause of Stalinism, that activity had helped to make its emergence possible.

The seizure of power

Every insurrection entails a violent confrontation, a rebellion, requiring the participation of the masses. Even so, the October 1917 insurrection falls somewhat wide of this criterion. The element of rebellion was present, as was violence, and indeed both were implicit in the act of arresting a lawful government.

Yet violence, or its repudiation, was more significant as a threat than as an actuality. For their part, the masses did not directly participate in the insurrection, although their presence in the wings was an indispensable element in its victory.

The decisive act in general resembled less a military operation than an armed demonstration—and one of very modest proportions at that. Nevertheless, despite these reservations, "insurrection" may still be deemed an acceptable term to describe the events in question.

On the eve of October, social tension had been brought to a breaking point by the violence raging in the countryside and the army's refusal to fight. In this atmosphere, with violence, both actual and potential, hanging in the air, the Provisional Government was nonviolently overthrown. The antibourgeois insurrection occurred in a military scenario, as reflected, in fact, in the name of the committee that had led it. This fact is of crucial importance for a correct determination of the character of the insurrection, which was neither socialist, nor proletarian, nor even anticapitalist, but simply antibourgeois.

The insurrection was political in that it imposed a political solution on the violent clashes that had both come before it and accompanied it, but which had shown that the use of force alone was ineffectual for resolving social conflict. The insurrection brought to an abrupt end the deflection of violence into political issues. The insurrection had come the full round from the isolation of the Bolshevik party to the isolation of the Provisional Government and the political parties supporting it. Its dynamics may be brought out more clearly by distinguishing between its premises, its actual unfolding, and its effects.

Its premises or preconditions were determined by the specific constellation of social forces: first, the existence of powerful popular movements raising vital problems in forms that threatened to overturn the structures of society; second, a government unable to satisfy, control, undermine, or dissolve these movements; and third, a revolutionary political force capable of translating a valid strategy into efficacious action, the constant terms of which were intransigent opposition to the government and its camp and unconditional support to the popular movements. The Bolshevik party figured in only the last of these three premises, although in so acting it was not itself immune to serious inconsistencies. Nevertheless, these factors were of such force that their confluence was able to transform the destructive violence of the social upheaval into the political ascendancy of the Bolshevik party.

The overthrow of the Provisional Government had another political aspect which was reflected in the particular way events unfolded. The peasantry aside—absorbed as it was in its war against the feudal order, it paid no attention to the insurrection—the other social classes as well as the army found themselves little more than observers from the sidelines in this final battle, which in reality was a battle between two opposing political institutions. It was the nature of the forces it faced and the means it employed that determined the political nature of the insurrection. It is a significant fact, generally disregarded, that the Provisional Government had been dismissed by the eminently political decision of the Second Congress of Soviets before being arrested without a shot being fired by the twenty-five men under Antonov's command—but not without the fact being recorded in official minutes written *in loco*.

Finally, the political nature of the insurrection was especially in evidence in its immediate effects. Depriving the bourgeoisie of its political advantages—but not of its property—the insurrection enabled the Bolshevik party to assume effective political power, but without economic underpinnings. The political nature of the insurrection unfolded progressively, from being of overriding influence in the prelude to events, of decisive importance in their actual course, to a being a restrictive factor in the questions that arose in its aftermath.

In revolution, a victory that stops at the frontiers of politics can easily become a pyrrhic victory. The Bolsheviks had given their unconditional support to the demands of the vast popular movements: peace, land, wages, and food. They gained power by defending the immediate interests of the populace, and then kept power by sacrificing these immediate interests, defined in terms of the existing situation, to the long-term interests of society, defined in ideological terms. This sacrifice is one of the fundamental features of Stalinism.

One aspect of the October insurrection that was replete with consequences was the narrowness of its scope. With the partial exception of the workers, the popular movements hardly associated the satisfaction of their demands with the overthrow of the Provisional Government. The soldiers and peasants had been losing their confidence in this government only bit by bit through their own first-hand experience. Thus they were more or less inclined to favor its overthrow, which for them had nothing to do with the suppression of the political power of the bourgeoisie or, worse still, the abolition of the bourgeoisie as a class. The Bolshevik party invested the overthrow of the Provisional Government with a range of other meanings of an entirely different order from what it meant to the principal movements in the revolution. If the insurrection was to have the same significance practically as that with which the Bolsheviks had endowed it theoretically, then the party had also as far as possible to assume responsibility for it. But an insurrection brought swiftly and resolutely to a successful conclusion by the Bolshevik party alone had necessarily to be an action that was fast and sparing in the extreme. "The final stage," observed Trotsky, ". . . occupied exactly twenty-four hours. . . . During this period the Military Revolutionary Committee openly employed arms for the conquest of the city and the capture of the government. In these operations, generally speaking, as many forces took part as were needed to solve the limited problem—hardly more than 25 or 30 thousand at the most." "The tranquillity of the October streets, the absence of crowds and battles, gave the enemy a pretext to talk of the conspiracy of an insignificant minority, the adventure of a handful of Bolsheviks."

In a country numbering tens of millions, the Bolshevik party had carried off one of the most radical actions in history by bringing it down to manageable limits. To succeed, it had counted on the unwavering trust of the masses, and the effective impotence of its adversary: the Provisional Government had become nothing more than a shadow. The party had taken the diffuse energy of the social conflict and, by concentrating it in time and space, limiting the number of direct participants, and restricting it to a single political level, succeeded in turning the tide of history. The work of the Bolshevik party, the insurrection itself, was a miniscule event rounded with premises and effects, both of momentous proportions.

One underlying effect of this achievement must not be overlooked: the insurrection had for all practical purposes solidified the Bolshevik party's autonomy even before it established itself in power. At the time – and the observation bears repeating—this was a contingent autonomy, for it was the popular movements of the revolution that had eroded the power of the bourgeoisie, enabling the Bolshevik party, when the time came, to suppress it with an absolute economy of means, paving the way for its utter autonomy in the exercise of power.

The redefinition of the role of the party occasioned by the victory of October entailed a necessary redefinition of the role of the proletariat as well. The party's autonomy with regard to society was both condition and consequence of its autonomy with regard to the class it had effectively replaced. The tendency for these two roles to diverge, one of the results of the revolution, was transformed upon the seizure of power into a tendency for them to become complementary: the party could become a dominant force solely on condition that the class be reduced to a subaltern force. At the same time, the roles themselves became increasingly more fixed, noninterchangeable, and nonnegotiable.

In October, as in February, one character of the revolution clearly predominated in each case, but in neither case did change go beyond the political sphere. But if the two insurrections were bounded by the same limits, they differed in their mechanisms and their tendencies. The violent but incoherent action of the masses in February ended with the constitution of a new power that contrived to restore the old. In October, the resolute, cohesive, nonviolent, and minority action of the Bolshevik party ended with the establishment of the party itself in power, with monopolistic and indeed irreversible tendencies. Further, whereas it had been the principal aim of the power established in the aftermath of February to contain change within the political domain, such containment was an obstruction for the power that came upon the scene in October.

The autonomy manifested by the Bolshevik party in the October revolution contained the possibility of smashing the bourgeoisie, something that the autonomous class struggle had as yet been unable to achieve through its own momentum. This "revision" was situated in a reality that had been barred to Marxist scrutiny; a reality, namely, where the defeat of the bourgeoisie was the work not of the working class, even underdeveloped, but of a party well suited to the task. Bettelheim, correctly refusing to attribute credit for this defeat to the "intentions" of the Bolshevik party, nonetheless draws the peculiar conclusion that "henceforth analysis must focus on social classes" and indeed goes on to center his attention on a phenomenon that was peripheral to the reality under examination. As a consequence, he overlooks an identifying trait common to the revolution, postrevolutionary society, and Stalinist society alike, reaching its apogee in the last: namely the replacement of the diffuse social energy of class struggle by the concentrated forces of a political organization. So long as the revolution pursued a predominantly antifeudal course, it retained a predominantly class, i.e. social, content. But as soon as its antibourgeois character gained ascendancy, the content of the revolution became predominantly political; a metamorphosis took place, in that the social conflict had now acquired a political dimension. Out of this conflict emerged a power that, in separating itself from the class from which it had emanated, cut itself off from society as well. Society's material conditions provided no basis for its conferring any legitimacy on power, and the power that stepped into the role of dominant class became the term of reference generally in class struggles, which thereby became struggles for or against the constituted power. This is why in Stalinism there is no social conflict that is not at the same time a political conflict.

In modern societies, social classes are represented by political parties, which are granted relatively broad prerogatives to this end. Not only did the Russian revolution give these prerogatives maximum scope, it also carried the social conflict into a political domain where it was no longer able to find legitimate expression. The social conflict, waged between two immature classes, had the force neither to renovate existing structures, nor to render them functional to the purpose of choosing between the alternative of capitalism or anticapitalism that had been placed upon the order of the day. The path toward industrialization thus remained blocked, the abolition of the autocracy having merely replaced one barrier by another just as total. To remove this barrier the social conflict had to be carried to the political level where it assumed an autonomous form. Thus class struggle, though making the insurrection possible, did not make it a reality, and no study that focuses on class struggle alone will be able to resolve the enigmas of the antibourgeois insurrection. The power, in turn, created by the insurrection only modelled itself after class relations rather than, in fact, reflecting them.

The historical roots of a power of this order go back far beyond the revolution into Russia's remote past. For centuries before it finally collapsed, the autocracy had itself been a political institution exercising the function of dominant class not only on behalf, but even in place of, the Russian feudal estate. The autocratic character of Stalinism was thus fed by a tradition in which this form of power expressed a peculiarity of the existing class relations: the inability of the possessing classes to assume directly the position of dominant class. Of course, given the progress in productive forces, the monopolization of social control by political power was used by the Tsarist autocracy and the Stalinist autocracy in totally opposite ways. But both modelled themselves after the class structure, with a vast bureaucratic apparatus, vertically differentiated, of unparalleled endurance, each withstanding the severest of historical tests. Of course the longevity of Stalinism does not compare with that of the Tsarist autocracy, which extended over centuries. But Stalinism's potential for survival on a historical scale must not be underestimated: indeed, it brought Russia industrialization, victory in the greatest war in history, the status of a world superpower based on an undisputed military might, and forty years of outward expansion without general war.

Thus separated initially from the working class, and then isolated from the class structure in general, the power that issued from the antibourgeois insurrection set the stage for its possible degeneration into Stalinism.

Power

The victory of October brought a new power into being, and its character would be the consummate expression of the character of the insurrection. Inasmuch as it is the most direct source of Stalinism, it is worth dwelling on the historical roots of this power.

Aside from its antifeudal credentials, another aspect revelatory of the new power from the standpoint of its future degeneration into Stalinism is the functions specific to it and the way in which these functions shaped the structures of power.

Once established, antibourgeois power was abruptly transformed: from a strategic goal, it became a real structure which, if it were to last, had to be functional. Apart from the forces driving it, two antinomies joined forces to shape its effective character: on the one hand there was the contradiction between the functions forced upon it by history and the tasks the new power set itself; on the other, there was the contradiction between the functions it did in fact exercise, and the structures of power. Like any revolutionary power, antibourgeois power was so indeterminate upon its establishment that to say it was poorly structured would be almost an exaggeration: rather it seemed almost totally to lack structure. Its metamorphosis into a monolithic power took place with a rapidity that testified to the force of pressures to which it was subjected by functional exigencies, as imperative as they were ill-formulated and difficult to steer. The gravity of events magnified these pressures considerably, but the events themselves were transitory, while the basic functions endured to become more formidable than ever.

The central function, and indeed the very raison d'être of the new power, was to initiate a process of industrialization able to provide a material basis for capitalism to take root and thrive, but also to initiate the first stage of a transition to socialism. This function was not merely one of choice; it followed quite consistently from the antibourgeois character of this power. Industrialization initiated by an antibourgeois power must necessarily be anticapitalist. In order to prevent the development of productive forces through industrial growth from taking its natural course, i.e., toward the establishment of capitalist relations of production, power was compelled to add a secondary function to its central one: the conversion of political privilege into the most powerful lever of the economy. Its economic impact had to be mighty, but it also had to have a clear direction. Theoretically, anticapitalist industry could plausibly be built with a number of different models of economic organization. The economy could be wholly anticapitalist or mixed; if the latter, it could combine a form of social proprietorship with small-scale private farming, or it might add controlled forms of limited capitalism to both of these, and so forth. The other ancillary function of power was to elaborate an economic strategy that was theoretically defensible and in accord with practical conditions.

Of all these functions, the one most immediately pressing was that which required political power to extend itself into the economic domain. This caused the structure of power to contract; thus, the general tendency toward monolithism had roots in objective circumstances that merit more attention than usually accorded them.

At the time of its accession, the new political power and the economic and social structures were mutually autonomous. The political relations introduced by the new antibourgeois power did not mesh with the relations existing in and, in fact, dominating both the economic domain and the society at large. If power was to extend its dominion into the economic and social systems, so as to allay this discordance, its autonomy in their regard was not sufficient; their total subordination was required. The same assymetry of autonomy and subordination describe power's relationship to the working class and to the class structure in general. Unlike a social class, power assumed this function of the agency of change—ordinarily the function of a dominant class—not by becoming part of the class structure, but by removing itself from it. Power situated apart from society and social classes became power above society, and above its classes. These pitfalls aside, the path to the role of determining factor in economic relations was direct.

A product of anticipatory revolution, this inversion in relations of determination had consequences of its own. Rather than being the precondition for social and economic changes comparable in magnitude to the political change it had brought about, antibourgeois power had directly to effect or even impose such changes itself. Anticipation gave birth to a power alien to prevailing economic conditions, whereas it should have been simply the expression of these conditions. Encharged with determining conditions which in the natural course of things should themselves have played the determining role, power assumed more and more the quality of an expedient. Of the two functions, that of expressing the relations of production and that of transforming them, it was the latter that would be decisive in shaping the structure of power.

Once economic and social relations had been brought into line with political relations, this inversion, an aberration, should also have disappeared. But Stalinism accomplished this realignment while preserving and even exacerbating the unfortunate effects of its having been lacking in the first place.

There was no strategy guiding the historical decline of Soviet power into supercentralization. Lenin, who never tired of repeating that the supreme question of the revolution was the question of power, had been supremely uninterested in the institutional form this future power would take. It was not until the eve of

24 October that he asked himself "Who must take power?" and answered "It is of no importance for the moment whether it be seized by the Revolutionary Military Committee or by 'another institution'"; that agency would declare that it would hand over power only to the true representatives of the interests of the people. "'Another institution': These words placed between enigmatic quotation marks," reflected Trotsky, "meant in conspiratorial language the Bolshevik Central Committee."

Indecisive, yet sensitive to the popular forces whose support was essential to them, the Bolsheviks took up this ticklish question for consultation with their representatives at the Second Congress of Soviets, where they formed the majority of delegates. "When the Bolshevik delegates to the Second Congress of Soviets were questioned on their views as to what the future form of government should be," Schapiro observes, "the overwhelming majority of them replied 'All Power to the Soviets' and some of them more specifically that power must be vested in a coalition of all 'democratic parties.'" Thus the task of initiating the first anticapitalist industrialization fell spontaneously to a political organization which to accomplish that task was forced to assume the prerogatives of a dominant class, although it was unprepared either to acquire or to use those prerogatives effectively. The party had a monopoly of power in its hands with which to dominate society, yet its hands were also tied by the burden of having to fulfill this function while lacking the means to do so. Trapped in this contradiction, the initial bearer of power, the Bolshevik party, shrank into insignificance and a new figure moved in to wield power in its stead: the providential leader and his apparatus.

The transformation of the internal structures of power took place within the context of its external relations with the society at large. First and foremost, this transformation had been designed to permit power to fulfill the function of dominant class, i.e., to lead society onward, molding anticapitalist relations of production as it developed an anticapitalist industry. Adaptation of its structures to this function meant pruning what was unnecessary, making the structures of power more compact. The power of the soviets was soon reduced to the power of an ineffectual alliance of political parties, then to a coalition between the Bolsheviks and the Left SRs, followed by a vertiginous stride into monolithism; the one party boasting of open debate and free discussion was transformed into a solid rock of silent unanimity. And ultimately, the monolithic party was for all practical purposes reduced to its providential leader; further than that the process could not go.

The process of contraction set in quickly, in the midst of great confusion. Initially the Congress of Soviets acted in a dual capacity: as a source of power, and as a local executive authority. The first of these capacities was destined to remain altogether provisional, the formal role of source of power being reserved to the Constituent Assembly, which would be convoked and dissolved in the same stroke a few weeks after the insurrection. The Bolsheviks' attempt to form a socialist coalition government under their leadership failed; the only takers had been the Left SRs. The chaotic structure of the new power accurately reflected the diffuse nature of the original conflict, but that structure was ill-suited for the well-defined functions it was called upon to play in the postrevolutionary period. Under the imperative of fulfilling these functions, the structure of power became less and less differentiated, and this tendency was further intensified by untimely contingencies, the disaster of three wars—the world war, the civil war, and the war of intervention—the famine, the defection of the SRs, the failure of war communism, and the defeat of the revolution in Europe.

The dual power of the bourgeoisie was one of the causes of its downfall; it was superseded by the monolithism of antibourgeois power, which enabled that power to survive, if in degenerate form. Bourgeois power had succumbed by permitting too many hands on the reins of power; antibourgeois power would survive—and degenerate—by contracting until it was ultimately embodied in a single person. A functional and structural inertia was at the core of this degeneration. The function of dominant class had been transferred from an immature proletariat incapable of fulfilling that function to a power which then fashioned for itself the structures appropriate to the task. Over the course of time the conditions responsible for the immaturity of the proletariat were gradually eliminated in their broad features; there was no longer the need for power to fulfill its substitutive function, and its structures, custom-fitted to their purpose, became more and more irrelevant and ill-matched to meet new needs. Yet they persisted and even became more entrenched. Initially a necessary function had produced structures consonant with its purpose; now existing structures reproduced a function no longer needed by sustaining the myth of its necessity. Stalinism is not the domination of society by a new class; it is the direct and illegitimate exercise by power of the dominant role of the working class. The power born of October was not the power of a class, but at least it had been historically legitimate and revolutionary; the power perpetuated by Stalinist society is also not the power of a class, but it is historically illegitimate and regressive.

Revolutionary power did not degenerate beyond a certain point: it retained its antibourgeois character, conferred upon it by October, although henceforth in a socially barren form.

Anticipation

The anticipatory quality of the Russian revolution first became manifest in October. The revolution abolished feudalism and the autocracy with great historical delay; despite its early appearance, the anti-imperialist character of the revolution corresponded to a reality that had reached full maturity; the antibourgeois character alone was achieved before all its necessary premises had been established. A discussion of the antibourgeois insurrection that took no note of its anticipatory nature would therefore be radically lacking in completeness.

It had become practically a revolutionary commonplace that the longer the bourgeoisie delayed in carrying out its own revolution, the more likelihood there would be for that revolution to be transformed into a proletarian revolution. Indeed this notion antedates not only Lenin but also world imperialism, and even Marx and Engels had observed in the Communist Manifesto that the 1848 uprising in Germany would be "but the prelude to an immediately following proletarian revolution." Ernest Mandel points out that "This prognosis can be said to have been demonstrated to be incorrect empirically, but it was correctly formulated"; taking the Russian revolution as an example, he explains that Marx and Engels' formulation "rejected the mechanistic interpretation later prevalent among the Mensheviks and held by a 'classical' Marxist like Plekhanov, according to which a backward country like Russia also had to pass through all the stages of the bourgeois capitalist process." The dispute seems to imply a strategic free choice. The possibility of anticipation is posited, yet remains vague and undefined (stages would be jumped over, but how many? which ones? at what pace?) and totally unconnected with real processes. The possibility of anticipatory revolution had not been invented merely as a strategical expedient; rather, the possibility derived from an awareness of changes that had come about in social and historical reality. Unequal development had become an irreparable fact of world history, as imperialism spread and eventually embraced the globe. A major opportunity would be afforded to backward countries to escape the effects of the imperialist law of unequal development if the general economic law dictating a correspondence between the relations of production and forces of production could be suspended. Anticipatory revolution meant abolishing capitalist relations of production just at the time when the productive forces should have served as a springboard for their development.

From a more general standpoint, the substance of imperialism consists of asynchronous development. To imperialistic asynchronism, whose principal meaning is unequal development, anticipatory revolution counterposes a contrary asynchronism. Countries possessing none of the preconditions for development simply dispensed with them in their initial stages and embarked upon development nonetheless. The inversion was universal. While imperialist asynchronism held back the level of productive forces, anticipatory asynchronism drove the organization of the economy relentlessly forward at an ever faster pace. Rather than organizing the economy to fit the state of the productive forces, anticipation undertook to mould the productive forces into a fit with the new economic order. The end result had been hammered into being before the preconditions for it had been born.

The law of correspondence assumes a natural order in which the productive forces give rise to a class stratification specific to their state, and the functional articulation between classes is based on relations of production crystallized in a stable and defined economic system, with political and legal structures ensuring that this economic system with the social stratification peculiar to it is reproduced. Eroded at the base by imperialism, this presumed natural order was utterly subverted by anticipatory revolution. First, anticipation transformed the political and legal structures which were to have provided the basis for subsequent social and economic changes, promoting the transformation of productive forces. At every point, anticipation inverted the relations of determination, with determinant becoming determined, and vice versa. Revolution merely gambled on the consequences of these changes before they occurred. Anticipatory revolution throws the law of correspondence into disarray; it is a countervailing force to the law of unequal development.

Practically, anticipation brought about the transformation of a belated revolution, predominantly antifeudal, before it reached completion into a predominantly antibourgeois revolution before capitalist relations of production had matured. Anticipatory revolution transformed successively the basic structures of society in an order contrary to the order of their relations of determination. Through this inversion, each structural transformation became an anticipatory act of its own. Anticipation reversed social time.

Every revolution entails an immense contraction of historical time, and anticipatory revolution incomparably more so. Determined and determinant became confounded, even exchanging roles. In the Russian revolution the flow of history was accelerated to such a degree that it turned back upon itself. The drama inherent to any revolution was enhanced by the unwonted drama produced by this inversion.

Anticipation is a category of subjectivity. But specific historical conditions must create the objective possibility of anticipation before it can be taken up by the subject. The past lingers on while history is propelled into the future, and between the two the present pales and recedes from view. The natural order of things is suspended. The energy amassed by the leap over stages vibrates in the immense tensions produced by the long period of stagnation. The law of inertia leaves physics and enters social life. To emerge from its inertia, history must be driven forward in earnest, quickening its pace impetuously, and anticipatory revolution is one of the most radical forms for this. Overcoming stagnation became an objective necessity, in turn creating the objective possibility of anticipatory revolution, and whether that possibility is realized depends to a crucial degree on the subjective factor. Anticipatory possibility is studded with antinomies, objective and subjective, demonstrating to what extent the antinomic necessity of the world imperialist system has had a hand in its creation.

In the presumed natural order of things (a mere convention, however indispensable for analysis) social classes are the vehicle of objective necessity. But the link they forge between objectivity and subjectivity is seriously strained by anticipatory revolution. In a sense history had set the stage: the bourgeoisie was in a state of objective degeneration even before it had reached maturity, creating the potential for anticipation: the subjective role of the proletariat had been defined even before the class had emerged from underdevelopment. Of these two cornerstones of anticipation, the former was provided by history in its workings, and the second was fashioned by the hand of men. The uneven development of societies in the grip of imperialism was reflected in the time allotted by anticipatory revolution to the natural processes of history. The early maturation of the proletariat took place more slowly than the early decomposition of the bourgeoisie. The lag left society without a social class capable of serving as an effective vehicle for the most urgent objective necessity of all, namely of assuming the role of dominant class. Necessity and possibility rely on different social mechanisms. Necessity is realized by the spontaneous action of a determinate social class, but anticipatory possibility is realized through the deliberate action of a social force capable of elaborating an adequate strategy and of carrying it out. This role was beyond the proletariat: its lack of aptitude for theory generally, which Lenin never tired of stressing, was compounded many times over by its underdevelopment. Thus anticipatory revolution magnified the role of the subjective factor even as it rendered the natural bearer of that role less and less capable of fulfilling it.

Not finding its due subject in the working class, anticipatory possibility turned to the party. The party's lack of preparation for the role increased the chance of a new transference, and from a social force, anticipatory possibility became embodied in the person of a social actor. As the objective function of the subjective factor grew in importance, the number of social structures suited to the exercise of that function diminished. The narrow path from class to party and from party to omniscient leader was merely the outward reflection of the categorical shift from the necessary to the possible, and from the possible to the providential.

Thus anticipation added a new and dominant character to the revolution, despite the fact that several of its natural premises were inadequate or even lacking. In broadening the ambit of characters assumed by the revolution, anticipation crossed paths with contradictory necessity. Whereas the contradictory nature of the revolution derived from its several characters being present at the same time without regard to their hierarchy, its anticipatory nature played upon its various characters successively as they moved into ascendancy. The category of anticipation regards the revolution as a diachronic phenomenon, extended over time, and defined by the direction and pace of its unfolding.

Anticipation reached its apogee, and, as it turned out, its limit, in the October insurrection. The most elusive aspect of anticipation is its degree. It can be of profound historical consequence whether anticipation exceeds the limit of the possible, or whether it is not carried far enough. The problem has indeed received little attention in the specialized literature, and most often it is ignored entirely. In a text which in other respects was quite fundamental, Lenin gives the problem only passing comment: "What if to create socialism it were necessary to have achieved a specific cultural level (even though no one might be able to say what a specific cultural level is since it differs in each of the Western countries, even the least influential), and what if on the contrary we propose to acquire through revolution the preconditions for the specific level so as then, made strong by a workers' and peasants' power and a Soviet regime, to get moving and catch up with the other nations?" In stressing how vaguely defined this requisite level is Lenin seems to be suggesting the existence of a natural order of things susceptible of amendment which the Bolsheviks were resolved to modify or even to overturn.

There are in fact no criteria for defining the limits of the rational either as regards the purported natural order of things or its rectification, anticipatorily undertaken. "The factor of time is decisive here, and it is difficult in retrospect to tell time historically," wrote Trotsky a propos of the revolution. And elsewhere: "The laws of history have nothing in common with pedantic schematism." "The possibility of skipping steps is by no means absolute. Its degree is determined in the long run by the economic and cultural capacities of the country." Marcuse takes a purely descriptive approach: "The Soviet system," he remarks, "appears to be another example of a latecomer skipping several stages of development. The skipped stages are pure absolutism and liberalism, free enterprise, and freedom of competition—an old culture of the middle classes, with their individualistic and humanitarian ideology." Was this leap too modest, was it excessive, or was it of just the right magnitude? Marcuse does not commit himself.

But anticipation was surely exaggerated in Lenin's strategic conception of it: he defined anticipatory revolution as socialist, claiming for it powers to transform that were palpably greater than those it actually had. However, anticipation was also efficacious, in that by accelerating history it carried the antibourgeois character of the revolution to its completion before the bourgeoisie had played out the whole of its historical potential. Finally, anticipation was truncated in that the changes it wrought were restricted to but one region of the globe.

The society born of anticipation faced a quite unwonted problem: once the anticipatory revolutionary act had been carried through to its completion, how was a social structure to be created on this historical virgin land?

First, anticipation met a natural barrier in the practical task of moving from the destruction of one society to the building of the new. Social structures were haphazardly transformed: transformations were swiftest and most radical in those structures to which anticipation had easiest access, rather than in an order that would have ensued had history pursued its natural course.

Over the long term, and for the world at large, the disconnectedness in the changes wrought by anticipation gives rise to structural disjunctions. Antibourgeois political structures, anomalous relations of production, and underdeveloped productive forces coexist in apparent synchronicity, whereas in reality each of them belongs to a different era. The more severe these disjunctions, the more narrowly they verge on incompatibility and the greater is the danger of their dissolving into formlessness. The problem therefore of restoring cohesion was of utmost urgency for postrevolutionary society—indeed, as urgent as it was insoluble.

Efforts in this direction in the postrevolutionary period would be turned by Stalinism into their contrary. For Stalinism, the disjunctions and structural inchoateness of postrevolutionary society became a fact of existence, and the problem therefore became not how to overcome this condition, but how to render it functional. Hypertrophy of the structure of power, the most accessible to anticipation, secured it absolute dominion over every other structure of society. It then proceeded to establish an effective form of proprietorship and of relations of production without precedent, and on this basis the country embarked upon the first anticapitalist industrialization in history. Structural disarticulation became the functional condition of the social order, and defense against retroaction provided an objective basis for the continued autonomy of power. But it also prevented the veritable revolution that had taken place in productive forces from effecting any significant change in the fundamental structures of power and proprietorship. By throwing the correspondence between the forces and relations of production into disarray, the October insurrection benefited Stalinism, which was later able to throw the determining spheres of social life into a state of upheaval, while holding the others in the most rigid immobility.

By rendering the disarticulation of social structures permanent, Stalinism remained a syncretic society. As such, it was able to make great strides, although in the end they were limited and transitory, and to control the crisis that it was compelled constantly to reproduce. Considering its historical circumstances, this syncretic society has demonstrated a capacity for persistence and reproduction that was hardly to be foreseen.

As a final point, the objective foundations of anticipatory revolution were laid by the historical backwardness into which imperialism had driven most of the countries of the world. This type of revolution was therefore in no sense a universal model, but was rather specific to the imperialist era and moreover, a genuine possibility only for those countries at the periphery of the system. In countries at the center, a revolution aspiring to reproduce this model would be utterly illegitimate and doomed to either defeat or to tragic degeneration.

Incomplete realization

The incomplete nature of the Russian revolution spared none of its characters, but was particularly telling in its anticapitalism. This incompleteness was of course most evident in the discrepancy between the historical functions ascribed to the revolution by Leninist strategy and those that it had actually accomplished; but it also went much further: none of the fundamental characters of the revolution were in fact completely achieved. Feudalism had been abolished; but no coherent stable postfeudal economy, serving as a springboard to a higher level of productivity, proved to be in the making. For a long period, its anticapitalist character was unable to move beyond its intermediate antibourgeois stage, and it freed itself from imperialist domination only to engender a new and likewise oppressive imperialism later on.

We are thus brought back to the original conflict. Because it was so diffuse and weakly structured, none of the revolution's basic characters was able to generate the energy necessary to remold society's structures to its own ends.

The antifeudal character transformed economic and social structures but not the political structures; the antibourgeois character did the opposite; and the anti-imperialist character roused society to rebellion against the international monopolies, only to subjugate it to the Stalinist monolith. All in all, such partial transformations demonstrate that the anticipatory revolution was infinitely more qualified to fulfill the negative functions history had bestowed on it than its positive ones. The incomplete nature of the Russian revolution was the consequence of anticipation, and therefore bore the marks of negativity, and its capacity to negate was far greater than its capacity for providing viable positive alternatives.

The October insurrection abolished the class rule of the bourgeoisie with the aim of establishing the class rule of the proletariat as a prelude to the abolishment of class society in general. But the anticipatory revolutionary process fell short of achieving its end: the class rule of the bourgeoisie was effectively abolished, but the proletariat as a class did not move in to rule in its stead; nor could all class rule be abolished before the necessity for it had been eliminated. Class rule had been made an impossibility before it had become dispensable. The antinomy between the necessity of class rule and its impossibility created a hiatus in the presumed natural order of things, and class rule became rule by a party or leader.

A revolution may be incomplete but what kind of society will it bring into being? Here is how Bettelheim describes it: ''The existence of a defeated capitalism was clearly also the existence of a defeated bourgeoisie and a proletariat: these two classes continued to face off although their social conditions of existence had been altered profoundly. The first and fundamental alteration of the conditions of existence of these classes was tied to the fact that the bourgeoisie had lost power. In concrete terms, this meant that the bourgeoisie no longer dominated the old political and administrative apparatuses. . . . It also means that the capitalists lost the capacity to 'dispose at will' over the means of production.'' Indeed, although a few enterprises were legally expropriated, many came under the direct attack of the workers' organizations, whose offensive ranged from mere intervention in their management to the illegal confiscation of premises, and sometimes also of the proprietors themselves.

The October insurrection may be defined as an anticapitalist struggle that ended in victory over the bourgeoisie. Although of patently historical dimensions, the victory was limited on two counts, each replete with implications. First, the political transformation was not extended into the economic and social domains; secondly, political change was itself diverted from its end: institutional power took the place of class power. The proletariat had been prevented by its internal antinomies from leading the revolution, and now the same antinomies took from it any chance of becoming the ruling class of society. Trotsky provides the following insight into these internal antinomies in a commentary on the origins of the Russian proletariat: ''From the absence of conservative traditions, the absence of castes within the proletariat itself, and the freshness of its revolutionary spirit, from these things, along with other forces, came October and the first workers' government in the world. But from thence also came illiteracy, a backward mentality, shoddy organizational habits, the inability to work systematically, and the lack of cultural and technological education.'' These flaws prevented the proletariat from seizing power, and also prevented society from establishing an anticapitalist order. Every advance toward the socialization of productive forces is contingent on their development, and the proletariat is the living productive force in an industrial economy. Therefore it was not primarily the level of consciousness or state of organization of the proletariat, but its backwardness as a productive force which made socialism and even anticapitalism an unattainable goal and prevented postrevolutionary society from maintaining momentum enough to carry it beyond its antibourgeois project.

After October, the main obstacle to crossing the threshold between the antibourgeois character and the anticapitalist character of the revolution was posed not by the bourgeoisie, but by the classes to which it owed its defeat: the proletariat and the peasantry. Incomplete capitalism was the outgrowth of the momentary incapacity of the proletariat to replace the bourgeoisie in the economic management of society, and of the peasantry's spontaneous leaning toward capitalism in the postfeudal period.

With an anticipation of such proportions, the revolution could install a political power capable of hindering if not preventing the bourgeoisie from reaping the benefits of its proprietary holdings. Supported by the élan of the workers this power would be able to expropriate the means of production from capitalists, but not itself assume proprietorship over them and put them to productive use. In other terms, aided by the proletariat, power was able to confiscate but not to socialize capitalist property. As Lenin conceded in *Left-wing Communism, an Infantile Disorder*, ''Socialism differs from a simple confiscation in that one may confiscate merely by 'resolving' to do so, without being competent to take stock and redistribute rationally what had been confiscated, whereas without this competence socialization is impossible.'' On the eve of October, not only the class, but also the power supposed to represent it lacked this competence. But all in all the subjective shortcomings were no more than a reflection of an objective phenomenon in the last instance decisive: socialization was prevented by the backwardness of the productive forces, both living labor power and the means of production.

Anticipation encountered a new limit: it had invested the proletariat with a function it was not yet prepared to exercise, i.e., proprietorship, but over a property still organized in terms of the old capitalist society. This limit also served to draw the line between the anticapitalist character and antibourgeois character of the revolution, and indeed was important enough to stamp the revolution as incomplete. Anticipatory revolution was incomplete because in the society born of it capitalist property had been outlawed, but social property remained beyond reach. The state of economic limbo that ensued threatened to undo society at its seams, and objectively paved the way for the advent of Stalinism. Stalinism was the social consequence of the antinomy between the political capacity to expropriate capitalist property and the economic incapacity to appropriate it. Anticipation created this antinomy.

Failing in the first step, i.e., the step from antibourgeois power to a productive anticapitalist economy, the new society could not then go on to undertake the second, i.e., the advance toward socialism. Stalinism took this first step, but it did so in a manner that was to bar the way totally to the second. It drove society headlong into technological development, at the price of a total and lasting paralysis. Its solutions to the most pressing problems caused by uncompleted anticipation were partial, transitory, short-term and incoherent, but through a reduction of social life to a state of immobility, they would be made to appear total, definitive, lasting and infallible. Stalinism was the social assimilation and perpetual enshrinement of the incomplete nature of the revolution.

The possibility of Stalinism

Stalinism was the product not directly of the antibourgeois insurrection, but of the society that was born in its wake. But whether by way of similarity or of contrast, some of the major features of the insurrection may indeed be found recapitulated in Stalinism, and to that extent the October insurrection may well be regarded as one of the historical events that made Stalinism possible.

The October insurrection and the advent of Stalinism are linked in a contradictory relation of continuity and discontinuity. Continuity was not only partial, it was also differentiated: linear in relation to some traits of the insurrection, compensatory in relation to the others. In its linear form, continuity appeared mainly in the economy and the structure of power, while in its compensatory form it was visible primarily at the level of strategy.

To clarify this point briefly, the insurrection bequeathed to Stalinism the necessity of a strategy without defining what that strategy should be. Compensatory continuity is reflected in the fact that the absence of strategy was reduced to travesty in the institution of providential leader. The providential leader compensated for a strategy that was as necessary as it was unattainable. So the growing, healthy revolutionary instrument was transformed into a monster: Stalinist power.

Strategy. The insurrection established the ascendancy of a minority over a majority, and of a political organization over a social class, signalling the triumph of strategy over spontaneous movement. Ironically, strategy acquired its historical endorsement at the time it was approaching the end of its resources.

Under Stalinism, ascendancy in the first two cases was maintained and developed to the point of excess; but with strategy beyond reach, its legitimating function was transformed to a substitutive one. The legacy of the October insurrection to postrevolutionary society was double-edged: it established the necessity of strategy, yet no strategy was forthcoming from it. Stalinism stepped into the breach to resolve this antinomy. How it did so may be recapitulated in the following points:

(1) Postrevolutionary society had been bedeviled by the fruitless search for strategy; Stalinism first abandoned the search, and then later barred its way entirely;

(2) The functional surrogate embodied in Stalin's person, which Stalinism offered in compensation, was plausible yet ultimately specious. It was plausible in that it defined a necessary objective: industrialization. It was specious in that it defined neither the means to achieve this objective, nor how that objective fit in with the development of society over the long term;

(3) Thus did Stalinism drift into an antinomy which also snarled its project of industrialization: namely, pursuit of a strategic end with improvised means;

(4) Ultimately the end yielded to the dead weight of these means, and strategy degenerated into mythology, while infallible revelation replaced the fruits of discussion;

(5) The social energy necessary to pursue this end derived less and less from solidarity in recognition of a common cause, and more and more from cowed obedience to a personified substitute for strategy under the ineluctable constraint of objective conditions.

The revolution, unfinished, strained toward completion on the back of a makeshift strategy. Over the long term, strategy was reduced to repression, and stagnation moved in to bind the revolution permanently in its stranglehold.

The economy. The interlude of war communism excepted, postrevolutionary society in essence conserved the legacy of the October insurrection: namely, anticapitalist aspirations ensnared in an antibourgeois reality. It proved incapable of effecting a lasting transformation in existing economic structures, or even of merely remolding them into a viable economic basis for industrialization. Put to the harshest of historical tests, postrevolutionary society cast ever greater doubts on its ability to survive through its inability to take economic questions in hand. A wide range of factors were responsible for this ineffectiveness: the absence of an articulate social strategy and the lack of a unified political leadership; the managerial ineptitude of the working class; the desperate swings between the anticapitalist élan of the insurrection, at the one extreme, and the engrained tendency of the peasantry toward a capitalist type of development at the other—all these things together created a nearly impossible task. It was thus that Stalinism intervened to transform this motley economy, sapped of its resources and adrift, into the barest of systems, yet expansive, and dedicated to a clearly defined end. Stalinism established its dominion over economic mechanisms by rendering them less vital. Its method was generalized expropriation, effected by administrative rather than revolutionary violence. Stalinism continued where the October insurrection stopped.

But the elimination of capitalism was a mere negative act; a positive

132 THE ORIGINS OF STALINISM

conception was necessary for building industry on a noncapitalist foundation, and to do just this Stalinism elected to place control over the means of production not in the hands of the workers who aspired to proprietorship (legally recognized) over them, but in the hands of a subaltern bureaucracy whose historical credentials for assuming such a function were infinitely frailer. To complete the picture, small peasant plots were confiscated in the countryside. The regime established its dominion over the economy by abolishing property in all its manifest forms, regardless of their social nature, and by establishing one single form of discrete property, over which it had virtually total control.

Manifest property implies the concordance between the effective use of property and its legal definition, while discrete implies a discordance between the two. Indeed, in Stalinist society, the law proclaimed forms of property that economically were nonexistent, while the economy had been reduced virtually to one single effective form of property that conversely had no existence in law. Reduced to its fundamentals, Stalinism was the direct, illicit appropriation of the whole of the nation's patrimony by the seat of power, and this at the same time was the recipe it used in performing to the extent it did as an industrializing force.

To develop industry, capital had to separate the producers from the means of production. This was primitive capitalist accumulation, and the peasants were the first to be drawn into its vortex. Under Stalinism the means of production were alienated not from a class, but from society as a whole. This is generalized primitive accumulation. As a corollary to this generalized expropriation, a conspiratorial proprietorship was installed over the means of production, the historical antecedents of which are by no means easy to disentangle.

Stalinism connected to the October insurrection in a variety of ways. While it transformed its antibourgeois legacy into a noncapitalist reality, it only prolonged and deepened the division between power and class. Preempted first in the seizure and then in the exercise of power, the proletariat was ultimately also substituted in the exercise of proprietorship. But in this it merely shared the lot of all the other social classes, Stalinism thereby accomplished one of the most thorough transferences of function in history, transforming class structure and the structure of power alike. Once a defining attribute of social classes, property now became one of the essential prerogatives of power. Social classes, their roles already enfeebled, experienced a qualitative change in them in that now property relations underwent a restructuring as well.

Stalinism demonstrated the limits of the use of force as a principal or even exclusive means to shape social structures. With force at their origins, Stalinist structures were able to function, but not to evolve nor to adapt to changed conditions. The sheer inertia and inflexibility of Stalinist structures derives from the paralysis of society's principal economic function: primitive accumulation continues in a never-ending cycle, although the need for it has not existed now for decades. Society has been deprived of effective proprietary control over the means of production, whereas the revolution should have placed that function directly in its hands.

Primitive accumulation, becoming universal, ravaged every element of the economy capable of holding it in check, even enabling it ultimately to be superseded. Deprived of any instrumentalities that would have enabled it to evolve, it was reduced to reproducing itself indefinitely.

Power. Stalinist power transformed the economy of Russia, but it did so by absorbing the economy, rather than by assuming control over it. It thus ceased to be a class power and became a proprietary power. The loss of this utterly fundamental quality of class was in fact only the epilogue to a historical process defined by three principal considerations.

(1) The separation—even as the broader context was marked by a convergence of interests—of the Bolshevik party, the nucleus of future state power, from the working class, made the victory of October possible;

(2) The separation continued following victory, but now the new power and the proletariat began to show divergent interests. At core, the divergence concerned the exercise of proprietary rights: although not yet equipped with the necessary skills of management, the workers set about forthwith appropriating the means of their productive labor, and immediately encountered the resistance of the regime;

(3) Stalinism carried the separation between class and party further, on to a new level, subordinating the class to the seat of power. A mutation had taken place, brought about by the fact that separation had in the meantime begun to fulfill a basic economic function; appropriation of the means of production by the proletariat had not been merely postponed for a future agenda; its very possibility was henceforth ruled out by the fact that an appropriation of another sort had taken place.

This epilogue to the revolution reveals how Stalinism was swept along by a historical tide that carried it beyond its own limits. Stalinism had altered the interstices of power, and at the same time demonstrated the limits of a social order that was merely anticapitalist. The strict separation between producers and the means of production was palpable proof that anticapitalist industrialization of the Stalinist variety was based on the same mechanism as capitalist industrialization: primitive accumulation.

In its conduct toward the working class, Stalinism seems to have been guided by a number of tacit assumptions, namely:

(1) A class that had over an entire decade demonstrated its inability to administer the precarious economy of the postrevolutionary period would certainly not be able to manage an accelerated anticapitalist industrialization;

(2) It could effectively assume this function only by extricating itself from its proletarian condition. But emancipation, inaccessible to the class as a whole by reason of its immaturity, could be granted by the regime to the most active elements of the class by coopting them into the bureaucratic administrative apparatus. Rounding out the picture, to this conditional access to management was added an unconditional barring of all access to proprietorship;

(3) With its most advanced elements declassed, the working class found itself once again debased to the status of mere object of the economic process. The process leading from separation to substitution ends logically with the alienation of the class as a whole;

(4) This being the case, the role formerly played by capital becomes the role of power, seated between the worker and his means of production and incorporating the separation between the two. This redistribution of roles became the foundation of a new social and economic order;

(5) The abolition of capitalist property was but an ephemeral precondition of Stalinist industrialization, whereas the separation between producers and the means of production was the permanent condition of its continued movement;

(6) Initially a product of historical circumstances, the immaturity of the proletariat became a necessary and permanent condition for the continued functioning of the social order.

In 1917 the proletariat was unable to assume direct responsibility for either the seizure or the exercise of power. But regardless of the proletariat's limitations, the power called upon to represent it would become totally and irreversibly autonomous with regard to the class. The temporary limitations of the class produced a regime that in the end would perpetuate them. Stalinism, the very possibility of which was contingent upon the immaturity of the class, was able to perpetuate itself only by ensuring that this contingency would last. In the end, the regime ceased representing the class to represent solely its immaturity. Its legitimacy no longer derives from the desideratum of eliminating the backwardness of the class, but from the reality of its efforts to perpetuate that backwardness. Originally a natural but passing effect of history, the immaturity of the proletariat became the functional precondition of the regime to which it had given birth.

The distribution of roles established between the proletariat and its regime had originally been expected to evolve; instead they became mired in a state of utter fixity. A dynamic society became a society of ritual. The immobility so characteristic of Stalinism had its roots in the forced immobilization of the proletariat. The Stalinist system rests on its ability to prevent the proletariat from translating its force of numbers and its ever-growing technical competence into a better social, economic, and political condition for itself and the commonweal. The objective premises of its immaturity regressed, but their consequences lingered on, becoming ever graver.

The cult of personality. The role of the providential leader is constant in its necessity and variable in its manifestations. Its necessity in this instance was determined by the structure of the prerevolutionary conflict and by that of the postrevolutionary society following it; the variations depended to a high degree on the actors who fulfilled this role. This distinction is based on the fact that, despite the variety of actors performing the role, it invariably remains central in social organizations of the Stalinist type.

In revolutionary periods, history has frequently caused the emergence of a providential leader. The Russian revolution is distinguished from others not by the fact that it created this role, but because it created a society incapable of doing without it. In my view, this particularity is an effect of the anticipatory nature of the revolution. This anticipation, a deliberate asynchronism, also gave rise to some unintended asynchronisms. One of them, for example, was that the anticipation imposed on the subjective factor a historical burden that existing institutions and actors are still incapable of bearing. There is a disarticulation between the necessary function and the existing structures, which concerns the social classes and political organizations. One solution would be to await the natural maturation of these factors, all the while attempting to urge it on. Another solution would be to take recourse to an immediate substitute. Stalinism is an example of this latter solution. The providential leader represented a perverted satisfaction of the necessity for the subjective factor to play a decisive role in the anticipatory revolution and in the society produced by this revolution. Society invested the providential leader with the potency that history held out to him without granting it, and which consequently assumed superhuman dimensions. Imposed by this asynchronism, the personification of the subjective factor took place independently of whether it did or did not find the appropriate actor. Anticipation modified the objective role of the subjective factor, above all thanks to the fact that its realization necessarily presupposed a strategy. The extent to which the actor corresponded to the requirements of the role may be evaluated in terms of two criteria: the validity of the strategy that the actor adopted, and his own capacity to make this strategy socially operative. Up until the October insurrection, Lenin showed himself to be the appropriate actor for this role: it was he who had worked out a valid strategy, and was able to bring the party and society to pursue that strategy without allowing himself to be maimed intellectually or morally by the immense weight of this role.

In Stalinism, the role of the providential leader was imposed by the same general necessity, which however operated under greatly changed conditions. The most significant of these changes were:

(1) After more than a decade, postrevolutionary society had not found the forces necessary to transform its frequent vicissitudes into a true evolution. There was only one subjective initiative that could lift it from the morass. This initiative had to be expressed in a strategy which neither the interested classes, the political forces, nor the existing leaders could determine;

(2) Guided by necessity, Stalinism replaced strategy by action that immediately yielded results. Under such pressure he established anticapitalist industrialization, subordinating producers to the regime. The counterpart of this subordination was the placement of political power above society. History shows that all regimes aspiring to put themselves above society have the tendency to undergo a metamorphosis into personalized power;

(3) His reign suggests that Stalin was better equipped to seize this role than to fill it.

Stalin's victory against his adversaries, who were of a superior theoretical stature, was in large measure due to his indifference to theory and his empiricism. This helped him to understand that the way out of stagnation could not await the discovery of an optimal strategy. Given this priority, an apparent strategy is better than no strategy at all. The strategic vacuum, with its paralyzing effects, was eliminated on the orders of the leader, which while not claiming to be a strategy was indeed the only strategy possible. By destroying the old Bolshevik party and free discussion, Stalin destroyed an organization that was incapable of either assuming the role of the subjective factor or conferring it on someone else. In its place, he built an organization destined merely to second the actor who effectively filled this role.

Justified not by the exigencies of history, but by the superhuman gifts of the actor, the role of the providential leader became incompatible with any competition. That is why the destruction of the party, punitive, adaptive, and preventive at one blow, was rounded out by the destruction of its best leaders. Thus repression seemed to emerge from the antinomy between the necessarily decisive role attributed to the subjective factor and its incapacity to fulfill that role. The extent of the repression would depend largely on the relationship between role and actor. The less capable the actor is of fulfilling this role, the stronger will be the tendency to inflate it, on the one hand, and legitimate it by repression, on the other.

The disjunction between the role and the actor was possible owing to their different origins: whereas the first was imposed by a necessity diverted from its path, the second was due to chance. Before October Lenin had been a product of chance, acting in the name of a controlled necessity. Stalin remained a product of chance, acting in the name of chance, i.e., an uncontrolled necessity. The regression of the leader also signified a change in the relation between possibility and necessity: it was chance, and no longer possibility, that became preponderant in relation to necessity.

In terms of the institution of the providential leader, Stalinism may be defined as the social order that reduced the decisive role of the subjective actor to the decisive role of the leader. The sources of the "cult of personality" lay in the historical origins of this society, and not in Stalin's psychological makeup. What that can help explain is the form assumed by this cult, and indeed the variation to this form can weigh extremely heavily on the life of society. It was not the role of providential leader, but the actor who filled it, that turned this dominating institution into an instrument of repression, mere oppression, and even manipulation.

The anticipatory nature of the October insurrection determined that this role would emerge, and its perversion was made possible by the absence of three things: a social strategy, an organization capable of implementing that strategy, and an authentic leader able to be the animating force for both.

Stalinism is not the creator, but the creation of the absence of this triad.

The compensatory function. Of all the traits of the revolution, the one that contributed the most to the advent of Stalinism was its incompleteness. Stalinism was able to wrest society from the impasse into which it had fallen by dint of the revolution's incomplete nature, but it was unable to restore it to the path of historical evolution. And so one dead center replaced another. The new one was technologically more advanced yet socially more backward, and, above all, much more difficult to dislodge. Stalinism moved in by way of compensation for the unfinished work of the revolution, above all the incomplete fulfillment of its anticapitalist character.

The defeat of proletarian revolutions in Europe and Asia meant that the anti-imperialist thrust of the revolution would necessarily remain incomplete. Post-revolutionary Russia continued to stake its hopes on world revolution, which never came about. Stalinism gave it a way out of this impasse by offering positive compensation: the attempt to build socialism in one country became an overriding principle. Behind the mere phrase lay something more essential, deriving from Stalinism's very nature: namely its trait of taking an unbridgeable barrier, inherited as a dead weight from the past, and transforming it into a positive value. Dreams of world revolution gave way to the sober realization that the aspirations of October would have to be confined to the national dimension. Industrialization gave this realization an economic content and hence a new and unexpected vitality. Socialism in one country would soon become socialism for one country, from which Stalinism became inseparable. The incomplete achievement of the revolution's anti-imperialist character was compensated by a policy which under Stalinism would give rise to a new Soviet-style imperialism, some aspects of which would bear the unmistakeable characteristics of Stalinist techniques. Accommodation to necessity, where no other alternative existed, was marketed as strategic innovation. Effective over the short run, this solution in the end would have consequences as serious as they had been unforeseeable.

The antifeudal character of the revolution also remained incompletely achieved, as evidenced in Stalinism's inability to organize postfeudal agriculture viably, coherently and productively. The expropriation of small peasant plots is the most trenchant example of how Stalinism dealt with the unresolved problems handed down by the revolution. The solution was alien, and even opposed to the real trends taking place in society. The instruments of administrative constraint and sheer force would therefore necessarily become its principal means, while its principal effect would be the installation of a structure hand-molded to the expediencies of power. But Stalinist agriculture did herald a number of advantages: as its internal structures became more coherent and its links with the structures of power acquired stability and definition, it had fair prospects of surviving on the strength of the combined effects of mechanization, inertia, and institutionalized constraint. But these advantages were nullified by a congenital evil: artificially imposed, Stalinist agriculture could never become productive. In the end, therefore, this capacity for survival became transformed from a potentially positive quality into a veritable bane, for like the social order of which it was a part, Stalinist agriculture could endure only on condition of rejecting all change.

Stalinism was antinomic as a historical movement. Its remedies enabled society to move beyond some of the consequences of incomplete revolution, but with regard to others it turned back the clock of history grievously. The fate of agriculture is revealing of the social techniques of Stalinism. The structures of power adapted the structures of the economy by obstructing the spontaneous workings of economic laws, i.e., by sacrificing economic efficiency over the long term to immediate social and political advantages. Thus Stalinism's response to the incomplete achievement of the revolution's antifeudal character was an accommodation that was itself incomplete, as manifested in an agriculture more capable of reproducing its own structures than in producing for the society at large.

Economic policy in agriculture was too flawed for its effects to be limited to the economic sphere. Although aspiring to create the most advanced type of post-feudal agriculture in existence, it was unable to dispense with mechanisms that had themselves been fundamental to feudalism. First, there was the form of agrarian ownership: vague and ill-defined, it was regulated more by convention than by law. Second, there was the growing subordination of economic relations to extra-economic relations backed up by the direct use of force: centralized determination of the uses of the productive forces of every agricultural unit regardless of how proprietorship might be formally defined; compulsory levies instead of exchange relations based on processes of sale and purchase; the practice of imposed prices linked to no economic realities, etc.

The decisive factor in diverting postrevolutionary society down the fateful path of Stalinism was not the incomplete achievement of the antifeudal or anti-imperialist character of the revolution, but the incomplete fulfillment of its anticapitalist character. The incomplete nature of the anticapitalism introduced by Stalinism was most evident in the organization of property. Having abolished capitalist property, society found itself with a form of proprietorship that was neither social nor based on law, for the monopoly that exercised the absolute right of proprietorship had placed itself above society and beyond the law's institutions. Of course, when these changes took place the principal obstacle to the socialization of property was not Stalinism, but the underdevelopment of the productive forces. True to its ways, Stalinism surmounted this objective obstacle by shrinking from it. The result of this antagonistic movement was an anticapitalism based on mechanisms that were essentially capitalist: monopoly proprietorship and the methods of primitive accumulation. Yet, even with these mechanisms, Stalinism is not simply capitalism in a peculiar guise, no more than its recourse to feudal mechanisms makes it merely an industrializing variety of feudalism.

These oscillations had particularly profound effects on the revolution's principal motor force. Under the weight of its own works, Stalinist power degenerated into an autocracy whose rule was as absolute in the political as it was in the economic sphere. This total power, anticapitalist and monopolist, autocratic and antifeudal, would be capable of transforming the productive forces, yet itself remain unchanged. The product of antinomic historical currents, thus did Stalin-

ism shuttle back and forth over the watersheds of historical time. The technological progress achieved by industrialization was based on an anticapitalism of
precapitalist mold that combined monopolism with autocracy and extra-economic, essentially feudal regulation of the social relations of production. The structures established to bolster industrialization outlived the purpose for which they
were created. The artifices that enabled them to come into existence deprived
them of every possibility of evolving. They degenerated by the simple fact of their
persistence. After wrenching society from the predicament in which it had been
marking time since the revolution, Stalinism plunged it into a historical limbo
without perspective.

The compensatory function of Stalinism had to do not only with the characters but also with the more general hallmarks of the revolution, for instance, the
historical cadence that constituted the essence of anticipation. History had undergone several breaks in its rhythm within a very short period. In the first stage of
the revolution the cadence of history had been slowed by imperialist efforts to
drive economic backwardness to the point of utter stagnation. In the next stage,
revolutionary anticipation was accelerated even further by way of compensation.
Next occurred a backlash to this compensation: anticipation fell short of its goal.
A fourth stage found postrevolutionary society in abrupt retreat, incapable either
of transcending the limits laid down by the revolution or of living with them.
Finally, a fifth stage was marked by the emergence of Stalinism, which universally and prematurely abolished private property, and posed the goal of industrialization. Anticipation outdid itself. Industrialization thoroughly transformed
the forces of production, yet this had no impact at all on the structures of power
or of the economy. The last stage of the process after industrialization finally
exposed the regressive immobility of Stalinist society. The price of the anticipatory extravagance of eliminating private property was an inordinate regression that affected the whole of organized society. The effect was twofold: industrialization drew up short of society's ultimate goals, and the regressive
structures that appeared to bolster it along its way assumed the quality of perma-
nence.

These frequent breaks in history's cadence found a perfect compensatory
remedy in Stalinism: the suppression of all historical movement. Its premature
absorption of all forms of private property made Stalinism appear to be the
legitimate continuation of revolutionary anticipation, even as its regressive structures cast it in the role of the revolution's redeemer. The historical trajectory of
the revolution had come full circle: the stagnation imposed by imperialism was
eliminated by the revolution which in the end led to the stagnation that was the
legacy of Stalinism.

Stalinism also served to compensate for society's low level of cohesion.
Reflecting the weakly structured social conflict out of which it had come, the
revolution produced a weakly structured society with severely reduced chances of
survival. Structural disjointedness was pervasive: between the inherently antibourgeois power and the patchwork economy, and, further, between these two

structures and the productive forces, mired in underdevelopment. The changes imposed upon economic structures in an effort to put postrevolutionary society back on its hinges were many and frequent, and just as frequently short-lived. Stalinism moved in with the manifest objective of eliminating this state of affairs by absorbing the structure of the economy into the structure of power, prefatory to effecting a swift and thorough transformation of the productive forces. But the limits of this solution became increasingly apparent as time passed; for society's lack of structure was merely replaced by formlessness of another kind. Translated into material terms, absorption of the economy meant absorbing property, and this power could do only by placing itself beyond the law and above society. Disjointedness, far from being diminished, became even more pervasive. Not only the links between power and the economy, but between it and the society as a whole, lost every mediating term. Henceforth economic activity was regulated directly by the mechanisms of power rather than by those of the economy, and extra-economic constraint became absolutely dominant.

Stalinism was the boldest attempt undertaken by postwar society to eliminate the thorniest consequences of the incompleteness of the revolution. It freed society from the temporary limits it inherited from the revolution, but imposed on it new ones that would remain impassable for a whole period. The rigid structures of Stalinism moved in to replace the shaky structures of postrevolutionary society. In a first phase, their primary function was to abolish every basis for private property, paving the way for accelerated anticapitalist industrialization. Once this end was achieved, their function shifted, and they entered a second phase in which their primary function henceforth was that of ensuring their own perpetuation, thereby securing at the same time monopoly over property through power unseen. The more thoroughly they fulfilled this function, the less susceptible were the new structures of Stalinism to change. Thus the first phase was concentrated principally on breaking through the limits inherited from the revolution, and here Stalinism accomplished mainly positive works. In the second phase, which is still upon us, the main function has been to immobilize society within its new limits; here, in its new edition, Stalinism has become regressive. The offence of Stalinism, if one were to venture such a judgment, lay less in having existed than in having endured beyond the period of its positive accomplishments.

This same ambiguity marked the way Stalinism fulfilled its compensatory function in history, appearing as a belated product, both possible and avoidable, of the revolution, which solved some grave problems the revolution had left hanging, yet gave rise to others graver still.

IV. THE ANTI-IMPERIALIST CHARACTER OF THE REVOLUTION

Hypotheses

(a) The incomplete realization of the anti-imperialist character of the Russian revolution was a decisive historical factor in the shaping of contemporary neo-Stalinist imperialism;

(b) The revolution was anti-imperialist from the start, because it had been a direct consequence of Russia's integration into the imperialist system; in its end result, in which it showed itself to be the most insistent and least complete of the revolution's several characters, anti-imperialism was a most faithful expression of the antinomic necessity that had presided over the revolution from the outset. It therefore influenced the other characters of the revolution more than it was influenced by them;

(c) The anti-imperialist thrust of the revolution was conditioned by prerevolutionary Russia's singular situation within world imperialism, being at the same time both its victim and its beneficiary;

(d) The dual role of Russia in the world imperialist system had three principal aspects in 1917:

(1) Economically and politically the country was in the thrall of Western imperialist powers;

(2) Russian imperialism in turn was the oppressor of other nations;

(3) Russia itself participated in the imperialist war.

(e) The popular movement tended to reduce the struggle against imperialism into a struggle against the war, especially during the first months of the revolution. As a consequence, the principal bearer of the revolution's anti-imperialist character was of course also the war's principal instrument—i.e., the army; because of this, the anti-imperialist thrust of the revolution derived its momentum less directly from the society's stratification into opposing classes;

(f) In October, the Bolshevik party promulgated the Peace Decree, which marked not the international victory over imperialism, but the national defeat of revolutionary Russia;

(g) In a similar spirit, the revolutionary government granted the oppressed nations of the Russian Empire the right of self-determination, even to the point of separation. This was a historical event without precedent, but in a world dominated by imperialism the exercise of this right had paradoxical effects: the liberated countries rose up against their liberators;

(h) Leninist strategy was premised on the consideration that the circumstances of World War I had aggravated the consequences of unequal development to a point where a world revolution that was both anti-imperialist and socialist had become more possible than ever, and had similarly increased the likelihood that this revolution would begin in a backward country in the specific form of an anticipatory revolution, evolving its anti-imperialism into anticapitalism, but able ultimately to assume a socialist character only if proletarian revolutions were also victorious in the advanced countries. History would vindicate Lenin's prediction by negating its converse: it would demonstrate not that the victory of socialism was possible on a world scale, but that socialism on a national scale, in a single underdeveloped country, was impossible. Stalinism would be the historical instrumentality of this demonstration;

(i) The failure of world revolution put the Russian revolution in a situation that was antinomic on two counts: circumstances had reduced it to the national dimension by denying it the international validation it needed; secondly, it was compelled to adopt a pattern of behavior that was both accommodating to and destructive of world imperialist domination at the same time. In practice, the state treaties concluded in the '20s served the ends of accommodation, while the creation of the Comintern was done with subversive intent;

(j) Although not vanishing completely, this antinomy was attenuated considerably by a growing tendency for subversive designs to be subordinated to the needs of accommodation, an implicit acknowledgment of the reality that the international significance of the revolution had been eclipsed by its national dimension. Put at the service of a world revolution run aground in its initial national phase, the Comintern would do more to accommodate the Soviet Union, bastion of the revolution, to the imperialist system, than to undermine that system;

(k) Following the German offensive of 1918, which all but crushed Soviet Russia in its infancy, down to Hitler's aggression in 1941, history would cruelly and brutally demonstrate many times over to this country that it could not survive in a world ruled by imperialism if it flouted its rules, and these rules became altogether the prime regulator of Soviet behavior on the international arena;

(l) The society that came out of the Russian revolution was syncretic in two respects, themselves deriving from an incompatibility on two levels: namely between the precapitalist productive forces and the postcapitalist character of the new class structure, and between this society and its international environment, in which it could be forced to exist, all the while resisting adapting to it;

(m) Its gradual adaptation to imperialism, which it had aspired to destroy, was fostered by both external and internal factors. But the pivotal factor was

Stalinist industrialization, largely inspired by the capitalist model of primitive accumulation. Expropriation of the feudal lords and capitalists was rounded off by the expropriation of small peasant plots and the reestablishment of the separation between workers and the means of production. Stalinism is generalized expropriation: it converted the property vacuum created by the revolution into a vacuum of proprietors. The only social force able to assume proprietorship was the seat of power. A virtual monopoly arose, extending over power and property alike; this monopoly was the key internal factor upon which the USSR's adaptation to the external imperialist environment was premised. The real level at which this dual monopoly was exercised became a center of decision–making with unbounded powers. Real society became peripheral to this center, which totally eluded its control. Stalinism is the internalization of the separation between center and periphery established by imperialism on a world scale. Internal and external conditions join forces to transform the Stalinist social order into a new type of imperialism.

(n) Thus Stalinism represents the limits within which the Russian revolution had accomplished its anti-imperialist function, pushed to a grievous extreme. The revolution was unable to impose an imperialist peace, offer the people subjugated by the Russian Empire their genuine national liberty, or, above all, to carry the European proletariat along with it and thus truly become the historical prologue of the world revolution. And so revolutionary Russia freed itself from subjugation to the imperialist world, but did not abolish it;

(o) This is the primary meaning of the incomplete achievement of the anti-imperialist character of the Russian revolution. In general terms, the limit was reached when the international aspirations of the revolution foundered on the insurmountable barriers of national reality;

(p) Postrevolutionary society attempted to go beyond the national impediment upon which Stalinism was later to found its historic works. The function of Stalinism was to integrate the Soviet Union into the world system, not to create a countervailing force. With the world revolution delayed, postrevolutionary society was unable to free itself from a world dominated by imperialism without becoming isolated, and Stalinism could not escape its isolation without internalizing the rules of this world. Liberation, isolation, and reintegration were the way stations on a historical path that led from the anti-imperialist revolution to neo-Stalinist imperialism. The one circumstance above all others that turned the course of history along this path (thus serving as cause and not effect) was the inability of the Russian revolution to acquire an international dimension.

Definition

The anti-imperialist character of the Russian revolution invested it with the historical function of freeing Russia from imperialist domination, and from the backwardness that was a consequence of that domination. Because of the particular conditions at its start, the revolution displayed its anti-imperialist character first and foremost in antibourgeois trappings, but was able to move on to acquire a full-fledged antibourgeois thrust only by altering the face of its anti-imperialism.

This change is of utmost importance in the light of its later degeneration. Basically what it meant was that if postrevolutionary society was to steer its root anticapitalism toward socialism, freeing itself from imperialism would not be enough; imperialism would have also to be abolished. No merely national revolution would be able to assume a historical function of this scope. Abandoned to its own means, the Russian revolution was condemned at the outset to an incomplete achievement of the possibilities inherent in its anti-imperialism.

The abolition of imperialism, or in any event the undermining of its position of supremacy, had to be the work of an international anti-imperialist and anticapitalist revolution, of which the Russian revolution, according to Lenin's formulation, would be only the prologue. Its continuation on an international scale would have enabled the Russian revolution not only to survive, but also to assume a socialist character, and according to Lenin's analysis, this was the only possibility open to it for survival.

Thus to achieve the strategic objective of socialism, the revolution had to establish a continuity in two respects: internally, through the ultrarapid development of the productive forces and relations of production, and externally, through its even more rapid spread into the developed countries. It was this desired coherence through continuity, the gist of Trotsky's theory of permanent revolution, and this real and undesired coherence in discontinuity, that separated the Russian revolution from the world revolution and the development of the forces of production from the development of the relations of production, which is the substance of Stalin's empiricism.

The revolution proposed to establish Russia's relations with its international environment on a new basis, conformity to the objective conditions. Subjectively, i.e., in accordance with Leninist strategy, this meant restructuring that environment: it was not the Russian revolution that was supposed to adapt to the world outside, but the latter that was to be remolded by the Russian revolution, that is, in accordance with the model it proffered. Here the line between the revolution as a prologue to a new world order and the revolution as a model is altogether effaced. The prologue was followed not by different acts in the world historical drama, but by its own reiteration an undetermined number of times. The merger of anti-imperialist revolution with anticapitalist revolution was transformed from a mere possibility with positive potential into an invariable condition. Future revolutions were henceforth supposed to pursue strategic objectives that clashed with the historical and social premises that had brought them into being.

Obviously, the Russian revolution would be unable to shape its relations with the international environment with its own means; world revolution assumed more and more unambiguously the quality of its complement, brooking no alternative. The relationship was reversed: it was no longer the Russian revolution that was at the service of world revolution, but world revolution that was supposed to help the Russian revolution survive and carry the ultimate victory, i.e., the establishment of socialism.

Anti-imperialism was the one character of the Russian revolution whose full achievement did not depend primarily on the revolution itself. But its assumption of a socialist character was contingent on the achievement of its anti-imperialist character. Conversely, the incomplete achievement of the latter would necessarily entail the nonachievement of its socialist character. The two dimensions of the revolution implicit in the antinomic necessity that presided over its birth became manifest in its anti-imperialist character. They formed an antinomy that eluded virtually all attempts to bring it under control: a harsh testimony to the glaring disparity between its relative potency within the country's borders and its impotence in the world beyond. This relative effectiveness on the soil of old Russia would lay the objective foundations for Stalinist nationalism and that in turn would become the supreme form of the internationalism practiced by the international communist movement throughout an entire historical epoch.

Russia's dual articulation with
the imperialist system

Unlike the Western powers, England or France, for example, or the major colonial countries such as India or China, autocratic Russia was in the singular position of being at once both object and subject of world imperialism. Dependent on the Western powers politically and economically, Tsarist Russia was also the oppressor of a number of peoples, and never wearied of embarking upon new conquests. This dual and contradictory articulation with the imperialist system gave the Russian revolution a historical originality which, far from justifying the aspiration to become universal, on the contrary made its reproduction difficult if not impossible. Enthralled by fancies of new territorial conquests, the Russian bourgeoisie remained obdurate in its pro-imperialist positions, not perceiving that by so doing it compelled the revolution to turn against it and become antibourgeois as well as anti-imperialist.

Object. For analytical purposes it is perhaps useful to attempt to separate Russia's dual position of subject and object in the imperialist system; but the effective unity of these two roles appeared most clearly in her participation in the war, which was as much the consequence of Western pressures as of the enticing prospect of picking off the Dardenelles, which she had coveted since the time of Peter the Great.

Russia entered the war in a state of heavy dependence. France and England controlled 40% of the total capital invested in Russia, and even more in the most modern industrial sectors. Through a network of subsidiary banks, foreign capital enjoyed almost total control of heavy industry. A mix of industrial capital and finance capital put together abroad was foisted upon Russia's precapitalist structures.

Over half of the industrial equipment was imported. France's trade treaty, conceded to Russia in 1905 to shore up the autocracy, contained some revealing clauses. The value of Russia's exports was one third that of its imports, and the trade structures and tariff conditions augmented this inequality even further. Dependent and isolated Russia's industrial output remained prisoner to its inertia, perpetuating the country's state of underdevelopment. The aggregate length of railroad track suffices as a good indicator of the extent of Russia's technological progress at the time. Another industrially backward country, Germany, had 11.7 kilometers per 100 square kilometers; Russia had only 400 meters. In 1913 the per capita GNP was $1400 in the United States, $1250 in Great Britain, $975 in Germany, but only $200–375 in Russia.

Political dependence assumed forms no less total. France and England, with American complicity, had actively supported the autocracy against the revolution, but shifted their support to the various provisional governments after the tsar's fall in February 1917. Such protection had two conditions attached: continue the war and combat the revolution. But the provisional governments were as persevering as they were ineffective in pursuing these two ends, so there is no wonder over the interest shown by the Western powers that summer in Kornilov. On the eve of the putsch, the Commissar of the Provisional Government abroad, Svatikov, reported from Paris that during an audience granted him on August 23 by President Poincaré, he had been questioned broadly about the general situation. At about the same time, General Marks, Head of the British Mission at Petrograd, declared to his American colleague: "I am not interested in the Kerensky government—it is too weak; a military dictatorship is needed." When the putsch failed, Western sympathies turned again to Kerensky. At a state conference, organized in the hope of regaining his lost prestige, Kerensky read the telegram in which President Wilson "promised all moral and material support to the Russian government for the success of the common cause of the two peoples."

The purpose in citing these few examples is not to show how Western sympathies vacillated, but to demonstrate the unremitting efforts exerted by the respective powers to extend their grip from autocratic Russia, which had now passed into history, to the Russian revolution now in full flower. Russia could not be simultaneously the theater of a great revolution and a demesne of world imperialism. The October insurrection had confronted this question squarely, but had skirted its consequences: the first of these was that the Western powers adopted a strategy toward Soviet Russia that had one principal aim: to subjugate it anew. The second consequence, which followed from the first, was that Soviet Russia would oppose the collective onslaught of the imperialist powers by choosing a path that allowed ever less room to the methods and policies that had made prerevolutionary Russia into an imperialist power in its own right. The anti-imperialist thrust of the revolution was as rich in consequences for Russia's role as object of imperialism as for the role of subject once performed by Tsarist Russia.

Subject. Like the Turkish or British Empire, the formation of the Russian Empire anticipated the imperialist era. But Russia, unlike Turkey, had subjugated nations generally more backward than itself, and unlike England, it had not sought new territories across the seas. Its territory was compact, giving it strength and security, but the subordination of the periphery to the center within this compact empire also enhanced its vulnerability.

The instrument crucial to the growth of the Russian empire was also the autocracy's principal historical achievement: a centralized military force. The autocratic structures that had moulded this force hindered its conquests from becoming a factor of economic and social progress. The rise of imperialism was accompanied by a revolution in the technology of war. Because of Russia's inability to keep abreast of these developments, the contradiction between military expansionism and a stagnant economy in the end degenerated into a general crisis of the autocracy. The social structures that had made expansionism possible came to serve as shackles upon it. It had become clear with time that Russia was pursuing its role as an imperialist nation without having economic means to this end comparable to those of other countries cast in the same role. Expansionism became contingent upon its ability to generate a competitive military force from a noncompetitive economy. This, autocratic Russia failed to do. It may be added in passing nonetheless that everything that Tsarist Russia of the 19th century failed to do in this respect, neo-Stalinist imperialism has achieved in our era to no mean degree.

Before it addressed the question of world imperialism, the anti-imperialist character of the revolution focused on imperialism at home, where it had lately transformed economic underdevelopment into military underdevelopment, as amply illustrated by the catastrophic course the war had taken.

The mass anti-imperialist movement reduced the anti-imperialist character of the revolution to its lowest common denominator: the dual role of Russia was reduced to the role of subject, and that role was in turn reduced to one single issue: continued participation in the war. Thus reduced by the masses, the anti-imperialist movement was amplified anew by Leninist strategy along two lines: first, the revolution had not simply to end the war, it had to transform it into a civil war against the possessing classes. Second, the civil war was to grow into a revolution of the international proletariat against the world system of imperialism. Yet, although the war had become the dominant issue, the anti-imperialist movement could not afford to ignore the issue of the oppressed people of the empire, who represented 57% of its total population.

The need to subjugate this diverse and variegated mass with a firm hand had contributed in large measure to the creation of the oppressive structures of Russian autocracy; hence these structures derived their legitimacy from the need to maintain and nurture this aggregation of peoples and nations. This is presumably what Tolstoy had in mind when he said of the 1905 revolution: "If Russia is to survive, the Poles, Finns, Estonians, Georgians, Armenians, Tatars, and sundry other nationalities have to be bent to its yoke."

Thus the majority of the population of Russia had grown used to perceiving social conflicts in terms of national antagonisms. This was one reason why the flame of revolution was kindled less swiftly in non-Russian regions, and also one of the reasons why the peoples that formed independent states after 1917— Poland, Finland, and the Baltic countries—projected their hatred of the Russian autocracy onto revolutionary Russia.

The dialectic between object and subject.   To cease being an object of the imperialist system Russia had to break loose from its economic and political dependence. To cease being its subject, i.e., to cease being an imperialist power in its own right, it had to leave the war and dissolve the basis of its empire. In the Leninist view, the radical solution to these problems consisted in suppressing their terms. Russia would free itself from imperialism by destroying the twin pillars of its domination: within, the possessing classes, and without, the imperialist grip of foreign powers.

In ascribing this dual historical function to the anti-imperialist character of the revolution, Lenin's strategy was merely reflecting the reality of Russia's dual articulation with the imperialist system. The two roles were seen as two sides of the same coin. Russia's condition as subject and object of the imperialist system was one and indivisible, and the revolution could abolish it only by attacking both roles simultaneously.

Although indivisibly united in their function, these roles were contradictory and unequal in status. It is the very essence of imperialism to mete out and forcibly impose complementary and unidimensional roles. In this way it divides the world into center and periphery, rulers and ruled, advanced countries and underdeveloped countries, rich and poor. Although Russia did not contest the existence of this system, her place in it was contradictory to its essence: the roles Russia had simultaneously assumed were mutually exclusive according to the rules of the system itself. This incongruity made prerevolutionary Russia a special case of imperialism and would make postrevolutionary Russia a special case of revolution. The search for the historical roots of Stalinism can neither omit, nor neglect, nor underestimate this link, which transcends time itself. By virtue of its history, Russia remains a special country, and many of the unique features of its present cannot be isolated from those of its past. Russia's two roles in the imperialist system were not of equal status: its role of subject was dependent upon its role as object. But as subject, the autocracy was constrained to affirm the very national interest it was brought to violate as the object of imperialism. This is surely what Deutscher meant when he observed that "the Tsarist governments were too strongly dependent on Western finance capital to assert Russia's national interest against it." As military power became a function of technological power, Russian imperialist ambitions were progressively eviscerated of other substance by its thralldom to the European imperialist powers. Its backward economy, perpetuated by imperialist dependence, prevented it from building up the modern military forces it needed to realize its own imperialist ambitions. More than that, underdevelopment, devouring more than it yielded, deprived Russian expansionism of the economic stimuli that served as a driving force for the Western powers.

The war

Russia's dual articulation with world imperialism was also the reason for the ambiguous nature of its participation in the imperialist war. "The participation of Russia falls somewhere halfway between the participation of France and that of China," Trotsky observed. "Russia paid in this way for her right to be an ally of the advanced countries, to import capital and pay interest on it—that is, essentially, for her right to be a privileged colony of her allies—but at the same time for her right to oppress and rob Turkey, Persia, Galicia, and in general the countries weaker than herself."

Internationally the overriding ambition of autocratic Russia was to entrench itself as an imperialist power. But to do this it would have had to bring its own structures, both outside and in, in line with the times, and it was precisely this it was unable to do. The only recourse left, therefore, was to increase its economic, political and military dependence on its allies. The war brought the contradiction between Russia's two roles in the imperialist system to a head, and it was the war as well against which the main thrust of the masses in affirming the anti-imperialist character of the revolution was primarily directed.

Russia's military action began with several minor victories in skirmishes against Austria-Hungary, but these were offset on the German front by defeats, forcing a general retreat in the spring of 1915. The mobilization of 15 million men had brought havoc to the backward economy, yet they were still no match for an enemy that was incomparably better equipped. Lacking food, clothing, weapons, ammunition, and qualified commanders, the Russian army suffered the greatest losses of all the belligerents: 40% of the Entente's total casualties, or 5.5 million men. Reeling from these losses, the army at the front and the society behind the lines underwent rapid disintegration. The rage welling up from the very base of society threatened the highest rungs of the autocratic hierarchy. The overthrow of the Tsar put an end to a frantic situation which had seen the arrest of the Minister of War, amidst accusations of German sympathies directed more and more openly by the State Duma and the general staff against the court.

These were the events and processes that culminated in the February insurrection and the Tsar's downfall, after turning popular feelings against the war. It was not the war itself, but the fact that it had been lost, which was the most direct cause of this decisive turn in the anti-imperialist movement of the Russian people, and indeed this distinction is indispensable for a correct understanding of that movement. The war was execrable to the masses of Russia not because of what it signified socially, but because of the way it had fared militarily. So motivated, the popular movement very quickly swept away all the remaining obstacles before it.

The liberal government propelled into power by the February insurrection changed the direction of the war, but not its pursuit. On March 23rd, Miliukov, Minister of Foreign Affairs of this government and the leader of the party in power, presented the war program of the new regime to journalists. It was the same as the old one: annexation of Constantinople, Armenia, and northern Persia, and the dismemberment of Austria and Turkey. But in 1917, instead of rekindling the enthusiasm of 1914, this program provoked vehement protests among the populace.

By this time the war had passed beyond all reviling and had become a deadly catalyst of mass discontent. Because of the war, the anti-imperialist aims of the revolution became the single issue upon which all the social and political conflicts out of which the revolution was born came to focus. The first insurrection was the prelude to a period in which the issue of the war became the stumbling block on which each of the forces supporting the expansionist program, from the autocracy in February to the last Kerensky government in October, fell one by one.

Fueled by defeat, popular action against the war was also implicitly directed against imperialism. Radicalization came from two sources: the first of these was the practical demonstration, and, ultimately, the conscious appreciation of the fact that, with the exception of a radical minority, there was no organized political force that supported the popular movement against the war. It had become clear that the country could leave the war only if it abandoned the political forces supporting its continuation, and so did the main burden of the conflict shift its locus from outside to within.

The second radicalizing circumstance was one for which the Western powers themselves were responsible. After February they intervened publicly and quite boldly in defense of the war's supporters. The Kerensky government received military supplies from France and England and a loan of 75 million dollars from the United States in preparation for the June offensive, accompanied by the dire warning of the consequences of a separate peace. Thus, international imperialism had acquired a recognizable face in the eyes of the population.

These two circumstances conjoined to bring out an insupportable truth: in pressuring her to continue the war, international imperialism was demanding that Russia embark upon an imperialist mission not unlike that which earlier it had done its utmost to obstruct. The anti-imperialist movement, which had progressively narrowed its focus to the war as such, now assumed an anti-imperialist character in the fullest sense of the word.

The real state of affairs became more and more transparent, thanks to pressure from the allies. If Russia continued the war, she would become more an object or pawn of Western imperialism, and less its subject, i.e., one of its determining forces. The anti-imperialist movement began to grasp what was at stake in its true dimensions: at issue was far more than a temporary wartime alliance; Russia had to do no less than smash the historical fetters that had made it a pawn in the imperialist game.

Connections

The anti-imperialist character of the revolution interacted with all of its other characters, and even provided the anti-autocratic character with its substance, inasmuch as the overthrow of the Tsar was above all an episode in the struggle against the war. The two characters of the revolution did not simply intersect, they had a common axis, which like every axis had two ends. In February, the same issue, namely the war, created a temporary alliance between forces with totally opposing ends. The fall of the monarchy would enable it, so thought one side, to consolidate existing structures and continue the war with better success, while the other side counted on being able to transform these same structures and so put an end to the war.

The war's supporters wanted Russia to maintain its role as an imperialist power without reducing its role as object of imperialism. As the war progressed, however, and its consequences became ever graver, the incompatibility of these two roles became increasingly obvious; yet there was a real connection between them, reflecting in fact the necessary connection between the anti-imperialist character of the revolution and its other characters. Though the origins and functions of that character were external to the revolution itself, the anti-imperialist character had profound repercussions on the internal conflicts out of which the revolution was ultimately born. The antinomic necessity inherent to the imperialist world system acted on the Russian revolution in a very special way, forcing it to assume an anticapitalist function as a prerequisite for fulfilling its anti-imperialist functions.

The anticipatory core of the Russian revolution lies in the connection between these two characters: the anticipated achievement of its anticapitalist character domestically, compounded by the anticipated achievement of its anti-imperialist character internationally, constituted the fateful prelude to the final anticipation, namely its assumption of a socialist character.

From a Leninist perspective, the combination of anti-imperialism with anticapitalism is a general law governing revolutions in underdeveloped countries. The implication is that none of these countries could free itself from imperialist oppression without first liberating itself from its own bourgeoisie. To accomplish this dual aim, revolution must be led by the working class allied with the peasantry, with a revolutionary party modelled on Bolshevik lines at its head—conditions that are tantamount to the dictatorship of the proletariat. In a revolution of this sort, anti-imperialism and anticapitalism are inseparable.

History has demonstrated amply enough the validity of this strategy applied to Russia, but not that it is universally applicable, as presumed. Most of the colonized countries obtained their independence from imperialism without eliminating their own bourgeoisie, and indeed sometimes even under its leadership. Further, the limits of this independence have demonstrated that old age has brought imperialism not only new worries, but also new and sometimes appreciable advantages as well. It was no longer only imperialism that reproduced inequality; cumulative inequality also reproduced imperialism. The anticolonial revolution did not abolish imperialism for one fundamental reason: it may have destroyed the political premises for future inequalities, but it was unable to nullify the economic effects of those inherited from the past. The international structure of inequality was modified, not abolished, and became the source of a new contradiction: economic inequality contrasted with political equality. In the era of late imperialism, international inequality had narrowed its scope, yet its intensity remained undiminished.

This priority of politics over economics creates an imbalance in inequality affecting all countries that have had their anti-imperialist revolution, including those that have followed the Leninist strategy. This in general may be said to enhance the chances of industrialization, but does not render a closing of the economic gap relative to the center any more likely. It is of course difficult to determine to what degree this semi-success or semi-failure is due to the original strategy, or to subsequent Stalinist deviations. By all appearances, the elimination of imperialism will be the work not so much of the periphery as of the center.

The purpose of the foregoing was to evaluate critically, not to contest, Leninist strategy. Its fundamental premise, namely that an anti-imperialist character must necessarily join with an anticapitalist character to produce an anticipatory revolution, has proven neither generally valid nor generally inappropriate. For underdeveloped countries it represents merely a possibility, no more, but a possibility that is totally out of the question for countries at the center; Leninism is a strategy for anti-imperialist, not socialist, revolutions. But conversely, it was wholly legitimate under the conditions obtaining in Russia at the time, where the national bourgeoisie proved totally incapable of defending its own interests irrespective of its dependence on Western imperialism.

This dependence was confirmed for the first time after the revolution on the occasion of the famous events of April. On March 23, three weeks after the formation of the liberal government, the United States entered the war, rekindling hopes of a swift victory not only among the allies but among Russian liberals. But this mood, which set the tone of Miliukov's press conference, did not sit at all well with the general populace, who were convinced that once they had done with the autocracy, they had done with the war as well. The result was that the soviet was forced to disavow the government that it itself had installed. Four days later, to calm the atmosphere, the government published a declaration for domestic consumption which Paléologue, the French Ambassador, deplored for its "timidity" and "ambiguity." Indeed the declaration proceeded much more warily in its terms than the expansionist program laid out a few days before. The desired calm did not come about and the soviet compelled the government to send the declaration to the allies in the form of an official memorandum. Also drafted by Miliukov, the memorandum offered a résumé of the declaration which essentially annulled it, dismissing any conjecture to the effect that "the revolution which had occurred entailed a weakening of the role of Russia in the common struggle of the Allies. Quite the contrary—the universal desire to carry the world war through to a decisive victory had only been strengthened."

The memorandum was dated 18 April and printed the following day in the newspapers, provoking a reaction on a par with the February days in its violence. Under the motto "Down with the Provisional Government," armed soldiers, followed by the civilian population, surged into the center of the capital. Work came to a halt in the large factories, and after three days there was no longer any doubt that popular wrath was developing into an armed uprising. Hélène Carrère d'Encausse comments on the events thusly: "Both the government and the soviets observed then and there that popular demands had gotten out of hand and were imposing their own solutions: the urgent solution that ensued from the troubled days of late April was to transform a government that had been based on cooperation between representatives of the bourgeoisie and representatives of the soviet." The "semi-insurrection" put an end not only to dual power, which had been replaced by a coalition, but also to the bourgeois liberal government, once and for all. The Russian bourgeoisie had governed a total of seven weeks, only to lose, abruptly and forever, a power it had in fact never actually fully and firmly held in its hand. It had staked its all on Russia's imperialist mission, which effectively meant itself becoming an imperialist bourgeoisie before even having emerged from underdevelopment. Translated into political reality, this illusory mission cost it the power of government for all time. In April, without having the least idea of Leninist strategy, the revolution had already discovered the necessity of merging its anti-imperialist character with its antibourgeois character. The conditions that had made the Russian bourgeoisie a reactionary class before even having been a progressive class have been discussed elsewhere. But one point deserves restating: the position of the Russian bourgeoisie with regard to imperialism was determined by Russia's special position within the imperialist system. After February, it was the bourgeoisie that was responsible for keeping that position functional, and as a class the bourgeoisie had an interest in internalizing the two incompatible roles of being simultaneously the subject and object of imperialism. Leninist strategy had foreseen but had not determined this position, and it was this position, and not Leninist strategy, that for all practical purposes had left the revolution no other chance for victory than that of combining its anti-imperialist character with its antibourgeois character.

The revolutionary forces

Unlike the antifeudal or antibourgeois characters of the revolution, its anti-imperialist character had no class content: the movement that was its expression embraced the broadest layers of the population. However, three forces alternately assumed ascendancy over it: the army, the national movements, and the Bolshevik party.

The army. The war had carried the glaring contrasts between Russia's military ambitions and its economic and technical capacities beyond the breaking point.

The Russian Empire had required its army to undertake missions of a scope that exceeded the autocracy's capacity to equip and control it. The social force most directly implicated in these chimerical imperialist designs would also be the one most directly implicated in the anti-imperialist movement of the revolution.

Prior to October, the anti-imperialist character of the revolution was manifested not in the positions adopted by political forces, nor in large demonstrations, necessarily sporadic, but in a growing lethargy that had taken hold of the army. The army's defeatism on all fronts of the war was matched by its militancy on the fronts of the revolution. Indeed, its place among the front ranks in the confrontations that were decisive for the course and outcome of the revolution helped shape the course of history. The direct consequences of its refusals to act were of vastly greater import than anything it had been able to accomplish through acting, however feverishly, e.g., in June when it abandoned the offensive, in August when it refused to follow Kornilov against Kerensky, and in October when it refused to follow Kerensky against Lenin.

In the period prior to the peace decree, the army had been the principal social force sustaining the anti-imperialism of the revolution. How it fulfilled this role was defined by three parameters: its position in decisive moments, its internal divisions preceding polarization of the social conflict, and its ability to turn its anti-imperialism against the bourgeoisie.

The army's forward position. The forward position of the armed forces relative to civilian society showed up in key events after February as well as in the soviets. The first of these was the February insurrection. Begun on the 23rd of February, the demonstrations in Petrograd took an abrupt turn on the evening of the 26th. The mutiny of a small military unit altered the course of events, transforming the demonstration into an insurrection. This unit was the fourth company of the Pavlovsky Regiment, the tsar's bodyguard, and it was promptly followed by the rest of the regiment, including the reserve batallions and the student officers especially trained for repressive operations. Instead of obeying the order to crush the rebellion, the Preobrazhensky, Volinsky, and Lithuanian regiments joined it. The insurrection had begun, the Tsar was lost.

In April, the Finnish regiment began the demonstrations that ended in the overthrow of the first provisional government. Its soldiers poured into the streets, followed by the 180th Reserve Regiment, the Pavlovsky and Kekholmsky regiments, the soldiers of the Second Division of the crews of the Baltic Fleet—a total of 25–30,000 men. Comments Trotsky, "The slogan carried into the streets by the armed soldiers and sailors: 'Down with the Provisional Government!' [considered inopportune by the Bolshevik Central Committee] invariably introduced into the demonstration a strain of armed insurrection." The population of the capital, the proletariat included, merely joined hands with the soldiers. The official *History of the CPSU* acknowledges the preeminent role of the army and makes no mention of what the Bolsheviks were doing on this occasion. "The soldiers went out into the streets on April 20. . . . The workers began to join the soldiers,'' it tells us.

Toward June, in preparation for the offensive, the government adopted increasingly harsh measures: the most revolutionary units were sent to the front, the Petrograd garrison was transferred, and the most brutal forms of discipline were reintroduced, all of which provoked quite understandable agitation among the troops. ''The fermentation among the soldiers was a fact,'' observed Stalin at the time. ''Among the workers, the mood was not so resolute.''

The military units stepped up their pressure on the Bolsheviks to launch countermeasures. ''The initiative for the demonstration (called for in June) came from the military organization of the Bolsheviks,'' writes Trotsky. ''Its leaders said that if the party did not assume the leadership, the soldiers themselves would go out into the streets.'' And so the ferment of June spilled over into July. In contrast to February and April, on this occasion the Bolshevik party occupied only a marginal position on the battlefield. Far from taking the initiative, or leading it, it rather joined half-heartedly the spontaneous movement it had not been able to hold in check.

A few examples will help to show that in the historical process of radicalization of the revolution the army functioned as an autonomous social force, but also as a shock troop. It was regularly out in front in every crucial confrontation before October. Its fundamental apoliticism turned political relations upside down: it made politics without being aware of it, and its involuntary politics gave a portentous element of reality to Bolshevik strategy, which its adversaries steadfastly dismissed as utopian down to the very last. With each crucial confrontation, the army modified its perception of the anti-imperialist character of the revolution: having first reduced it to the war, it gradually broadened its perception until it included the antibourgeois character in line with Leninist anticipation.

The army gravitated toward the soviets with an enthusiasm unequalled by any other social force. The soldiers' growing impatience with the oppressive structures of the army took a positive form in their unprecedented attraction to the democratic structures of the soviets.

The army's forward activities had a dual effect. The soldiers' vertiginous embrace of the soviets helped give the latter positive social sanction, just as their embrace by the Bolshevik party amounted to their political ordainment. But the soldiers not only overran the soviets numerically; they also became the dominant influence in them. As Trotsky observed: ''There were more than 150,000 soldiers at Petrograd, and four times more workers of all categories. Nevertheless there were five soldier delegates for every two worker delegates in the soviet.''

The army was ahead of other social forces on two counts: mounting an offensive against the old structures, and building new structures to replace the old.

As long as they were at core dominated by soldiers, the orientation of the soviets would be guided by the anti-imperialist character of the revolution. Pledged to peace, they had necessarily to oppose a government that had vowed to continue the war. The soldiers pouring into the soviets isolated the government from the two institutions on which it had staked its authority: the soviets and the army.

Dichotomization. The forward position of the army in the decisive struggles and in the soviets was not due solely to the way it successively assumed the characters of the revolution, but also to the way it experienced the revolutionary conflict. With its motley composition, paradoxically, the army gave a sharp turn to both the internal conflict rending it and the external conflict that placed it in opposition to civil society.

Held together by harsh discipline and exposed in a most direct way to the atrocities of the war, the army was of all the social institutions the least stable and the most heterogeneous. Within its ranks were men coming from different classes and social layers, from different regions of a country that embraced a whole continent, as well as from many different and often hostile ethnic groups. The armed forces were the meeting ground of the revolutionary tradition of the sailors and the repressive traditions of the Cossacks, while the hopes of the troops of the front line diverged from those of the soldiers behind the lines; the men in the army reserve were not the same as those on active duty, and the officers and junior officers corps were of a stamp different from that of the troops. This diversity seemed to carry structural differentiation to an utter extreme, making conflicts of high definition impossible.

The actual turn of events proved otherwise. One of these diversifying factors gained the upper hand over all the others: namely, the conflict between the troops and the command. This conflict was of such violence that the split took place in the army before it occurred in civil society. And so, despite its extreme heterogeneity, the army produced the most highly structured conflict of the young revolution. The glaring professional and administrative failings of the command were costing soldiers' lives. To curb the soldiers' ire, the military leaders applied the most barbarous punishments: torture applied to the genitals, horrible and cruel executions which every officer had the right to command, etc. The military hierarchy tried to reassert its authority through repression just at the moment when the civilian hierarchy was rapidly losing it, and endeavored to make up for its inability to wage war competently by making unrestrained use of its right to repress. The soldiers' response was predictable: acts of insubordination multiplied and grew in scope, from mere individual desertions to collective actions, to counter the repression. The convulsions shaking the army crystallized into a conflict that divided it neatly down the middle. The force of the conflict matched the bitterness of the antagonism: the command tried to force the soldiers to die in a war it was incompetent to wage, as it had already amply demonstrated. Rejecting the war was a radical refusal to carry out the orders of this command. Thus the conflict that polarized the army was not at bottom a class conflict. The exigencies of belligerence absorbed class relations and made the army into the most direct and determined vehicle of the anti-imperialist character of the revolution. Class relations were not annulled, but rather engulfed by relations of war. For this reason, troop action became anti-imperialist not because of the antibourgeois character of the revolution, but rather vice versa: the troops were swept by the anti-imperialist revolution into an antibourgeois position.

The added virulence of this conflict made it more socially productive as well. Not only were the troops conspicuously in the vanguard in the social conflict and in public assemblies, they had also effected a radical transformation, ratified in law, in their relationship to the command at a time when the population at large was merely demanding new civilian authorities and nothing more. In the turmoil of the February days, the Petrograd Soviet issued the famous Order No. 1 under the direct dictate of the soldiers, prescribing: elected committees in all units; the right of soldiers to be elected to the soviets—the only institution authorized to control their political activity; weapons henceforth to be under the control of company and battalion committees, rather than officers; strict discipline of soldiers on duty and full civil rights off duty; the military salute and the use of titles of rank no longer obligatory, etc. In Trotsky's eyes Order No. 1 was "the only estimable document of the revolution in February, a charter of freedoms of the revolutionary army."

Order No. 1, acclaimed by one camp, rejected by the other, carried the conflict from within the army into civil society. The troops, supported by growing numbers of the population, demanded that the order be respected; the command, supported by the authorities, blamed the order for their most recent defeats on the front. With forces thus aligned, the troops would very quickly move toward the Bolsheviks and the command toward the attractions of a military dictatorship.

The division in the army accelerated the division in society. Any hope the government had of restoring order in the country and continuing the war was an empty rhetorical exercise if it had no control over the army. As soon as the troops raised the anti-imperialist banner they virtually paralyzed the political power of the bourgeoisie without this ever having been their conscious intent.

The soldiers had no choice but to withdraw from this power the trust they had spontaneously accorded it at the time it was established. Determined to sacrifice the revolution to the war, bourgeois power could obviously not afford to tolerate an army that had just sacrificed the war to the revolution. Their radicalism drove the troops into objective opposition to civilian authorities, but their political awareness of that objective fact emerged only later, gradually, abetted jointly by the authorities and the Bolsheviks.

The lines between the conflict within the army and the conflict within civilian society blurred, and events would soon find the two squared off one against the other. It became apparent that the troops, whose primary aim was stopping the war, i.e., fulfilling the anti-imperialist character of the revolution, would necessarily be propelled further to smash the bourgeoisie, i.e., achieve the revolution's antibourgeois character, which thus became their secondary aim, and abruptly the army found itself involved in transforming an imperialist war into a civil war. Ignoring the strategy that this implied, the army was by no means itself a neutral element in it. Thus did the Bolshevik party succeed in converting a staunchly revolutionary act, which it neither initiated nor led, into political capital.

A veritable fury descended upon the troops following the collapse of the Galician offensive in June. Kerensky appointed a new commander in chief, Kornilov, who immediately launched a sweeping wave of repression. The principal target of the vendetta was the garrison in the capital, which responded in kind by the "semi-insurrection" of July on the initiative of the machine gunners. The convergence between spontaneous troop actions and Bolshevik strategy spread, in Trotsky's view, from the issue of the war to that of power: "By its conduct during the days of July 3–4," he wrote, "the garrison had created an absolute possibility for the Bolsheviks to take power," but in doing so they were less responding to Bolshevik appeals than they were following the logic of their own ends. The resulting alliance of interests was nonetheless, in Trotsky's eyes, an identifying trait of the October insurrection. "The first task of any insurrection," he writes, "is to bring the troops into it . . . The absolutely originality of the October insurrection was that, thanks to a fortuitous coincidence of circumstances, the proletarian vanguards succeeded in bringing the garrison of the capital over to its side even before the uprising began." Even as they followed their apolitical impulses, the troops nevertheless effected some crucial political changes: the anti-imperialist rebellion became a struggle against the bourgeoisie, which, in turn, became a pro-Bolshevik insurrection.

The oppressed nations. The anti-imperialist character of the revolution was reduced to the issue of the war by the army while for the oppressed nations it was the issue of their own independence. For them, the prospect of a war of national liberation rather than a civil war ensuing from the imperialist war was more relevant to their purpose. Initially at least, the various social forces assimilated the anti-imperialist character each in their several ways.

In its oppression of the nations that had been annexed by the empire, Russia had acted as an imperialist power par excellence, rather than as an object of imperialism. But even when the role of subject was defined so clearly, Russia remained too unsure of her footing to enable a sufficiently articulated and defined conflict to emerge. If the army anticipated civil society in the progress of the revolution, the national movement can be said to have been its rearguard.

Like the army, the oppressed nations were a heterogeneous grouping, but they differed from the army in the extent of that heterogeneity, as well as in the stability, variety, and internal complexity of its elements. Whereas an army is a transitory social grouping consciously molded to a specific purpose, a people is a natural society complete unto itself. The nations of Central Asia lived in a different historical epoch from those in the western regions of the empire.

Though all shared the common aim of national emancipation, their several short-term goals were as disparate as the social elements giving voice to them: where this was the clergy, the proclaimed end was recognition of the Islamic religion; the nations with intellectuals and civil servants as their spokesmen an alphabet and a national language; and peoples led by their bourgeoisie called for national sovereignty. The further advanced the social differentiation in an oppressed nation, the more intense tended to be the clashes among its classes over the definition of emancipation. Class stratification at the periphery was often not so rigorously defined in terms of the contrasts between city and countryside; this was one of the more important reasons why at the periphery, more so even than in Russia, the peasantry was so reticent for a time about embracing the soviets.

Before irrevocably altering the fate of these nations, the revolution deepened the internal divisions already rending them; the discussions of emancipation no longer concerned mere principles, but decisive historical events. The internal disarray was compounded by the confusions engendered from without by the duplicitous policies of the provisional governments on the national question.

There was a tendency for a legitimate hatred of autocratic Russia to pass over into an illegitimate hatred of the Russian revolution, and for the interests of the revolution to be confused with those of the forces that happened at the moment to be leading it.

The movement of national emancipation may have matched the army in the heterogeneity of its structures, but its behavior, extremely erratic and confused, placed it in a totally different category politically. Even as it exacerbated class conflicts at the center, the revolution ran the risk of submerging them in national solidarity in the borderlands, where the anti-imperialist and antibourgeois characters of the revolution, rather than merging, tended to pursue their several aims to the point of mutual opposition. "This inevitable national disguise of social contradictions," writes Trotsky, ". . . adequately explains why the October revolution was destined to meet more opposition in most of the oppressed nations than in Central Russia." The Provisional Government left no doubts that for it the well-being and any future betterment of Russia were contingent on maintaining its dual articulation with the world imperialist system; it was pledged therefore to continue the war for the purpose not only of preserving, but also of expanding substantially the Russian Empire. Through a kind of intrinsic logic, the anti-imperialist position of the Bolsheviks was exactly the converse of the above. Its radical stance on the imperialist system and the war required Bolshevik strategy to adopt a radical solution to the national problem as well. Before October, i.e., before the logic of the strategy had become debauched by the burden of its own practical consequences, it would have been absurd, and moreover politically fatal, to militate for the downfall of world imperialism while trying to keep Russian imperialism alive. The consequences of October would for a long time obscure the transparency of this syllogism.

The Bolshevik party. The national policy put into effect by the Bolshevik party immediately after October was manifestly unique in history. A multinational state had accorded the right of separation and effective independence to sundry peoples, not as a consequence of their revolt or of international pressures, but because of fidelity to its principles. But this principled policy was ill-suited to the real world in which it was to be applied, and would have consequences unfavorable for its protagonists, and in some instances for its beneficiaries as well. The revision of their national policy forced upon the Bolsheviks by the international environment would become one of the cornerstones of Stalinist imperialism. Indeed there was a certain ironic obverse symmetry between the two: its national policy lost Poland, Finland, the Baltic countries and Bessarabia for Russia after October, only to have Stalinism regain them, wholly or in part, twenty years later.

Before the revolution and during it, the Bolshevik party not only opposed defense of national territory in a war that nonetheless continued, it also preached the dismemberment of this territory by virtue of the right of self-determination even to the point of secession, which it supported and which it would respect. And if these demands were not radical enough in a country with strong chauvinist traditions, a third, necessarily following from them, went even further: the overthrow of the world imperialist system. The international environment would have to undergo radical change for Russia to afford to be indifferent to its own national interests; but if that environment was to remain as it was, those interests had necessarily to be refueled. Their all too brief eclipse was followed by a long period when they would be pursued almost with a vengeance. The fatherland would be resummoned from temporary oblivion, glorified beyond bounds by a pervasive chauvinism, legitimated by class, and its banner unfurled in internationalism's name. Stalinist slogans, such as the "capitalist encirclement of the beleaguered fortress," were an accurate rendering of the USSR's dire predicament internationally, but a serious and critical transformation was necessary for this society to internalize its outward plight. Whereas formerly the right of oppressed nations to secede from the empire had been openly proclaimed, now, abandoning a besieged fortress was regarded as rank desertion. Secession yielded its place to annexation, and working principles gave way to unprincipled maneuvers.

Their out-and-out unqualified anti-imperialism, inappropriate to the outside world, entailed considerable political risks internally for the Bolsheviks: opponents of the war, defenders of the separation of other nations, they rashly left themselves open to vehement accusations of treason. Lenin himself had to go into hiding in July 1917, accused of being a German agent. Though without effect on the world outside, the Bolsheviks' intransigent anti-imperialism caught the ear of Russia, and abetted substantially by the mistakes of its adversaries, the Bolshevik party in the end found itself the sole credible opponent to the war and to national oppression in the eyes of the population. This gained for it if not the support, at least the approving neutrality of the masses, which later on, in October, enabled it to act with a now legendary effectiveness.

The Bolshevik national policy was no improvisation; it had firm roots both in Russia and internationally. Marx and Engels themselves consistently stressed the interaction between national and class relations after publication of the *Communist Manifesto*, and it was in that same spirit that the founding congress of the Russian Social Democratic Workers' Party in 1898 had proclaimed the right to national self-determination, which the Second Congress in 1903 would include in the party program. That particular article, written by Lenin, was received with critical reservations by such leading political figures as Plekhanov and Rosa Luxemburg, as well as by the major European socialist parties (particularly the Austrian).

Lenin's radical stance on the national question put the Bolshevik party in a singular position both domestically and internationally. Standing virtually alone, its popularity had ballooned; yet within the party Lenin's position was a constant source of friction that would never wholly subside. It cropped up again when the right to separation became a practical question, and was redoubled in the '20s, this time over Comintern strategy. In the end, the radical stance on the national question eroded whatever cohesion there was among the Bolshevik leadership, and Stalin moved quickly into the breach, ultimately to replace that leadership with the monolithism unique to his name.

The Bolshevik dilemma did not oppose duty to love as in classical tragedy, but rather one duty to another: duty to the revolution and duty to one's country. Though conceding the antinomy of these two commitments under imperialism, Leninism was obliged to attempt their reconciliation. Lenin therefore insisted that the slogan "self-determination to the point of secession" should not indicate preference, but simply a guaranteed possibility. In his own words, the distinction meant "that Social Democrats of oppressor nations should insist on the 'freedom to secede' while Social Democrats of oppressed nations should insist on 'freedom to unite.' " The national question was complex, as reflected in the paradox that a party that boasted perfect unity among its members was on this point asking them to take different positions. Party monolithism was refracted through the spectrum of nations.

Over the long term these conciliatory initiatives would run aground on chauvinism, the ideological basis of neo-Stalinist imperialism and an integral part of every nationalist version of contemporary Stalinism. The objective isolation of the Russian revolution and its subjective incapacity to control its consequences were at the root of this theoretical debasement. It was this imposed solitude more than any other single factor that reduced this country from the harbinger of world revolution to the fatherland of the world proletariat.

Out of this cosmopolitan devotion, legitimate enough, to a fatherland transcending nations—a devotion as inestimable as it was undesirable (for the prospects of a successful world revolution)—sprang the one enduring world mythology of our era. Captivation with the first victorious socialist revolution has been so thorough that even more than a half century of Stalinism has not been sufficient to lift its spell completely.

Two important aspects may be distinguished in the historical process leading to the perversion of this devotion to the birthplace of revolution: the first was the estrangement of the fatherland of revolution from the revolution itself; the second was the shift of the boundless devotion inspired from the revolution to its fatherland after that separation had taken place. The formidable energy generated by revolutionary militancy was rechannelled into Soviet patriotism, imbuing Stalinist chauvinism with an unequalled potency and creating a new national messianism, socially sanctioned, casting present-day Russians in the role of the chosen people.

The anticipatory nature of the revolution had created dysfunctional effects from the outset, owing to the disjunction between the revolution's premises and the functions it came later to assume, and these effects took a particularly crass form in the nationalist distortion the anti-imperialist character of the revolution was later to undergo in the national liberation movement.

The three cardinal issues on the order of the day at the historical juncture of the Russian revolution, i.e., the war, the national question, and imperialism, were inseparably intertwined, and Bolshevik policy accordingly embraced them all integrally as bearer of the revolution's anti-imperialist character. It would be a mistake, therefore, to separate its national policy from its policy on the war, or toward international imperialism.

The Russian revolution, far from simplifying the problems of the war, complicated them immensely. Before February, the war had been waged ostensibly for the defense of the fatherland, although in reality in defense of the autocracy. But once the monarch was otherthrown, defense of the fatherland became for many defense of the revolution. This was indeed brought out quite clearly in a manifesto entitled "To the peoples of the entire world" adopted by the Soviet on March 14, which Trotsky called "the triumph of a new republican social patriotism in a French mould." The manifesto was adopted unanimously, i.e., with the support of the Bolshevik faction of the Soviet as well. Lenin described it as pure "wordmongering" and added that "the defeat of Russia is the lesser evil." *Pravda*, controlled by Stalin and Kamenev (both of whom voted in favor of the manifesto) declared on March 15 in an editorial that "all defeatism died the moment the first revolutionary regiment appeared in the streets of Petrograd." Two days later, Lenin sent a warning letter via Stockholm saying, "Our party would fall into eternal discredit and commit political suicide if it admitted such an imposture. I would even prefer an immediate break with anyone in our party before I gave in to social patriotism." Thus Lenin compounded the risk of isolating the Bolshevik party from other socialist parties, both Russian and foreign, with the risk of isolating himself within his own party. This was especially evident in his "April Theses" proclaimed on his return from emigration at the Finland Station, before even he had consulted with his comrades.

The Theses were published in *Pravda* on April 7 under the title "The Tasks of the Proletariat in the Present Revolution" and began with a stunning declaration: the establishment of the Lvov government did not alter the imperialist character of the war being waged by Russia, and hence allowed not the least concession to "revolutionary defensism." For the war truly to acquire a character of "national revolutionary defense" three conditions would have to be fulfilled:

—power would have to pass to the proletariat and the poorest layers of the peasantry close to the proletariat;

—all annexations would have to be renounced in fact and not merely in words; and

—there would have to be a total break with capital and its interests.

These three conditions expressed in the most succinct terms possible the essence of Lenin's view of the war and hence of the anti-imperialist character of the Russian revolution. The nature of war is determined by the nature of the society it serves. This meant that Russia could not wage a war that was not imperialist as long as the bourgeoisie was in power. To defend the revolution, therefore, the war had to be turned inward, against the bourgeoisie itself, and not continued abroad—and this was the task not only of the Russian proletariat but of the proletariat of all the belligerent countries. There was but one way to put an end to imperialist wars, whether actual or potential—namely, by putting an end to the imperialist system that engendered them.

The role of the Bolshevik party as vehicle of the anti-imperialist character of the revolution was manifested first and foremost in the achievement of that character, and this role has remained substantially operative down to this very day.

Realization

The various characters of the revolution reflected the principal functions that were imposed or granted by history, and which it was able more or less adequately to fulfill. The more complex these functions, the more differentiated could be the manner of their fulfillment.

The anti-imperialist character of the revolution was achieved gradually, over a period of time punctuated by the following historical landmarks: the decreed peace, the peace obtained, national autonomy, and world revolution. All these aspects together created the premises for Stalinism.

The relationship between the Russian revolution and world revolution, or what is the obverse side of the same thing, the relationship between the former and the world imperialist system, defined the terrain on which the anti-imperialist character of the revolution played itself out. The Russian revolution traced a path from general incompatibility with imperialism as a world system to limited confrontation with the imperialist states within that system, until finally, after numerous oscillations, the anti-imperialist focus shifted definitively from external to internal opposition. Over all, the anti-imperialist character of the revolution remained incompletely achieved, although it left a lasting mark on the society born of the revolution—at first restricting it, but later leading to its degeneration.

The decreed peace. The peace decree marked the birth of the new power;

it substantially strengthened the credibility of the new regime within the country, and at the same time had far-reaching international repercussions; in the end, however, it was not able to avoid plunging Russia into a military defeat without precedent. What it effectively brought to Russia was not a democratic peace but the harshest annexationist peace. The anti-imperialist thrust of the revolution had dominated the reality of the war; now, the illusion of a democratic peace dominated the anti-imperialist strategy of the new power.

The priority of the war was manifest in this document, which had been designed to put an end to it. The peace decree was the first act of the Bolshevik government, and indicated both the order of its priorities and that of its intentions. The priority of peace was so high that the government issued the decree even before it had formally constituted itself. In his brief introduction to the report on the decree, Lenin asked the delegates for permission "to go on to read the declaration that should be proclaimed by the government that you are going to elect."

The revolution at its apogee produced its first historical document, a government decree, before having even produced a government. Lunarcharsky was able to announce the resignation of the Kerensky government only toward the end of the first session of the Second Congress of Soviets, where Lenin appeared in public for the first time since July, emerging from the clandestinity forced upon him by the accusation of his being a German agent (sent to propose peace with Germany under conditions that were far from propitious). In doing so, he assumed a tremendous political risk in a situation that seemed to have no clear way out, while the SRs and the Mensheviks washed their hands of the matter and left the congress (where they had been a minority in any case). After having ventured some objections and observations, the delegates in attendance unanimously approved the peace decree. Its principal points were:

1. Immediate commencement of negotiations for a just and democratic peace;

2. Definition of the concept of "just and democratic peace," including the following criteria:

a. a peace ardently desired by the working classes of all the belligerent countries;

b. it must be concluded immediately;

c. it must prohibit the seizure of foreign territories, the forced annexation of other nations, and war indemnities.

3. A definition of annexation as the "adjunction of a small or weak nation to a large or powerful state, without the desire or consent of that nation precisely, clearly, and freely stated." The definition would apply to any annexation regardless of the time and place in which it occurred or the degree of development or underdevelopment "of the nation incorporated by force within the boundaries of the state in question." Finally, the annexed nation was to state its will by "free vote, and only after the complete withdrawal of the troops of the annexing nation or the more powerful nation." If all these conditions were not rigorously ob-

served, the incorporation of one nation by another "constituted an annexation, i.e., an act of conquest and oppression."

The contrast between the original anti-imperialism of Leninism and the imperialism of contemporary Stalinism could not be illustrated more clearly.

4. An immediate agreement on a truce of at least three months, to enable negotiations to get under way;

5. A declaration that the worker and peasant government of Russia would carry on all these negotiations openly, in accordance with its resolve to abolish all secret diplomacy and to publish all treaties concluded or ratified between February and October 1917.

6. A specification that these conditions were not final and that the worker and peasant government was prepared to examine any other proposal for peace.

Most of the objections and observations concerned the last point: the delegates feared that this flexibility might be interpreted as a sign of weakness by the imperialist powers. But the weakness was a reality, graver even than the worst expectations, however much the delegates closed their eyes to it, and the Bolsheviks saw it clearly.

There were quite a number of formal irregularities in this first historical document of Bolshevik power. It sometimes refers to itself as a decree, sometimes as an appeal, or sometimes as a declaration. Its formal legal identity emerges in general form from the universality of its political aims: it proposes no less than total achievement of the anti-imperialist character of the revolution, as spelled out in Bolshevik strategy. Its approach is synthetic: the war, national self-determination, and the world imperialist system are seen as interrelated. The international situation is linked to the internal situation in each country, the implication being that anti-imperialist revolution is linked to the anticapitalist and antifeudal revolutions as well. The solution it propounds is based on two postulates more or less implicit throughout the entire document:

—imperialist war can be ended or prevented only by abolishing the international imperialist system;

—the international imperialist system can be abolished only by beginning with its national roots within every country, whether developed or not, i.e., by anticapitalist revolutions within national confines.

It was an appeal for nothing less than international revolution, but by the same token the radicalism of the decree was too sweeping to avoid a loss of political substance. In every great revolution, new social relations burst forth to destroy the legal relations of the old order, and how real this contradiction can be is reflected in the unique intensity of this document with which the Russian revolution aspired to transform the world—though possessing not the least material means to do so.

A decree is properly a written statement, a decision issued by a sovereign authority, establishing the rights and duties of those under its sway. But the peace decree fits such a definition poorly. First, it did not decide but proposed; the issuing authority was not only not sovereign, it was also uncertain; and those it addressed were not in the least dependent on it. Its lack of legal precision was no more than a reflection of the de facto confusion of the powers presiding over the adoption of the decree: the government that signed it did not yet exist; in announcing the resignation of the Kerensky government, Lunarcharsky did not proclaim the establishment of a new government, but said simply, "The congress takes power in its hands," and continued: "The congress resolves that all power in all places shall be handed over to the soviets." This was not power already in existence in search of an institution fit to assume it, but an institution searching for a mock institutional facade for a power it already in fact possessed. The institution was the leadership of the Bolshevik party, and the illusory devolution of its power would remain a lasting trait, later carried over into Stalinism.

The decree's propositions were addressed simultaneously "to the governments and to the peoples of all the belligerent countries and in particular the conscious workers of the three most advanced nations." "Everywhere," added Lenin, "the governments and peoples are in disaccord, and we must help the people to intervene in issues of war and peace." The Russian revolution began its project to overturn the social order of the countries by overturning the legal order in international relations. That order made the legal guarantee of national sovereignty contingent upon imperialist domination. The Russian revolution not only turned the practice of imperialism against itself, it also tried to give that practice a juridical legitimacy. Even interference in the internal affairs of other nations, legally justified as a weapon in the anti-imperialist struggle, would become an instrument of Stalinist imperialism, summed up fifty years after the adoption of the peace decree in the famous "Brezhnev doctrine."

The decree was just such an act of interference, first addressing governments and people together in the same appeal, and then going on to distinguish first the workers and then the "conscious workers" among these. These workers, the text emphasizes, will "through their multilateral, resolute, and energetic activity help us to affirm the cause of peace and at the same time free the working and exploited masses of the population from all servitude and all exploitation."

The appeal to the people was an appeal to peace by the proletarian revolution. It was also the first official recognition of the fact that the Russian revolution stood in need of world revolution and, further, it was the first official bidding to the international proletariat to follow the model of the Russian revolution.

In its very first documents the Russian revolution showed its disdain for the legal norms of the international system that it aspired to destroy. But its readiness to disregard bourgeois legality would soon degenerate into an inability to respect legality in any form. In placing itself beyond the existing international legal system, revolutionary Russia placed itself beyond every legal system. Its extralegal behavior internationally would become more callous and hard-handed as power accrued, an evolution in large measure due, it must be conceded, to the aggressive behavior, utterly lawless adopted by the imperialist countries toward Soviet Russia from the very moment of its birth.

Domestically, extralegality became the main instrument for placing the relations of production on extra-economic foundations. In a state of penury, the law's limited efficacy makes the unlimited exercise of power not only possible but necessary.

The peace decree was a consciously perpetrated legal heresy, and in the sweeping nature of its proposals and its utter lack of means to implement them, it was tantamount to no less than the programmatic incomplete fulfillment of the anti-imperialist character of the revolution.

The peace achieved. The first major effect of the decree was that the soldiers abandoned the army with a zeal that showed no more regard for formalities than did the decree itself. And so the achievement of the anti-imperialist character of the revolution began with the dissolution of the social force principally embodying it.

The great majority of the soldiers saw this very first step toward the achievement of the revolution's anti-imperialist character as their last step. The army's predominant role in the anti-imperialist thrust of the revolution ended with a peace that was no more than a proclamation, but that alone was enough to hasten the army's dissolution and the reabsorption of its members by the civil society from whence they came.

No European government accepted the truce proposed by the decree, and no people overthrew their belligerent government to conclude an immediate peace. But the wave of sympathy for the Russian revolution washed high and spread throughout the world. Every revolution of modern times has divided the world into opposing camps, thereby acting as an international catalyst to the social conficts wracking nations internally; but with the Russian revolution this influence had a depth and persistence without precedence in history. The enthusiasm it fired around the world was due first of course to its radicalism, still but a promise, but also to the uniqueness of the period, pregnant with fateful events, which within a dozen years or so saw World War I, the first victorious revolution against all possessing classes, and finally the most devastating economic crisis in recorded history. The proclaimed aspirations of the revolution gained the sympathies of broad segments of society extending beyond narrow intellectual circles into the productive layers, with the proletariat heading the list. The proletariat projected its national class interest onto this foreign land in a more direct manner; from one day to the next, the material proof of the possibility or, indeed, the imminent achievement of a release from bondage had been thrust onto the world arena.

The wave of sympathy and solidarity set off by the peace decree did not lead to world revolution as the Russian revolution had hoped. Still, if we may believe Trotsky (despite his tendency to adduce arguments to support his theory of permanent revolution), "Soviet power would not have held out twelve months without the direct support of the world proletariat. The revolutions in Germany and Austria-Hungary annulled the Treaty of Brest-Litovsk within nine months. The mutinies in the fleet on the Black Sea, in April 1919, forced the government of the Third Republic (French) to abandon extending its operations into the south of Soviet Russia. The English government evacuated the north in 1919 under the direct pressure of the British workers.'' Counter, perhaps, even to their own interests, the millions of sympathizers of the Russian revolution stopped short of imitating it. The peace decree brought neither European revolution nor peace; on the contrary, it merely gave new fuel to the war, driving Soviet Russia to the brink of an abyss. The Western powers ignored the proposal to begin peace negotiations and, rebuffed, the Russian revolutionary government promptly began sounding out the central powers. The armistice was signed on December 2, substantially enhancing the credibility of the Bolshevik government within the country, if not outside it. At Brest, the Germans negotiated with representatives of the Petrograd government and of the Ukrainian Rada at the same time. The conditions they posed were crushing, on the order of an ultimatum. On January 8 Lenin presented to the Third Congress of Soviets a report, later entitled ''Theses on the immediate conclusion of a separate and annexationist peace.'' The ''just and democratic peace'' envisioned by the decree proved to be an empty hope. The report was rejected both by the Congress of Soviets and by the Central Committee of the party. Lenin's peremptory abandonment of the best hopes and dreams was counterposed by two other positions, themselves mutually irreconcilable. For some, revolutionary war against Germany was the only answer; for others, the key was the imminent revolution of the German proletariat. While the debate went on in Petrograd, at Brest the Germans presented a formal ultimatum on January 27, which Trotsky, instead of stalling for time as agreed, rejected out of hand. The Germans immediately launched an offensive, and within a few days occupied all of Estonia and Lithuania, as well as a large part of the Ukraine, even threatening the capital.

Both peaces, the ''just and democratic peace'' envisaged by the decree, and the humiliating peace of Brest-Litovsk, proved to be mere illusions. The country found itself in precisely the absurd situation Lenin had described in his report in favor of the decree: ''The war cannot be ended by only one of the parties involved.'' The first limit on the achievement of its anti-imperialist character lay with the fact that the Russian revolution proved unable to stop the war. The peace decree had presumed that the Entente would enter into the proposed peace negotiations; instead, the Entente flatly rejected the proposal, promptly suspended all aid to Russia, and went on the attack against its former ally. The decree had reckoned with a proletarian revolution in Europe, and in particular in Germany, but when that proved slow in coming, Lenin was compelled to admit before the same Congress: ''There can be no doubt that the military faction has gained the upper hand within the German government.'' The peace decree had depended on a truce which none of the belligerents acknowledged, but which the Russian army regarded as an accomplished fact, stamped, sealed and definitive.

In contrast to the events leading to October, which validated all predictions, those implicit in the peace decree were undone by events. The document lays bare two areas where Leninism was not equal to its task: international problems and the leadership of a society prematurely become anticapitalist. The contrast between the hopes it aroused and the actual events it precipitated reveals a peculiar dualism inherent in Leninism: it is both a revolutionary strategy and a revolutionary utopia. But these two aspects were revealed successively rather than simultaneously: as a strategy it was outstanding in the struggle for power, but it was utopian in the exercise of that power after it had been gained. The discrepancy is, however, irrelevant in the external world, where Leninism has regularly offered more of a utopian vision than a strategic guideline for action. Further, this lack of adequate strategy not only explains the desperate international situation into which Soviet Russia was plunged so soon after its birth, but also its erratic and inconsistent behavior subsequently, in the international arena, which ultimately led to its becoming an imperialist power. The incomplete achievement of the anti-imperialist character of the revolution was in large measure due to the incomplete nature of Leninist strategy.

The incomplete fulfillment of this character was also ultimately reflected in the changes the Russian revolution effectively imposed upon the imperialist system, and in the nature of the peace ending World War I. The historical fact that put an end to this imperialist war was not an anti-imperialist revolution, either international or Russian, but the military victory of one imperialist alliance over another. The peace may have altered the balance of forces and created new alignments within the imperialist system, but it changed nothing in its essence. The Russian revolution had no influence on the terms of the peace, although it was forced to bear a good share of its costs. The war began as an imperialist war and likewise came to an imperialist end, and as such entailed a mortal threat to the anti-imperialist revolution.

With Soviet Russia surviving and maintaining its anti-imperialist posture, imperialism ceased to be a world system spread literally over the face of the globe, although it remained the dominant world system. After various attempts, all failures, to destroy by force the new and threatening historical factor limiting its hegemony, the imperialist system ultimately succeeded in assimilating it.

On February 21, 1918, three weeks after the launching of the German offensive, the Council of People's Commissars issued an appeal, drafted by Lenin, entitled "The socialist fatherland is in danger." And so in February the Bolsheviks accepted a defensive war which in January they had opposed, working to kindle patriotic sentiments that they had consistently rejected throughout the whole of their party's existence. If they were forced to conduct a war, fielding a reluctant population while lacking even the most elementary means to that end, then a popular levy was necessary and the war had to be not a revolutionary but a patriotic one. Thus the country of revolution, scarcely born, found itself countering imperialism not with the hope of socialism, but with a call to arms in defence of the fatherland. Instead of the revolutionary unity of the international proletariat looming up defiantly to bar its way, international imperialism found itself faced with the nations of old peasant Russia, their ranks closed in unity around the state of yore. History itself had lifted up this strange blend of war, imperialism, and the national issue into the light of day.

The about-face was due not to Bolshevik inconsistency, but to the international isolation in which the Bolsheviks found themselves and to the burden of war they did not have the resources to assume. Carr says: ''The great Russian empire, when the Bolsheviks took possession of it, was in a process of rapid disintegration—the result of internal turmoil and of defeat in war. The immediate effect of the revolution was to accelerate the process.'' To temper a process that eluded their control, they cloaked new symbols and institutions in allusions to the past.

The February 21st appeal was followed by the establishment of a new army on the 23rd under the direct fire of the German invaders. The Soviet state created the Red Army with a call to arms in defense of the fatherland; a quarter century later, a second such war would transform it into the most powerful military force in the world.

The efforts of the Soviet regime in Febuary 1918 were concentrated on both preparing a military response and securing a truce. The Germans imposed humiliating conditions: annexation of Estonia and Lithuania, creation of a Ukrainian state under Germany, enormous indemnities, and the demobilization of the army—which the government had not yet even had time to mobilize.

On March 6, three days after its signature, this disastrous peace was taken up for debate at the party's Seventh Congress, the first to meet after the seizure of power, and convened especially for this purpose. The new treaty was approved by two-thirds of the delegates present. A few days later, the Fourth Congress of Soviets was held to discuss the same issue. After having presented the reasons for their disagreement, the Left SRs announced their wholesale resignation from the government. The Bolsheviks, already isolated internationally, were now isolated in the national arena. The party—or more precisely its Leninist nucleus—was the only factor to accept the political price of this suicidal peace. The end of World War I was followed by Leninist revolutions in three of the defeated countries, but in none of those that had emerged victorious. The revolutions in Russia, Germany, and Hungary were sparked in large measure not by imperialism as a system of domination, nor even by the imperialist war, but by the fact that these countries had been defeated in this war. Even for these social revolutions, therefore, national roots ran deep.

Unfortunately it was in the order of things that the international politics of the Bolsheviks was unable to alter the consequences of the nation's defeat; quite the contrary: those consequences would leave deep scars on the internationalist politics of the Bolsheviks. The imperialist war had been brought to an end, but the peace that followed, to which the Bolsheviks were forced to subscribe, was counterrevolutionary, not anti-imperialist, and positively damaging to the nation. As a result, the nation again assumed its somber priority. The desperate reinvocation of the fatherland in 1918 would play a key role in the later evolution of Soviet imperialism. It is to this that Bukharin was evidently alluding in his warning to the Fourth Congress of Soviets: ''The peace we are being asked to accept may perhaps save Soviet power, but it will kill the world revolution in the process. A decision to sign this peace is a vote for a national option.''

From the same tribune, Lenin rejoined that world revolution would prevent the implementation of the peace treaty.

The peace may have enabled the Soviet republic to survive, but it was nonetheless a prime stumbling block to the achievement of the anti-imperialist character of the Russian revolution.

With its very first step, the young revolution attempted to establish control over its international environment; with its second, it adapted grimly to the impossibility of doing so. Historical necessity brusquely exposed its inherent antinomy, abruptly choking off what it itself had brought to pass.

There was no connection between the internal and external aspects of this historical event, and between the two the revolution led a divided existence: victorious on the national level, internationally the revolution was weak to an extreme. The strain produced by this contradiction had a critical threshold beyond which the very existence of the new power was imperilled. The revolution had but one choice if it wished to survive: to accommodate to the very international environment it had originally aspired to transform. The inability of Soviet power to control its international environment was matched by an inability to control its own accommodation to it, and it traversed the inglorious path from a disastrous peace to affirmation of the fatherland over world revolution, and finally to neo-Stalinist imperialism. Of all the tendencies that rent the Bolshevik party from within after Lenin's death, Stalinism alone was able to transform these constraints into a party program. Stalinism's strength, which carried it to victory, lay in the fact that it was itself the unwitting expression of the objective necessity that others had aspired to control.

The national question. The Russian revolution chalked up some remarkable achievements in dealing with the national question. It not only proclaimed, but also permitted the exercise of the right of self-determination even to the point of separation. Poland, Finland, the Baltic countries, i.e., the most developed countries of the empire, took full advantage of this right. The Soviet regime, faithful to its principles, but also confident that the spread of its sway internationally was imminent, immediately ratified the independence of these new states. With, first, the German offensive and later the war of intervention, it became clear that this profoundly revolutionary act had won Soviet Russia less the gratitude of the peoples concerned than the hostility of their new governments. "It soon became clear," writes Carr, "that the demand [for separation] could be sustained only with the support of foreign arms and foreign money, so that those whose pride had revolted against dependence on Petrograd or Moscow found themselves the satellites and hirelings of Germany or the Allies or successively of both. The view that bourgeois nationalism was an instrument for the dismemberment of Russia on the behest and in the interest of foreign powers became difficult to refute." The anti-Sovietism of the countries touched by the revolution was one of the major sources of future Soviet chauvinism.

The tergiversation of the Baltic nations, and especially of the Poles, in 1918 played into the hands of imperialism, which found in these new sovereign nations an optimal base from which to launch its attacks on the new Soviet state. The right of separation proved to have effects completely opposite to those intended. Again antinomic necessity prevailed: to meet one of its requirements, it contradicted another. The consequences of this complication led both the Soviet government and the nations that had not yet finally decided on their status to adopt a much more cautious approach to the question of separation. Furthermore, the peace imposed by the Germans amounted to a de facto annulment of the separation upon which the nations of the Western territories had earlier so eagerly seized. During the debates on the peace, the Bolshevik partisans of "revolutionary war" saw quite clearly the paradox of the situation that had been created: the same government that had guaranteed these nations their rights of separation had by its signature abandoned them to the occupation of German imperialism for an indefinite time onward. Lenin's assessment of the situation was succinct and to the point. In his "Theses on an annexationist peace" he declared: "The interests of socialism supersede the right of nations to self-determination."

The world revolution. According to the Leninist view imperialism had become a world system that could not exist without causing world wars of ever greater atrocity. World War I had therefore to be ended in such a way as to prevent its even more horrible repetition in the future, and this meant the abolition of the world system that unfailingly produced them.

The historical mission of abolishing imperialism belonged to the international proletariat. This it would do through world revolution, and indeed, in view of the unparalleled intensity of the antagonisms underlying the events that swept over the face of Russia between February and October, world revolution indeed seemed to be knocking at the door.

Lenin's predictions with regard to this scenario were in part borne out, but also partly belied by the actual course of events. The first confirmation was the Russian revolution, which was also an uprising against imperialism as a system and as the cause of the war. On the other hand, the proletariat of the advanced countries did not rise up as predicted in an anti-imperialist world war. The net effect was a compounded misfortune: the Russian revolution was unable to assume a socialist character, and the end of World War I became one of the direct causes of World War II.

Thus Leninism was borne out by the effects of the world peace, but not by the outcome of the revolution, which proved to be an isolated episode rather than the first stage in a global process. War and revolution in reality were not the symmetric couplet that Leninism had supposed; and as regards world revolution, Leninism remained a roughcast utopia.

For instance, in 1908 at a meeting of the Internationalist Socialist Bureau, Lenin declared: "One would have to be blind not to see that the social revolution is progressing in Great Britain." In 1911 he wrote to Paul Singer: "The working masses in Germany and in other countries are joining the army of the revolution in increasing numbers, and this army will be deploying its forces in the near future.'' In 1912, in an article on the successes of American workers, he declared: ''The revolution is approaching in the United States.'' Finally in 1918 he wrote: ''Bolshevism has become the theory and tactics of the international proletariat throughout the entire world.'' But as history would show, this class was less disposed to smash the imperialist system than to better its predicament within it. Its penchant to adapt would make reformism as tenacious a phenomenon as its rejection by the Bolsheviks was vehement.

The strategy elaborated to abolish this system would have to be replaced by a strategy that would permit adaptation to it. With this fateful shift in aims Leninist strategy drifted toward utopia, and postrevolutionary society, deprived of its rudder, ran aground on the historical reef of Stalinist imperialism. When they first came to power the Bolsheviks believed that their revolution, now a historical reality, was merely the prologue of the world revolution to come. The term prologue, used frequently at that time, was significant in two other ways, one suggesting that the Russian revolution was only a stage in a world historical process, and the other suggesting that in the unfolding of that process the Russian revolution would precede world revolution. The second became a fact; the first remained an assumption. But the overarching implication is that the two revolutions linked together temporally and sequentially. The problem is thus reduced to the question: how long will the interval separating the prologue from the rest of the performance last?

The question was not mere casuistry: ''If the European revolution continues to delay,'' warned Lenin in his report on the annexationist peace, ''the gravest of defeats awaits us.'' ''Indeed,'' he says further on, ''the German revolution is in a process of growth, but not as we should like it, not as quickly as Russian intellectuals would be pleased to have it, not at the pace that our own history had assumed in October.'' The length of the historical period separating world revolution from the Russian revolution was determined by the latter's anticipatory nature. Within the Russian revolution proper the effect of anticipation was not the same for each of the revolution's characters: anticipation went much further in achieving, for example, the antibourgeois character than it did in its anti-imperialist pursuit. This same prospect sustained the belief that world revolution would spread more quickly in the relatively backward countries than in the more developed countries. ''World socialist revolution,'' observed Lenin on this last point, ''will not begin in the advanced countries as easily as it began in Russia.''

Leninism predicted three transformations, equally imminent:

—the Russian revolution would be transformed into a world revolution;

—the world revolution would lead to the abolition of the imperialist system;

—the abolition of imperialism would enable the anti-imperialist Russian revolution to become a socialist revolution.

These three transformations could take place only all together by virtue of the specific way the Russian revolution and world revolution intermeshed.

Unable to unleash a world revolution, the Russian revolution was able neither to bring about the collapse of imperialism nor itself to acquire a socialist character. These two historical limits reflect the dependence of the outcome of the Russian revolution on the world revolution.

The mere delay of world revolution reversed this relation, and world revolution became dependent on the revolution in Russia. By the end of 1918 Soviet Russia had survived the worst; the crucial breathing spell it gained was not due to world revolution, but to the German command, which preferred to wait until after the harvest to occupy the Russian steppes. The revolutions in Europe occurred later, in isolation, and were not destined to last. In November 1918 revolution broke out in Germany; enthusiasm was enormous. On October 1, Lenin sent a letter to Sverdlov in which he wrote: "The international revolution has moved so much closer in a single week that it is very likely to become a reality in a matter of days." At the same time, Lenin called on Sverdlov, the Secretary of the Central Committee, to organize aid for the German workers, "military aid included." "By the spring," Lenin went on to say, "we must have an army of three million men ready to come to the aid of the international workers' revolution."

These considerations point up the dependence of world revolution on the Russian revolution. The latter would crystallize this priming function into lasting forms, which Stalinism would later develop to surfeit. These forms were:
—military aid;
—imposition of its own model;
—political control.

Lenin would later reiterate again and again the duty of the victorious proletariat in a single country "to attach itself to the oppressed classes of other countries, rousing them to insurrection against the capitalists—if necessary even using its military forces." In the particular case, by aiding the German workers, Soviet Russia would also be doing its internationalist duty and meeting its own national interests. Under the pressure of imperialist encirclement, however, national interests and international duty little by little became separate issues.

Soviet Russia established relations with bourgeois governments, expecting proletarian solidarity. Treaties were signed with Turkey, Poland, Estonia, and later with Germany and Sun Yat-sen's China. "From the end of civil war," remarks Schapiro, ". . . the Russians were pursuing two parallel policies which were on the face of it incompatible. One was the furthering of world revolution, . . . the other was the consolidation by normal diplomatic means of trade relations and alliances with the capitalist powers." The establishment of relations with bourgeois governments had a dual aim: to prevent new military interventions against the young republic and to facilitate the procurement of machinery, equipment, and specialists indispensable for economic reconstruction and industrialization.

Thus the Bolshevik government was attempting to eliminate imperialism and win its confidence at the same time. The discontinuity between the Russian revolution and world revolution produced this ambiguity of policy. Internationally, Soviet policy was at one level directed toward maintaining regular relations with the same governments which at another level it was working to overthrow. The disjunction between the internal and external conditions in which postrevolutionary society had to live reflected this ambiguity. To overcome this disjunction would have meant transcending the bounds defining the revolution's anti-imperialist aims.

From isolation to internationalization

Nineteen seventeen had hardly passed than the Russian revolution found itself alone and isolated, all but crushed under the weight of general hostility; yet within the next half century, societies of a Stalinist type would emerge in a significant number of countries on four continents.

There is no disputing that the way out of isolation was the work of a Stalinist USSR; less clear, however, is the relationship between the spread of the Stalinist system around the globe and the imperialist evolution of the USSR. The abundant literature notwithstanding, a number of problems attendant on this theme have not yet been satisfactory resolved. For example:

• To what extent did those countries that have adopted the Stalinist model also opt for a Leninist model of revolution to reach that point?

• What precisely is the relationship between Soviet Stalinism and the forms Stalinism has taken in other countries?

• What are the qualities peculiar to neo-Stalinist imperialism, in the light of this relationship?

A few general observations on each of these points are in order.

The Leninist revolution and the Stalinist system. If a Leninist revolution necessarily leads to a Stalinist social system, Stalinist society should be the necessary outcome of Leninist revolutions. On the other hand, if this is a spurious necessity, then hypothetically Stalinist society could just as easily emerge from any one of a variety of social transformations. Another hypothesis, the most common, holds that the social similarities among these countries are due essentially to the pressures of the USSR.

Before examining the connection between revolutionary upheavals and the societies resulting from them, we must examine the similarities (and hence the differences) between different revolutions and between different societies. To compare the Russian revolution with other events of its genre, a usable definition is necessary. In the Leninist sense, such a definition must include at least the following criteria:

(a) a Bolshevik-type party in the leading role in the revolution;

(b) a worker–peasant alliance under the leadership of the party;

(c) transformation of an imperialist war into civil war;

(d) transformation of a bourgeois democratic revolution into a socialist revolution;

(e) establishment of soviet power.

One or more of these criteria will of course not be found in other revolutions. None of the criteria, for example, can be discovered in the historical premises of a Stalinist society of the type to be found in Cuba. Indeed, far from being led by a Communist party in the Comintern mould, Castro's revolution merely ignored it; the civil war did not ensue from an imperialist war; to the extent that the term is applicable, the alliance that carried this revolution to victory was an alliance not of workers and peasants, but of the popular masses and a militant intellectual elite; finally, the Cuban revolution has never established soviets.

Cuba is the most telling example, if less conspicuously so; yet some of the same criteria have been absent or have played but a minor role in the revolutionary transformation of other countries that ultimately have ended up with the same social system. They came to Stalinism by ways that diverged appreciably on one point or other from the Leninist description of the Russian revolution. This revolution attempted to carry its message to other countries without at the same time being able to transmit the historical premises that, presumably, alone made that revolution possible, namely: it was the first, and for a long time the only anti-imperialist revolution; it was victorious in one huge country that was egregiously underdeveloped; that country was enmeshed in the imperialist system through a dual and contradictory articulation; and it was a country with a divided tradition of both revolutionary and reactionary tendencies, reflected in spontaneous form in the physiognomy of its political parties, and in conscious form in Leninist revolutionary strategy.

But, however diverse the paths, the epilogue remains by and large one and the same. Despite dissimilar historical premises, geopolitical conditions and revolutionary strategies, the social transformations that have taken place in China, Hungary, Cuba, Ethiopia, Albania, and of course in Russia have invariably given rise to societies of the Stalinist type. Actually this diversity of paths appears important only if the criteria Lenin used to define the Russian revolution are applied. But these refer to strategy, not to the internal nature of revolution. Though crowned with success, this strategy remained a strategy of lavish anticipation, aimed at catapulting Russia, basically a feudal country, directly into socialism. The strategy may have been an accurate, if partial, expression of the revolution, but it was at variance with its nature. Most importantly, however, whether the strategy was a departure from the inner essence of the revolution, or, on the contrary, enriched it, the fact remains that it achieved its aims, albeit perhaps incompletely, and fulfilled the revolution's principal characters, and above all its anti-imperialist character.

The strategy of the Russian revolution was primarily determined by its immediate historical conditions, while its nature was a product of the general necessity, common to all underdeveloped countries, of overcoming the imperialist barrier to industrialization. Insofar as its immediate historical conditions transcended its strategy, the Russian revolution was and remains a remarkable event, if a solitary one, while as regards its general nature, it has proven its relative universality, i.e., its plausibility for any underdeveloped country.

To stress the point one more time: three qualities mark the Russian revolution as a revolution apart. It was anticipatory, it was strategic, and it was antinomic. But since then these three qualities have also been present in the revolutions that have taken place in almost all countries that were later to embark upon the path of Stalinism. The general implication of this is that, though a variety of strategies may have been used in these revolutions to impose a range of characters upon them—with the anti-imperialist and anticapitalist characters being the most constant—these revolutions were anticipatory insofar as the anticapitalist character was prematurely achieved. What history teaches, therefore, is neither the uniqueness nor the universality of the Russian revolution, but rather its international plausibility for underdeveloped or backward countries. That which has reproduced itself constantly as a factor of relevance is not the subjective strategy of the Russian revolution, but its objective conditions. With all the diversity of historical premises and political strategies, a Stalinist social system has invariably emerged from revolutions objectively similar and above all anticipatory in nature. More precisely, a social order of the Stalinist type tends to be the outcome wherever the legitimate attempt is made to move from victory in anticipatory revolution to an accelerated anticapitalist industrialization with no valid strategy or theory to accomplish this end. The salient element of the pristine Stalinist model as adopted by other countries is consequently not the egregious repressive force used to expropriate the peasantry, but the conception and the means of industrialization employed: anti-imperialist and anticapitalist industrialization through primitive accumulation in which the means of production—as yet underdeveloped when expropriated from their former owners—were not appropriated by society but by revolutionary power, which to perform this function placed itself beyond the reach of all social control and established the dual monopoly described in the foregoing.

This spontaneous tendency toward Stalinist economic, political, and social solutions has merited little attention; what interests analysts most in the spread of the Stalinist model is Soviet military intervention. But it is just as important to understand the limits of that intervention as it is to appreciate its influence. A composite approach, which covers all the functional aspects of the process, both external and internal, would seem to be more productive than a one-sided approach of whatever kind.

One initial point must be clear: military occupation or even pressure by the Soviet Union alone is not sufficient to bring about an anticipatory revolutionary transformation of existing social structures. Taking advantage of its military presence in Eastern Europe after World War II, the USSR gave major support to political and social forces struggling for this cause, but that support would have borne little fruit if objective conditions had not urged such a transformation—objective conditions implying the demonstrable lack of a viable alternative to anticapitalist and anti-imperialist industrialization. To have achieved that end, the political and social forces concerned would have had to have been able to use this support to activate a genuine popular movement against the political influence and ultimately the economic privileges of the possessing classes, including of course capitalist private property. Thus, though strongly influenced under certain circumstances by Soviet pressure, anticipatory revolution cannot be the direct result of that pressure. Under such special conditions the strategy of revolutionary forces will be substantially different from that of the Bolsheviks in 1917, but the nature of the social transformation will nonetheless be similar.

Once established, this historical scenario gravitates spontaneously to the Stalinist model, i.e., toward a system in which social ownership is defined by a monopoly on power. External pressure, which both economically and politically remains ambiguous in its results, is nevertheless able to bring more weight to bear in effecting an anticipatory transformation of social structure than in driving that transformation further toward its subsequent degeneration into Stalinism. That such a disjunction is possible is amply demonstrated by the existence of countries that are at once Stalinist and anti-Soviet.

All these observations apply to countries that are underdeveloped, although Czechoslovakia may be said to represent a special case. (The GDR, with its special geopolitical situation and the substantial external support it receives, is a separate problem, but does not detract from the general argument.) In Czechoslovakia there was no spontaneous internal tendency, but an alliance between external pressures and an inclination toward blind imitation, which forced upon this highly industrialized country the pre-industrial structures proper to Stalinism, plunging it into a political and economic doldrums from which it has never recovered. The fate of Czechoslovakia demonstrates the pernicious consequences of forcing the Stalinist model upon industrialized or highly industrialized countries.

The same factor that condemns Stalinism to failure in developed countries makes it ultimately intolerable in countries that have been wrested forcibly by it out of their economic backwardness. Rendered obsolete by its very achievements, Stalinism is implicitly rejected in attempts to reform it. Such reforms need only to begin to threaten the one institution fundamental to Stalinism—monopoly on power and proprietorship—and the risk of Soviet intervention multiplies beyond measure. The upshot is that if Soviet neo-Stalinism resorts to imperialist methods, it is due to the desire less to propagate its model than to preserve it. It is this priority more than anything else that distinguishes neo-Stalinist imperialism from all other imperialisms.

Unity of process—diversity of effects. Movements aspiring to anticipatory revolutions possess an impressive body of critical theory of the society they wish to destroy, yet only an apologetic ideology of the society they wish to construct. Abandoned to historical currents whose significance eludes them, these societies are swept up by a process beyond their control, fatefully dashing them from the triumphant heights of revolution into the abyss of Stalinism. This process has passed through the same principal stages in any country where it is set into motion.

If the forces of production are underdeveloped, expropriation of the possessing classes creates a real vacuum of proprietorship and, its natural base suspended, the economy is plunged into dangerous disarray. The way thrown open by revolution leads not to industrialization, but to economic collapse. A triple necessity is then imposed on these societies: to institute a definite form of proprietorship (other than a restoration of private property); to get the economy under way again; and to embark upon anticapitalist industrialization. The result is that these societies veer spontaneously, beyond any theoretical control or social strategy, toward the formation of Stalinist-type monopolies.

A brief historical lag is enough for the formula to be effective: the three goals are achieved. Yet, instead of disappearing after having fulfilled its mission, monopoly only grows stronger. It is able to survive beyond its social function first, because of the attachment of its historical agents to the power they wield, but also because of the surprising inertia of this social system: the hidden cost of a short-term effectiveness is a lasting paralysis of the mechanisms of social change. The illegitimate persistence of this regime obstructs the social appropriation of its technological achievements. The obverse side of the rapid transformation of productive forces is the entrenchment of the relations of production characteristic of monopoly proprietorship. And so it is that a temporary solution, improvised originally to meet a momentary crisis, was transformed into an autonomous mode of production.

Before sinking into its new crisis, Stalinist improvisation bore all the outward features of strategy: it defined its goal—industrialization; the requisite condition for pursuing that goal—anticapitalism; and persuasive means for achieving it—monopoly expropriation of the means of production by power. But the resemblance to strategy proved to be a specious one, for the definition that Stalinism gave to each of these criteria, and hence implicitly to itself, was false in substance. Stalinism represents unchecked submission to necessity, which is mistaken for a theory and a strategy, and in this sense is a preeminent form of false consciousness specific to the modern era. Anticapitalist industrialization based on monopoly proprietorship over the means of production becomes equated with the construction of socialism, and this subjective confusion, together with the objective paralysis of the mechanisms of change, leads to a perpetuation of the initial structures. Stalinism's inability to change alters its very historical nature: anti-capitalist industrialization obstructs the transition to socialism; the phase in which the transition to socialism becomes possible becomes itself an obstacle to that transition; a fanciful socialism seals off the path to true socialism.

This process repeats itself in general form from one country to the other, suggesting that the epistemological source of Stalinism is to be found in the discontinuity between the strategy that had guided an organic revolution and the arbitrariness that governed anticapitalist industrialization. A vital task of theory would be to transform this cumulative historical experience into an authentic strategy for societies born of anticipatory revolution. To be historically productive, such a strategy would require resolution of the following theoretical problems:

• What would be an effective anticapitalist alternative to monopolization of the expropriated means of production by the center of power?

• If such an alternative cannot be found, is it possible to create effective institutions capable of bringing this monopoly, and hence this power, under the genuine control of society?

• With or without such institutions, how could this monopoly be made sufficiently flexible or sufficiently vulnerable to prevent its ossification and to facilitate its abolishment once it had completed its industrializing mission?

The solution to these theoretical problems would have to be based on the practical history of Stalinism as it exists in fact. This history has a first stage, the emergence of the new social order; a second stage, that of industrialization; and finally a third stage, its crisis, in which Stalinism becomes neo-Stalinism. At the root of this crisis lies the conflict between monopoly proprietorship over the means of production and the pressing need to develop them further. Industrialization once completed, monopoly now serves to obstruct the transition to a new stage in which the fruits of that industrialization may be reaped. What is unique to the situation is that the same social grouping that provokes the crisis also keeps the social mechanisms capable of resolving it in systematic disarray.

Both the emergence of Stalinism and industrialization follow similar patterns, regardless of the country, although as a result of the crisis a certain differentiation is discernible as well. In some cases the crisis has erupted into the open despite all obstacles, while in other it is absorbed by social buffers. The variety of actions initiated by the body social has provoked an equivalent variety of responses from the authorities. The drive toward reform is almost universal, although in its specific features it varies considerably from one country to another.

At the moment the picture is one of difference in similitude. The Soviet model, being central, remains the most influential, but also one of the least flexible. Its rigidity is manifested not only in its own gropings at reform but, and indeed especially, in its attitude toward reforms attempted beyond its borders. At a critical threshold, defined by a range of criteria, its tolerance for this dynamic diversity stops. The first of these criteria is that reforms must not affect the monopoly on power and proprietorship; the second, that every change brought about by society, rather than forcibly imposed by the monopoly, is inadmissible; the third, that every attempt to subject the monopoly on power to genuine social control must be rejected; and fourth, that any reform affecting the military security of the USSR directly or indirectly is out of the question. Each time a reformist movement in any country approaches one or more of these critical points, the USSR responds with economic and political pressures, and with military threats and even interventions if necessary.

A general classification of the principal tendencies in these countries would distinguish three: rejection of all reform, as illustrated by North Korea; the failure of reforms, illustrated by Poland and Czechoslovakia; and the relative success of reforms, as illustrated by Hungary. The last case demonstrates the extent to which successful reforms are able to reduce considerably the tensions in social life.

But this statement of fact is not enough to justify the excessive optimism of some authors who mistake a reform of the Stalinist social system for a change in its nature. The reforms undertaken so far, even those that have been successful, do not warrant such an interpretation.

Two points are crucial to a placing of the discussion of reforms in a proper theoretical perspective. First, the zeal for reform manifested in these societies expresses, albeit in a confused, pretheoretical way, the objective necessity of their disappearance. Second, what successful reforms in fact demonstrate is the ability of these societies to effect a limited improvement in their functional performance without altering their basic structures, locked in immobility. The main trend of reforms, stimulated largely by trade with the West, has been toward a partial revival of market relations. Even in making such a concession, however, the center, with its monopoly on proprietorship and power, will have merely reshuffled the hierarchy of its instruments. Put succinctly, reform alters only the expression, not the substance, of the privileges of the monopolistic center. Still, the importance of such changes should not be underestimated, since social affirmation of the prerogatives enjoyed by the center entails in large part a shift of ground from repression to exchange relations, from extra-economic coercion to economic constraint.

Far from challenging the monopoly's supremacy, successful reforms reflect upon it positively in the popular mind. Clearly the population prefers an expansion of trade, which on the one hand would alleviate economic difficulties and diminish the use of repression, and on the other, improve the productivity of social labor and its living standards. To date no reform has ever been successfully imposed by a popular movement. Indeed one of the reasons for reform has been to prevent the emergence of such movements, and hence reduce the danger of Soviet intervention. In the process the monopoly regime becomes more flexible. From this vantage point, reform is, curiously, in a certain sense a product of the normal functioning rather than of the malfunctioning of the social order, and indeed ensures its reproduction as well as a measure of improvement in its performance.

To go beyond the mere attempt to streamline the Stalinist social system to a superseding of that system, reforms would have to aim first at reduction of the monopoly and ultimately at its elimination. If it were subject to institutionalized social control, the monopoly would find itself in a new position, namely, not of granting reforms, but of accepting them under the pressure of social forces pushing for change. Finally, and this is a *sine qua non* of their success, reforms would have to be based on a theory and a strategy aimed at a socialist resumption of the anticapitalism that was at the origins of the Stalinist social system.

Particularities. The historical merit of the Twentieth Congress of the CPSU did not lie in its critique of Stalinism, but in the fact of it having recognized for the first time publicly that such a critique was necessary. The Twentieth Congress opened the era of reforms and reformist movements in the countries under Stalinist rule, and a new era in the evolution of neo-Stalinist imperialism. The repeated confrontations between Stalinist imperialism and reforms of Stalinism over the past three decades are an eloquent expression of the conflict plaguing this social order. Neo-Stalinist imperialism preceded the reforms, but in recent years the reformist movements have played a key role in shaping its responses.

The events speak for themselves: between neo-Stalinist imperialism and that part of the world not under its sway there are no relations as explosive as those it nurtures with countries moulded in its own image. Since the Twentieth Party Congress, the USSR, avoiding any and all military confrontation with the members of the alliances opposing it, has made direct use of armed force against Hungary, Czechoslovakia, China, and even against Afghanistan, which was well on the way toward introducing a Stalinist social model. While the USSR does not break relations with capitalist or imperialist countries except in the case of openly reactionary regimes such as in South Africa, Pinochet's Chile, etc., and Israel, for all practical purposes it has done so with Yugoslavia, China, and Albania; a state of tension at times on the verge of erupting into the open has long marked its relations with Poland and Romania and, to a lesser degree, with North Korea. Of the dozen countries that make up this troubled family, only about a third— Bulgaria, the GDR, Cuba, and Vietnam—have managed not to engender uncontrollable situations. Among the eight countries that pose the most difficult problems for the USSR are some of its allies from World War II.

This paradoxical shift of the epicenter of conflict probably enabled the world to weather the Cold War and avoid nuclear catastrophe, but at the same time it also snuffed out, at least for the moment, the most promising attempt to transcend the Stalinist model, and in this way to promote a potential real transition toward socialism. Neo-Stalinism is thus less conciliatory to the prospect of socialism as a future reality than toward imperialism as a present one. The countries in the other camp cause it fewer worries than those that, while akin to Stalinism, resist becoming identical with it. For neo-Stalinism, capitalist imperialism is less unacceptable than an anti-imperialism that diverges from its own notion of what anti-imperialism should be.

This bizarre predilection is one more illustration of Stalinism's virtual calling to embody the revolutionary legacy while perverting it. The propagation of its likeness on a world scale, sanctioned by the watchword of anti-imperialist revolution, was transformed by Stalinism into a new imperialism, and the international aspiration of revolution was transformed into a virtual national obsession. Eastern Europe and East Asia are from this perspective a militarily attainable alternative to a world revolution that has remained perennially beyond the horizon. The young Soviet republic, assailed from all sides, dreamed of a political buffer zone of global dimensions, which later the Comintern proved unable to provide, and which finally neo-Stalinist imperialism replaced with a military buffer zone of continental dimensions. Fidelity to revolution became an embarrassment for it; the international spread of its model and control of its reproduction became political objectives that relied par excellence on military means.

A selective inventory of the peculiarities of this imperialism must include its readiness to resort to military force to resolve its disputes with countries organized in its own image; its compulsion to implant its own social and economic model anywhere it assumes control, and then in a form as close as possible to its own likeness, unlike Western imperialism, which tends to establish economies that are complementary to its own in those countries that come under its sway; its force of attraction for the underdeveloped countries, due on the one hand to the prestige, still living, of the revolution of which it is the heir, and on the other, to the prospect of an antifeudal, anticapitalist and anti-imperialist industrialization which by force of circumstance it has come to represent; the supplementary and gratuitous impetus given to its expansion by the tendency of countries that have carried off an anticipatory revolution spontaneously to adopt models not unlike the Stalinist one; its inordinate reliance on military means, due on the one hand to a historical experience of aggression from without, and on the other to the poverty of its economic resources; and finally its irrational tendency to supplant the workings of factors that would favor the spontaneous spread of its model with its own intervention or military pressure.

*　　*　　*

Stalinism is an indirect consequence of world imperialism, and a direct product of the Russian revolution of 1917.

The internationalization of monopolies also internationalized their own inner antinomy, which based the expansion of a market economy on the systematic perversion of its fundamental mechanism: equivalent exchange. As it became a predominant historical reality, this antinomy bent history itself to its needs: it became antinomic necessity.

Antinomic necessity, the principal moulder of international relations of the imperialist kind, also becomes the moulder of their negation. The negation of the imperialist system generates at its periphery stirrings toward anticipatory revolution. Once internalized by revolution, antinomy forges a simultaneity between a belated antifeudalism and a premature anticapitalism, the thrust of which is anti-imperialist. But so long as it is in the thrall of antinomic necessity, revolution is merely a possibility, which, if it is to become reality, requires the right conjuncture of events as well as subjective action ennobled by conscious purpose. With access barred to the spontaneity of history, anticipatory revolution necessarily requires a strategy and, moreover, must be plurivocal as well. But the very possibility of anticipatory revolution entails the probability that it will remain incompletely fulfilled, and therein resides its intrinsic antinomy. Plurivocal and incomplete, its necessary result was a syncretic society. The society is syncretic because it is ruled at one and the same time by both the imperative and the impossibility of matching up the existing forces of production with production relations different from those that had corresponded to them but which had been abolished.

Stalinism represents the transformation of a temporary disjunction between the forces and relations of production into a stabilized social order and ultimately into an autonomous mode of production.

Abstracted from its real conditions, the unbounded interplay of circumstance, chance, and historical agents, this sequence of successive determination reveals a pattern of continuous alternation between necessity and possibility. Antinomic necessity creates the possibility of an anticipatory, plurivocal revolution, which in turn necessarily gives rise to a syncretic society. The latter, abandoned to the spontaneous movement of history, renders the emergence of a social order of the Stalinist type highly possible.

Under the restraining hand of theory, antinomic necessity enabled the most radical revolution in history to erupt in the most backward country of Europe; but once that hand was removed, that self-same necessity led to one of the most oppressive social orders known to man. To understand this social order is to understand this necessity—not only what it is, but also how it functions.

A fruitful scientific study of the inner workings of Stalinist society must include a study of the circumstances out of which it emerged. The effort undertaken in this study to seek the seeds of Stalinism in the circumstances surrounding the Russian revolution is only a first step in this direction. The next step will be a study of the historical process that led finally to its birth.

ABOUT THE AUTHOR

PAVEL CAMPEANU was born in Bucharest, Romania, in 1920. He joined the Communist Youth League in 1935 and the Romanian Communist Party in 1940. From 1941 until 1944 he was imprisoned for antifascist activity.

Campeanu received a Ph.D. in sociology from the Stefan Gheorghiu Academy in 1960 and from that year until 1980 was head of the Opinion-Polling Department of Romanian television. He was appointed Professor of Social Sciences at the Bucharest Polytechnic Institute in 1950, then joined the Institute of Social Sciences at Stefan Gheorghiu Academy in 1956 and the journalism faculty in 1976. He is the author of numerous articles published in Romania and elsewhere, and of ten books, among which is a trilogy on audiences: *People and the Theatre*, *People and TV*, and (in collaboration with Stefana Steriade) *People and the Movies*. He has served as a communications expert with UNESCO, is a member of several international mass-communications associations, and lectures widely in North America and Eastern and Western Europe. Campeanu was awarded the Prize of the Romanian Academy in 1964 and again in 1977.